Powerpl

Toys as popular culture

Billion Dollar Batman: a multitude of toys contributed to the huge merchandising profits made around the Hollywood films *Batman*, *Batman Returns* and *Batman Forever*, the revitalised Batman comics and a television animation series. This was the epitome of 'total marketing'.

Powerplay

Toys as popular culture

DAN FLEMING

MANCHESTER UNIVERSITY PRESS

MANCHESTER AND NEW YORK

distributed exclusively in the USA by St. Martin's Press

Copyright © Dan Fleming, 1996

Published by Manchester University Press
Oxford Road, Manchester M13 9NR, UK
and Room 400, 175 Fifth Avenue, New York, NY10010, USA

Distributed exclusively in the USA by
St. Martin's Press, Inc., 175 Fifth Avenue, New York, NY10010, USA

British Library Cataloguing-in-Publication Data

A catalogue record for this book is available from the British Library

Library of Congress Cataloging-in-Publication Data
Fleming, Dan.
    Powerplay: toys as popular culture / Dan Fleming
        p. cm.
    ISBN 0-7190-4716-1. — ISBN 0-7190-4717-X
    1. Toys—Social aspects—United States. 2. Toys—Psychological
aspects. 3. Toys—United States. 4. Child development—United
States. 5. Popular culture—United States. I. Title
HQ784.T68F62 1996
155.4′ 18—dc20   95–43362
                                                          CIP

ISBN 0–7190–4716–1 hardback
ISBN 0–7190–4717-X paperback

First published 1996

00 99 98 97 96   10 9 8 7 6 5 4 3 2 1

Typeset by Carnegie Publishing, Preston
Printed in Great Britain by Redwood Books, Trowbridge

To Jenna and Shana,
playing between two cultures

Contents

Introduction

I still have vivid childhood memories of *Andy Pandy* and *Bill and Ben*. The BBC's own contribution, in the 1950s and early 1960s, to the imaginative lives of children such as myself was to offer a reassuringly safe and circumscribed space which we entered with wide-eyed and essentially passive pleasure. Parents recall the relief of letting the TV set take over on those occasions – the 'parental' supervision of the BBC proving characteristically reliable. But it was my Lone Ranger toys that I actually played with (I don't recall having any toys associated with the BBC's own children's programmes, although my parents say they bought me some). Saturday afternoon could easily degenerate into my brother and me acting out gunfights and brawls in front of *The Lone Ranger*. Seeing us arranging our little plastic Lone Ranger figures on top of the TV set must have alerted our parents to the fact that the TV was about to play a very different role – not a maternally quietening one but something potentially much more unruly.

I can still almost physically recall the feeling of security and comfort that came from *Andy Pandy* (in which puppets came briefly alive to play in a reassuringly familiar home, before returning to a big toy basket). It seemed capable of keeping the terrors of the adult world at bay. I imagined myself having that big basket to creep back into. It felt safe to be there in front of the TV set. But *The Lone Ranger* (a US import based on the legendary exploits in the old West of a masked ex-Texas Ranger who devoted himself to righting wrongs) seemed to take the terrors of the adult world by the scruff of the neck and wrest them into something so exciting that it almost took my breath away. I had a toy Lone Ranger figure on a rearing white horse – that horse galloped through my childhood dreams for years. It was the single most potent image that I returned to in fantasy throughout much of my childhood, and my stomach still turns over just a little when I see a white horse. I have no doubt now, looking back, that it was a symbol of power and confidence out there in the world, and as such was very different, in the imaginative life of that child, from the reassuring symbols of retreat into the safety of domestic and familial sureties. I remember how delicately these two things were balanced in my own mind – I clung to the reassurance of those safe BBC studio sets populated by friendly puppets and surrogate parents; but I loved that white horse with a passion.

Of course, *The Lone Ranger* was 'reassuring' in its own way. Things always turned out all right in the end, the utterly predictable narrative structure taking care of that, and the unruly adult world was always policed by a law best enforced through the properly restrained use of violence – combined with a heavy-handed paternalistic moralising. It is not too difficult to see what was going on there: if the child was venturing out of Andy Pandy's garden and away from maternal supervision, he was going to be told a story about how power really does operate out there in father's world. Alright, but what about that white horse? Why do I remember crying quietly in bed at night because I yearned for that horse to be real instead of just a little plastic toy on my bedside table in suburbia? And when I played with those toys the predictable narrative resolutions did not come automatically. There was always a tension (this was what made it fun) between the scripting of play, derived from the familiar TV stories, and a more open-ended relationship with those imaginal resources.

There has, of course, long been a similar tension at work in our conceptions of childhood generally. Later in these pages I refer to the 'ascetic' child as the cultural product of those historical forces that assembled and exploited notions of childhood innocence, in particular through a nineteenth-century cultural construction which invoked Romantic imagery of a lost natural innocence to set alongside the industrialising unnaturalness of the adult world. This construction became the focal point for moralising about what 'good' children (and also 'good' women, in a conflation of imagery) should be allowed to do, to experience and to be. This was an exploitable construction in very many ways: it contributed to the maintenance of a stable, private domestic sphere in which women and children knew their place, it provided an often spurious sense of moral balance at a time of industrial, capitalist development. The largely imagined moral imperatives of family life acted as a counterweight to the actual social immoralities of the public sphere. But, mostly, a moral notion of the child's innocence as a defining feature of the human essence could be linked to a belief in the naturalness of a social order in which protecting that innocence translated into moral policing tied irrevocably to the dead weight of the way things were. Thus conceived, the child was an invention around which turned a whole structure of power and of illusions on which that power depended in order not to be recognised for what it was.

The force of that invention was in a direct relationship with the degree to which the child was feared for being precisely the opposite – not good, not innocent, and indeed prototypically human in the sense of growing up to be capable of every human vice and excess. That was the dangerous terrain on to which Freud stepped, but it has also been, perhaps, the inevitable recognition at the heart of the adult's making of a culture for the child (from literature to TV and toys). To be always making children's culture for them, because they cannot make it for themselves, is to run the risk of recognising that they always grow up to be us in any case. Their culture is merely what we want it to be. So it is difficult to pretend that they are somehow better than we are and that the culture of childhood reflects that better state. We make that culture, after all, so we are always teetering on the brink of realising that we are making only a reflection of our nostalgia for the way things never were.[1]

This endless dynamic, operating between Andy Pandy and the Lone Ranger, between childhood innocence and the corruptions of the world, is something entirely of our own making. Children have to do the best they can to grow up within that dynamic, because that is what we have given them.

A distinguishing feature of the approach taken in the book is that the dynamic is viewed as a 'systematic' one. In other words, the historical and semiotic production of contemporary children's culture is found to be highly organised. The book is concerned with the basis of that organisation in its detailed form – especially in toys understood as such forms. There has recently been increased attention, both public and scholarly, focused on the nature of children's culture, but much of the academic work to date has been concerned with texts (TV programmes, films, comics).[2] Today's toys are much related to texts, the latter becoming advertisements for the toys in many cases. But once that has been said, it can be difficult to find anything else to say about the relationship when we only approach it via the texts. Toys become merely 'spin-off' consumer products, dependent on those texts. Taking it the other way round and starting with the toys, we find that there is a great deal to say about these objects: about how they carry narrative traces derived from the texts, about how they function as objects, about how they are related to each other in often complex semiotic patterns, about how the history of toys has structured those patterns of meaning.

The approach taken here is focused resolutely on the toys themselves. It uses, from time to time, the language of object-relations theory from psychoanalysis, but without becoming a detailed 'application' of a particular theory or set of theories. Rather, a style of thinking found in Erik Erikson and Alice Miller (and distinct from the Freudians' theory-building) offers a backdrop to this study and usable vocabulary, without a fuller theoretical treatment being attempted. (I therefore do not discuss the relationship between these useful but relatively 'minor' theorists and the absent 'major' figures such as Klein and Winnicott.) The accompanying photograph perhaps says all that needs to be said about why this should be so. I wanted to write a book about the toys without having them completely disappear *in advance* into a (very adult) theoretical discourse. As I worked I began to see an intersection between, on the one hand, the child as an object delineated by the culture we make for it, and, on the other, the semiotic system which toys become recognisable as when relocated within popular culture generally.

When toy manufacturing giant Hasbro asked girls what they saw when they closed their eyes at night and, time and again, got the answer 'horses' (in their early 1980s market research prior to releasing the My Little Pony range), it led to nearly 200 million chubby little plastic horses with brushable manes being sold. It led to an animated TV series. It led to comics. It led to girls having another (relatively rare) opportunity not to cross-identify with boy's culture, without simply playing house around doll-children and tea sets. The ponies are not ridden. They can sometimes fly. They glow with energy. They are what many little girls see when they close their eyes. The videos and comics tell stories about them that are simply sunny soap operas, tales of domestic conviviality, of sisterly affection and the inevitable overcoming of disruptions through sheer feminine niceness. But the power of the pony can soar above those textual closures. As such it is a power to make and re-make meanings. The idea of the child as (re)constructor is indispensable here. This book is on the trail of such power, but it is not going to be a power without constraint.

Darth Vader, Pocahontas and Me: the author amidst some of today's most popular toys. From left, Luke Skywalker (*Star Wars*), Squatt (*Mighty Morphin' Power Rangers*), Disney's Lion King, two Power Rangers, Pocahontas and her raccoon friend Meeko, Megazord (*Power Rangers*) and Darth Vader (Luke's father and villain from *Star Wars*). The rather insubstantial figure of Luke finds what it means to be a human male refracted through these images of the clever animal, the monster, the machine and the wild woman. Which figure the actual boy or girl identifies with remains open to question (although it is undoubtedly not the author)!

What prevents this approach from degenerating into a sort of vacuous populism (in which cultural resources are just a big playground where everybody has the power to make whatever meanings they want) is its sensitivity to the historical and semiotic structuring of the field of meaning in which today's toys operate.

Place Disney's Pocahontas, high on the list of Christmas 1995's most-wanted, amidst the Power Rangers, Lion King or Star Wars toys from previous years, and we do not have a playground on which these objects can mean anything a child wants them to. Each of the different object types here – human figure, animal, machine, monster – has a

Introduction

history and its own set of cultural reference points. Where these overlap, a systematic pattern of meanings becomes visible. It is that system which children can play with. And it is that system which this book describes in outline. Whether the feisty side of Pocahontas transcends the tendency to draw her back into a family romance with Luke Skywalker and Darth Vader is not a question with a predetermined answer.

Finally some brief acknowledgements. Two students helped with preliminary research on the toy industry – Paul Anderson at Robert Gordons in Aberdeen and Sharon Warren at the University of Ulster, Coleraine. John Izod, at the University of Stirling, encouraged an earlier version of the book – which unfortunately never saw the light of day but which remains detectable in these pages. Martin Barker at the University of the West of England read a draft and contributed greatly to its improvement. Anita Roy took hold of the thing and made it happen. Too many others to thank, young and old, told me about their toys. The Faculty of Humanities at the University of Ulster supported several invaluable visits to toy museums – despite some colleagues' scepticism about what the author might be up to there! Jasper contributed to many of the photographs by knocking something over just before the shutter clicked (all the photographs are by the author).

1

Cultural studies and children's culture

Toys mean a great deal to children and, as the process of being a child has everything to do with the kinds of people, women and men, which we become, it would seem not at all unlikely that toys have much to do with identity. Identity, though, is not easy to write about. Is one writing in an essentialist or an anti-essentialist way? In an extreme essentialist vocabulary people are their identities, there is no wriggling around inside identities, no hopping in and out, no weird out-of-body experiences that allow people to step outside their identities and take a long, quizzical look at them. We're stuck with them because there is no difference between us and them. They are who we are and they are real. In an extreme anti-essentialist vocabulary it is language, culture and society that we are stuck with and which constitute what we take to be real. The 'we' that we think we are is a product, an elaborate construction, fabricated out of words, texts and social arrangements such as the family. We may be no less fixed in place, but now it is a matter of being pinned to/by our socially constructed identities – so the idea of loosening the pins, of some space for movement, of a potential gap between identity and something else that we are, is at least thinkable (a thinkable impossibility?). Implications tending in one direction or the other dog the tracks of any writing that touches on such matters.

What will emerge from this study of toys and popular culture is the notion that identities are simultaneously essentialised and in motion. In one sense, therefore, I try to have it both ways: I need a vocabulary capable of using a word such as 'child' (never mind the gendered versions) without constantly apologising, either to the extreme anti-essentialist for erasing the complex construction involved, or to the extreme essentialist for my insufficient concern with the nurturing of its god-given uniqueness. Really, however, this is going to be an exploration and an argument that sides with the anti-essentialists. It is just that the extreme versions of this position lead to far too many objects

7

in the social field dissolving into their constituent parts. As a result, forms of understanding can drift away too much from forms of life to be effective any more, except in the academic seminar room.

There are fearfully strong essentialising forces always at work in us, in our cultures and in our social contexts, whatever and wherever any of those might be. To get a grip on them we do have to recognise the things, the objects, that such essentialising forces want us to mistake as simply there, fixed, natural. Seeing them does not mean accepting them as natural, but for convenience we may often have to talk about them as if their identities were not quite so problematic as, on another level, we really know they are.

Children, texts and toys

What can toys tell us about culture and vice versa? Toys tell us something about demand. In a colloquial sense first: parents know too well the insistent tug of 'I want'. There is more than individual desire here. Or rather, as individual desire is always articulated with socially constructed objects – the desirable – and with equally socially constructed ways of wanting – the routines of consumption – so there is, as the very engine of 'I want', an unmistakable 'massification' of demand. The child's demand is really a chorus, orchestrated but none the less breathed and felt as an individual desire by this child, at this particular moment. In fact toys are a wonderful place to look at the complex interactions between the desiring individual and the massified demand. It's all so visible here – the child appealing for satisfaction and the market providing the very vocabulary of appeal. Both are visibly and audibly present in the toyshop – neither can be reduced to a pale reflection of the other, without some deeply troublesome sense of having over-simplified what's going on.

The commodification and mass production of toys themselves is another, intersecting, set of processes. Some of its history will be detailed later in this book, but it is important to note at this stage that we have no reason for reducing either the mass market's orchestration of demand or the 'I want' itself to the status of a side-effect of commodification. Each has its own history, not always neatly synchronized with the others,' and each deserves distinct attention from us. So for example, the mass production of tinplate toys had much of the industrial revolution about it and relied on that machine revolution's inherent appeals, the appeal of the new steam engines and the new machines of land and sea. The toys were totems of the very revolution which included in its defining characteristics the processes of their own manufacture. (This would not happen again until computer games.) The role of popular culture in defining the desirable, particularly where toys were concerned, came later and was rather different, eventually having much to do with the new media. But even there things have to be held distinct: the popular culture that fed a boom in theatre and music hall toys was something different from television's global marketing of *Mighty Morphin' Power Rangers* (the former was more mediated by social class and parental taste, for one thing). And 'I want' spoken by a child of the late twentieth century, in a Western liberal context, depends for part of its effect on the changed nature of the relationships between adults and children at that time.

One can see a problem here. Either the sorts of term we are working with – let's take 'toy' itself – are inherently meaningful, in the sense of simply having an unproblematic meaning as unitary objects in the world, or they are not. Common-sense language certainly allows them such existences – indeed depends on doing so for the very way in which a trustable, everyday reality can be communicated about, no matter how much we might grant that linguistic usages have their own history and may evolve. It's a long, slow history and at any one point objects simply mean what they mean, don't they? It does not seem sensible to suggest that the word 'toy' is somehow fundamentally lacking in reality. And yet it doesn't really have that kind of given, unitary meaning. A plastic plaything is actually quite a complex object. Recognising it as a toy is precisely that – an act of recognition. Such recognitions depend on settings, prior experience, culturally-derived associations and so on. Indeed what one means by the act of recognition will itself vary – not least depending on whether one is a child or an adult, whether one has money to buy it or one hasn't, whether it appeals to one's tastes or it doesn't.

On the other hand, this then leads to its own difficulties. Every object starts to look as if it exists only as the point of intersection for a multitude of determining factors – not only settings, experiences and associations but representations (all the texts, written and pictorial, in which such an object appears) and in turn all the social, cultural, economic and historical factors that impinge on each setting, each experience, each association and each representation. We end up with vast interlocking chains of factors which together form a dense context out of which the particular object, the toy, derives its particular meanings at this point in time. The cultural critic-analyst can go on a brain-tangling pursuit of all these interconnections, but it can become something of an impenetrable jumble, so complex are the contexts in which we make even our simplest of meanings.

The toy is a good example, because it reminds us not to think the simple meaning out of existence completely. It would be so obviously crazy if we ended up unable to deal with the toy as a simple plaything, so thoroughly had we dissolved it back into its complex contextual ground. But it defies our over-subtlety. It pops back out from that ground and says 'play with me'! A lot of other cultural forms are less resistant to dissolution, won't pop back out at us precociously, so a cultural theorising that has replaced the objects with the maps of contextual interconnection has been very successful in recent years. That is harder to do here.

We can think, perhaps, of each object (whether toy, child or text) as sitting at the intersection of many roads, each carrying its traffic of meanings, events, experiences, feelings and so on. Ultimately this traffic is synchronised in some complex ways with the grander flows of the society, not least its economic arteries. But at our modest intersection there appears to be little going on of real importance. Given that things look fairly simple here, how are we to understand what happens at the point where this traffic intersects? What is a toy?

If this object's identity is not given, stable and intrinsically fixed in some unitary way, and if on the other hand it isn't to be dissolved back into the flows of intersecting traffic (your bodily memory of a cuddly bear, my fascination with the educational potential of Lego, Hasbro's marketing of their latest product, the local toyshop's post-Christmas sale, a Saturday morning TV show's merchandising, and so on), how are we to understand the nature of the object we are dealing with? The proposal here is that we should think of the object only partly as an effect of all those intersecting factors, lines, traffic or flows (there is an abstract visual metaphor here that is not quite captured by any one word). But, crucially, the object in turn generates effects amidst all that intersecting stuff; like a ripple back out from the point where the object has been formed. So the effects we are going to be interested in are simultaneously in the formation of an object and in that object's consequences within the processes that formed it. In a way, therefore, it might be better to talk about 'events' rather than 'objects'.[1]

Effectivity and a structure of feeling

The notion of effects, scores of them, back out along the traffic flows, effects rippling out from the particular effect (or object, or event) produced at one of the points where the flows intersect, is both teasingly abstract and yet very real in its consequences. It means that we can think about reconstructing some of those effects. We don't have to change the object to do so. If we can devise ways of recognising and grasping some of its effects, in our lives where they matter, we can stand some chance of remaking what we have grasped. Elsewhere I have tried to work out ways of doing this in classrooms, with photographs, TV soap opera, science fiction and so on. The ideal may be to break some of the long connective chains, or to block the flows, and to reconnect them in ways that . . . well, what is it precisely that we might be hoping to achieve?

This concept of effects (object as effect, plus ripples back out into the stuff that formed the object to produce other effects) has to be translated into very specific instances if it is to be of any use. The bulk of this book is such a translation. The reconstructive possibility is not the same thing as analysis. We can attempt to know some of these effects without trying to remake them. Indeed reconstruction may not depend on a prior analysis. It may be possible to so organise things, as I have suggested in a book about teaching, that reconstructive work can be done with the material which is to hand.[2] In fact a form of effective analysis may actually be embodied by, or produced by, the doing of it. The objective here is rather different; it is more deliberately analytical. We will return towards the end, however, to the question of reconstruction.

The first analytical step is to identify clusters of effects that underpin (but do not necessarily 'add up' to, in any simple sense) recognisable categories of social life. There is plenty of scope to do so, at various levels of generality or detail. In writing about classroom work I 'chose' eight such clusters. They happened to be: inner experience, living together, understanding the natural world, practical skills, physical well-being, expressive and appreciative activity, moral development and communicating.[3] These seemed to offer some real hope of grasping in the classroom things that matter to children, as well as 'traffic' in which they are caught up (ideas, beliefs, practices, values, representations, many of them in varying states of crisis these days). Here I want to focus in much more detail on a more specific cluster of effects – in short, on playing with toys. More general categories, such as the eight listed above, may be crossed by this one – it is not hard to see how all of those eight might be – but we will be trying here to remain in among the details that are specifically relevant to toys. So playing is the category of social life, or the 'mode of experience', in which we are interested, although our focus will be much more on the toys than on the activity of playing itself.[4]

This raises immediately the issue of whether observations of children playing are to be a part of the analysis. They should be. The difficulty is that techniques of ethnographic observation and interpretation seem insufficiently advanced to give us much purchase on the intersecting lines of cultural and other stuff that converge on the events of playing. Or maybe it is simply too much to expect that they should. So, odd though it may seem, this is a study of toys, children and popular culture that does not explicitly include observations of children playing, except the casual ones which none of us will have avoided. Perhaps the advantage is that, while observation too rapidly becomes absorbed by what is seen and heard, here proper attention can be given to the contexts within which what might be accessible to observation actually takes shape (indeed within which the very act of observation takes shape too). As what is available for observation will only be a specific kind of effect, an effect to which the contexts are by no means reducible, we should not be too apologetic for what we have chosen not to do.

In fact, one of the guiding principles here is that analysis should not give priority in advance to one kind of effect over another. Observable effects in play would be one example. Textual analyses, say of children's TV programmes, would be another. Toy manufacturers' marketing campaigns would be a third. The list could go on, but the point is that these things have to be interwoven. Some gaps may be left, but at least such spaces will be defined, in the best sense of that term.

The risk in not doing this is that we attempt to find too much in the prioritised effects – as when textual analysis becomes tortuously complex in order to say more than it is capable of saying about the whole cluster of effects and contexts in which the textual is actually located. In literary and film studies there has been a period of such over-reaching, of trying to squeeze too much out of texts when the sought-for results are more easily available elsewhere. So a detailed textual analysis of the *Mighty Morphin' Power Rangers* TV series will not tell us all we need to know about the toys, about what might be going on inside the young fans or about popular culture when it operates in this way. A corollary is that just because the texts seem uninformative that does not mean that there is nothing there worth studying. That is not to say that textual analysis simply needs to be complemented by another, secondary form of activity, contextual analysis. Or that when the texts seem insubstantial we should give priority to context instead. Rather it is that analysis of effects of the kind proposed here simply need not concern itself so much with such distinctions.

To recognise the 'content', whether textual or contextual, of our thoroughly encultured society, as well as to begin tracing in more precise terms what we might mean by 'effects', one can do little better than to quote Raymond Williams on such matters. In particular, this is Williams on the dissolution of a once key distinction between the unsettling stuff of a minority culture and the more generally reassuring platitudes of a popular culture, a distinction between Munch, Schiele, Pound, Beckett, on the one hand, and the once cosy world of Hollywood weepies, swashbuckling escapism and TV sitcoms on the other:

> The originally precarious and often desperate images – typically of frag- mentation, loss of identity, loss of the very grounds of human communication – have been transferred from the dynamic compositions of artists who had been, in majority, literally exiles, having little or no common ground with the societies in which they were stranded, to become, at an effective surface, a 'modernist' and 'post-modernist' estab- lishment. This, near the centres of corporate power, takes human inadequacy, self-deception, role-playing, the confusion and substitution of individuals in temporary relationships, and even the lying paradox of the communication of the fact of non-communication, as self- evident routine data . . .
>
> Yet what is much more decisive, altering the very terms through which the situation can be analysed, is the transfer of many of these deep struc- tures into effectively popular forms, in film and television and heavily marketed books. Apparently simple kinds of adventure and mystery have been transformed and newly marketed in highly specific representations of crime, espionage, intrigue and dislocation, mediating the deep assump- tions of habitual competitive violence, deception and role-playing, loss of identity, and relationships as temporary and destructive. Thus these

13

debased forms of an anguished sense of human debasement, which had once shocked and challenged fixed and stable forms that were actually destroying people, have become a widely distributed 'popular' culture that is meant to confirm both its own and the world's destructive inevitabilities.[5]

What has happened is that the artists who first encountered the awful forces of dislocation let loose in the past century, initially by destructive imperial and economic exploitation of everything remote from its own centres, expressed what they found (not always disapprovingly) as strangers in an ever stranger land. But as it became the only land, the only place available to live, so those themes of dislocation became first the knowing world-weariness of a cultural élite and then more generally the anthems of pragmatism and accommodation, of resignation and making do, a shoulder-shrugging 'so be it' (which suits the values of the stock-market dealing floor). Meanwhile the forms of a popular culture capable of speaking to the new masses became available as carriers of this nervy resignation, shedding many of their old stories of marriages made in heaven and heroes untroubled by self-doubt to be replaced by the more bitter content evoked by Williams. That content is re-formed into the templates of media culture, the genres and iconographies and narrative structures. Perhaps it is deeply over-simplified. But it is all the same culture now. What we have to study is Williams's 'effective surface' – a culture which is a vast rippling surface of effects, where somehow the novels of Martin Amis and the *Teenage Mutant Ninja Turtles* are formed out of the same stuff, vibrate with the same disturbances to that surface. One can still ask whether the Turtles or the Amis novel are qualitatively comparable, but the question will come belatedly, after they have been understood as effects or events on the same cultural plane.

From Cultural Studies to play

As terms are being used in quite a precise way here, it may be useful to summarise the basic set of propositions. In studying culture we are examining 'objects'. Here we will be concerned in particular with the toy and the child and with various texts, such as stories, comics and TV programmes, that relate in several interesting ways to toys. It is being argued that, in order to examine such 'objects' in a way that stands some chance of telling us how they interrelate culturally, it is necessary to think of them as effects, in a very specific sense. Each supposed 'object', rather than having a free-standing identity, needs to be understood as the effect of a complex intersection of determining factors. Part of the task of this book is to describe many such factors. But we are using the term 'effect' in a particular way: it entails the simultaneous generation of further effects back among the determining factors. This is a dynamic configuration of effects that we will be illustrating in concrete terms later. Abstractly, however, it is the specific manner in which we will be making sense of Williams's 'effective surface' as a way of thinking about contemporary culture.

This avoids two unhelpful approaches to our objects. The first would see them as unproblematically there, with self-evident meanings and identities that simply have to be described with clarity and precision. This would leave us with very little to say about contemporary toys (they are not all that complex as objects), but also with the feeling that we are missing a great deal of what is happening when toys exert their hold over children. Simply shifting the explanation on to a TV series, from which the toy is a spin-off, and calling it an extended advertisement, would then be to expect too much from our analysis of the TV series. There may be a great deal going on, when a child plays with the toy, for which a TV programme cannot be held responsible. Shifting again, and studying the child's playing as an activity of the developing organism will also be blinkered in its capacity to explain the cultural dimensions of actually playing with this as opposed to that toy.

Of course it can be suggested that simply adding together all these perspectives on discrete objects of inquiry has the end result of saying everything that needs to be said about them. To go back to the child's 'I want', however, is it fully comprehensible as simply the accumulation, the adding on top of each other, of a young organism's developmental urge to play, the promotional effect of a TV series and the inherent tactile or visual attractiveness of the toy as an object? That stacking up of pressures and appeals certainly says something about what is going on. Examining things just a bit more closely, however, soon reveals, as an entirely distinctive feature of children, toys and popular culture in their fascinating interrelationships, a certain unmistakable 'synchronisation' across those areas. When it all comes together around the Ninja Turtles or the Transformers, this powerful 'synchronisation' is clearly more than the sum of the parts – clear if for no other reason than that other similar parts don't stack up to the same effect. (Toy manufacturers and TV companies certainly wish that they did.)[6]

The other approach to be avoided goes to the opposite extreme. It dissolves the objects of study back into their contextual ground. So there aren't really children, toys or TV series at all. These are all produced by more fundamental structuring practices and processes, not least by language itself, and we mistake the name for the thing. Things may be there, but they are inaccessible to us. It is tempting to say, try telling that to a parent who has just tripped over a carelessly abandoned toy. It exists all right, and the little monsters who dropped it too. But that is to miss the point. There are complex networks of determining factors supporting every object – what they determine is what we recognise when we see that object. That always comes after the toe-stubbing encounter with reality, but supplants it almost instantly.

The problem with taking this dissolution of object into ground too far is that the specific television text gets too easily reduced to type, to genre, to repeated narrative structures, to iconographies. The specific toy gets reduced to commodity templates; the individual child to society's construction of 'the child'. Much of the liveliness of culture as it is lived comes from specific differences, from effects that outrun the levelling impact of shared structures.

We are, then, drawn to the idea of an 'effective surface' on which such liveliness is possible. Here each 'object' is an effect of intersecting determinations but simultaneously generates its own effects within those determining factors. In this way there is a surplus over and above the object and its determinations – a play of effects. I take this to be very close to the usage of the term 'effect' in Larry Grossberg's work, work which would be indispensable to a more theoretical elaboration of the approach adopted here.[7]

This play of effects is not then some postmodern notion of unanchored significations – the effects are organised by the specific relationships among objects and determinations. For this reason there will emerge clusters or constellations of effects, as a function of the underlying organisation of objects and determinations. So in thinking about toys, we will be dealing with some such constellation of effects. By definition that will also mean a configuration of determining factors – an organised network of intersecting determinations within which the clustered effects are being formed (or what Grossberg, after Foucault, calls a 'formation'). These constellations of effects can in turn be understood as contributing in complex ways to more general realms of social life, or 'modes of experience'.

Playing is such a realm or mode. We will be looking for the constellations of effects that play across it. And we will be closely examining specific effects within those constellations. It is unlikely that the effects simply add up in some way to the mode of experience called playing. Rather constellations of effects may further condense and accrete into what we might call social discourses, the material practices that fill and define the space of 'play' (how domestic life is organised to provide such spaces, how the toy industry and the media sustain it, and so on). Such social discourses are the sum of the effects.[8] Playing as a mode of experience needs some further explanation.

We may find it in Williams's notion of a 'structure of feeling', such structures being the affective accompaniments to cultural formations – what people feel when they live specific effects of culture. Crudely put, each constellation of effects may have its accompanying structure of feeling. Playing as a mode of experience is then a product of such structures of feeling, just as the social discourses that define play are the product of the constellations of effects (or formations). As Grossberg says:

> The most obvious and perhaps most frightening thing about contemporary popular culture is that it matters so much to so many different people. The source of its power, whatever it may seem to say, or whatever pleasures it may offer, can be identified with its place in people's affective lives, and its ability to place other practices affectively. For many people, certain forms of popular culture become taken-for-granted, even necessary, investments. As a result, specific cultural formations become 'affective alliances'. Their logic or coherence – which is often so difficult to define – depends upon their affective relationships, their articulated places within people's mattering maps. One cannot assume that such affective alliances satisfy needs created elsewhere, or that they create the needs which they in turn satisfy.[9]

The 'affective alliance' is another, more precise term for the 'synchronisations' invoked above, the powerful coming together that seems to exceed the mere stacking up of developmental urges, mass marketing and the manufacture of appealing objects. The convergence at a particular moment of all these things within a structure of feeling is what makes something matter to the child, and that mattering is not reducible to any one object (thus Grossberg's description of mattering

17

as a 'map'). Nor can any one object be identified as the source of the satisfied needs. The source is not within the child, for example, nor is it generated within the marketing objects (whether toy or related media texts) as some kind of pseudo or manufactured 'need'. Rather both need and satisfaction are effects of the whole shebang, the particular cultural formation and the particular structure of feeling that mirrors it. The particular coming together of effects is a dynamic occurrence within a specific structure of feeling.

This means that we have to handle terms such as feeling, affect, desire, demand and need very carefully, especially when we are trying to associate them with objects (as we inevitably are with children and toys). Grossberg again: 'Libidinal affect (or desire in psychoanalytic terms) is always focused on an object (whether real or imaginary), while nonlibidinal affect (affect for short) is always dispersed into the entire context of daily life.'[10] So the child's demand, the 'I want' with which we started, however libidinal at a precise moment of fixation on an object, has to be heard as also an effect of such a dispersal, and ultimately as an effect of Williams's structure of feeling.

As O'Connor says, 'The idea of a "structure of feeling" is often considered to be the major invention of Williams's sociology of culture', referring as it does to 'something like an emergent pattern of general experience'.[11] Williams himself used it in various ways when thinking about generations of artists, movements, styles or the link between a time's representational conventions and how people feel about them. Williams devotes a chapter to the term in *Marxism and Literature* (a chapter whose first few paragraphs overshadow everything that I have written here).[12]

In a marvellously suggestive metaphor Williams offers the thought that 'structures of feeling can be defined as social experiences *in solution*, as distinct from other social semantic formations which have been *precipitated* and are more evidently and more immediately available',[13] suggesting vividly that the more granular and readily detectable constellations of effects are accompanied by more liquid affective states. Williams's own description, from *The Politics of Modernism*, of the 'desperate images' that have migrated from a minority culture into the mass media, clearly goes some way towards describing the sort of state we are in. I want to focus now on a specific desperate instance, the *Mighty Morphin' Power Rangers*, and to cross its terrain of banality in order to re-connect with these preliminary remarks.

'Go, Go, Power Rangers!'

Shown six days a week on US television in late 1993 and 1994, and picked up in early 1994 by British breakfast TV and a satellite channel, the Power Rangers series at its peak was reaching 57 per cent of 6–11-year-olds in the United States:[14] 'PolyGram Video, one of 90 US licensees, has sold nearly 8 million videotapes since Thanksgiving. Grosset & Dunlap, the kids' division of Putnam, moved more than a million copies of its first four Power Rangers novellas in just two weeks, with eight more in the works. Fruit of the Loom has peddled nearly 7 million pairs of Rangers underwear since February. All told, industry analysts believe, sales of Ranger toys and other paraphernalia could approach $1 billion by [1995] – what the Turtles generated at the peak of their popularity.'[15]

In the UK the toys sold out within days of arriving in the shops from manufacturer Bandai in the run-up to Christmas 1994[16]. A cinema version in 1995 boosted interest again. The Teenage Mutant Ninja Turtles had been the last toy phenomenon on such a scale, and before them The Transformers. Along the way Jurassic Park, GI Joe/Action Force, Ghostbusters and others had momentarily peaked to almost the same commercial heights, but had not sustained the frenzy of interest. What the really major commercial successes in recent years have had in common has been an unsubtle blending of American and Japanese characteristics. Power Rangers achieved this in a very particular way.

Since the 1960s, and in particular the animated films of Tezuka Osamu who had watched Disney films at a school club as a child, Japanese television has developed several hugely popular genres of highly stylised animated or live-action series, mixing martial arts, science-fiction and traditional Japanese romantic adventure narratives.[17] Tezuka's *Astro Boy* (1963) offered a high-tech Pinocchio (a robot created in the likeness of a child killed in a car crash). Since then, in *anime* (animated films) and *manga* (comics), Japanese popular culture has explored its own distinctive universe of apocalyptic imagery (Tokyo is so frequently destroyed that Neo-Tokyo has entered common usage), robot–human hybrids, deformed characters, martial arts and traditional warrior-caste themes (ninja, samurai, etc.) and an ever-present fascination with technology. It is difficult, and probably unnecessary, to resist the link with the wartime experiences of the Japanese, especially as nuclear victims. Tezuka had actually started drawing *Astro Boy* in

19

the early 1950s, and thousands of pages of his earlier drawings as a schoolboy survived the American bombings. The protectively armoured robot-child rising from the dead is hardly an innocent image, set against such a background.

Conspicuous examples of this sector of popular culture have been the films and series *Mobile Suit Gundam* (1979–), with huge battling robots which are actually vehicles for human occupants, *Bubblegum Crisis* (1987–), with four sleekly body-armoured female vigilantes dealing with life in a post-apocalypse Tokyo, *Akira* (1987), Otomo Katshuhiro's internationally successful *anime* adaptation of his own *manga* about futuristic bike gangs in a decayed urban wasteland, and the notorious *Urotsukidoji: Legend of the Overfiend* (1987), with its sexually explicit animations of Monster Demons 'channelling their energies' (as the UK-released video packaging puts it) into the bodies of human girls (i.e. raping them). Among the live-action contributions to all of this, a special-effects-oriented series called *Kyoryu Sentai Zyuranger*, about lycra-suited young superheroes, is the sixteenth in a series of similar shows (called *sentai* or 'team' shows in general) that have been running on Japanese TV since 1975.[18]

In 1992 Saban Entertainment Inc. set about adapting *Kyoryu Sentai Zyuranger* for US television. This was achieved by taking the extensive special-effects sequences from the Japanese original and combining them with new material shot in the United States. The advantage of a series based around a group of masked characters was precisely that the two different materials could be intercut. In fact, in the process a slim male character from the Japanese original becomes Trini, the female Yellow Ranger in the first US and UK broadcast series. In their American form, the Rangers are a group of high-school students. Most of the new footage consists of contextualizing and incidental scenes from their high school lives. When they don their superhero suits it doesn't take long to get into the Japanese effects sequences which give the series its characteristic visual style and provide a showcase for the spin-off toys.

The basic story (or 'back story' in TV jargon) behind the Power Rangers is a simple one, but it is important to bear in mind that there *is* a story. The toys, like so many others these days, often seem incomprehensible to adults because they fail to understand that a story makes it all very precisely meaningful for children. There are some variations between the Japanese and US versions. Both have their roots in a galactic conflict between good and evil ten thousand years ago. Among the forces of good was the sorcerer Zordon (Barza in Japan) who battled with the witch Rita Repulsa (or Bandora). Zordon succeeded in having Repulsa imprisoned on a tiny moon of a remote planet (Earth), while she trapped Zordon in a time vortex (a tube of green light!). From his vortex Zordon can still exert influence through a robotic helper and a computer control headquarters, the Ranger Command Centre (a crossroads for many 'portals' to other dimensions), which he has located in a remote mountainous area of Earth to counter Repulsa's latest threat. This arises when she is accidentally released by astronauts from her moon prison and turns her malicious attention towards the planet below.

In the Japanese version, Barza has been holding in suspended animation his masked group of superheroes for just such an eventuality, but in the American version they are new teenage recruits, sought out by Zordon's robot assistant and on whom both special powers and technological assistance are bestowed. The latter centres around the Zords, or huge robotic vehicles. Each ranger has a Zord in the form of a dinosaur-like machine. These can combine to form Megazord (which can transform from a giant robot figure into a tank). Repulsa in turn has her assistance in the form of five bizarre villains: Goldar (Grifoza in Japan), a winged golden Pharaoh-like warrior; Squatt (Bukbak), a bulbous blue reptilian creature with protruding fangs; Baboo (Tottopat), a human-sized monkey with a twitch, bat wings and claws; Finster (Puripurikashi), a dwarfish, pointed-eared, grey-bearded monster-designer; and Scorpina (Rami Scorpion), a sleek, armour-clad *femme fatale* with a sting in her tail. Repulsa also has at her disposal the Putties, an army of grey faceless humanoid drones made from clay (and interestingly called in Japan *Golem*, the word for clay creatures that come alive in Hebrew folklore).

What each episode of the TV series does with these elements is highly formulaic. The teenage team is usually involved in something of marginal interest at school – an environmental clean-up campaign or a weight-lifting contest – when Repulsa launches her latest diabolical scheme. This often has some connection with what the kids are doing (such as an evil plan for global pollution) but is always an excuse for their instant change into masked superheroes and a protracted battle with Repulsa's forces. The battle goes through almost ritualised stages, from individual martial-arts conflict to engagement with the separate Zords, and usually culminates in the team's coming together to operate

1 The Power Rangers toys from Bandai were the big success of the Christmas 1994 and 1995 toy-buying seasons and were widely copied. On the left is the licensed toy of the Yellow Ranger, 16-year old Trini whose 'morph' form is a sabretooth tiger. On the right is a cheap, unlicensed Chinese copy of Red Ranger. The Bandai figures are beautifully jointed, right down to individual finger movements, allowing pleasureably tactile and dynamic handling of the toy which can be posed in a multitude of ways. Cheap copies were much less delicate and had a brutal, unyielding feel.

Megazord and save the day. Humorous sub-plots back at school centre around the low-level skulduggery of Bulk and Skull, the college bully and his henchman. Needless to say, the teenage team always get the better of the bully in the end as well. Little does he know, or the pompous college principal for that matter, that they have been saving the Earth in the meantime!

The persistent theme through all of this is the uneasy balance between individuality and teamwork. The American high-school kids ('teenagers with attitude', Zordon calls them) are individuals, their differences exaggerated in part by ham acting – the gymnast, the street-wise rapper, the muscle-builder, the shy intellectual and so on. But the masked Japanese fighters are a team, their identities wholly submerged. In fact Repulsa is always unsuccessful because she cannot get her unruly band of villains to work together properly. In high school, the teenagers can individually take the initiative, as Trini does with her environmental Cleanup Club. In superhero-mode they become a hierarchy, with Red Ranger in control (or White Ranger, who is lifted out of another *Sentai* show entirely and intercut!) and their ultimate destiny is to become cogs in the Megazord machine (called Great Beast God in the Japanese version). There is a basic kind of dialogue going on between these American and Japanese components of Power Rangers, and in the American producers' decision to effect this form of hybrid adaptation in the first place. As Schodt puts it:

> Japanese society is 'group-oriented' while America's is 'individual-oriented'. Japan's social organization is 'vertical' while America's is 'horizontal', and so on. Most of these generalizations are only differences in emphasis, but there are enough of them to keep Americans busy writing about Japan for centuries. And probably half the books about Japan are really books about America. For all its similarities to America, Japan is still the perfect mirror-image metaphor for America and the perfect place for us to form a new frame of reference . . .
>
> For Americans, Japan can be like a room of fun-house mirrors, where people enter, delight in the odd, distorted images they encounter, and then in the reflections see themselves . . .
>
> America and Japan are wonderfully complementary cultures, capable of great synergies.[19]

Mighty Morphin' Power Rangers is hardly an instance of great synergy, but it bears some of the qualities of the fun-house mirror that crazily intermingles self and other. There is a complex two-way intercourse going on between Japan and the US, culturally and in other ways. Japanese-American journalist Karl Taro Greenfeld's *Speed Tribes* dwells with fascination on people and scenes from the Japanese subcultures where this intercourse is most keenly experienced. Drifting appropriately into a form of journalistic fiction, he recreates the motorcycle gangs, porn video performers, glitzy TV soap-star-lookalike hostesses, and computer-obsessed kids.[20] Power Rangers is like the morning TV show which one of these people watches over breakfast: 'Right when the hero had worked his way through about a dozen evil underlings and had the black-kimono-clad Red Mask backed up, the phone rang . . .'.[21]

Power Rangers is speed-tribe stuff, without too many of the dark overtones. It is meant to be watched in much the same way as

MTV. Specifically we can borrow Goodwin's notion of precise visual hooks. In music videos there are the hooks that use close-ups of stars, the hooks that activate the 'scopophilic male gaze' (a theorisation of media voyeurism or pleasure-in-looking made familiar by Mulvey), and the hooks which 'carry an emotive charge or set of associations that connects with a musical motif'.[22] But unlike similar hooks in what we have come to know as classic realist texts, where the audiovisual organisation follows all the structuring rules of seamless editing, of spatial consistency and narrative continuity, in the music video there is a form of layering in which that horizontal consistency is much less stable. Instead the hooks may operate separately in a kind of vertical organisation that can seem to be 'fragmented' but is really just a different kind of structure.

Particularly in the Japanese-derived sequences, the TV episodes of Power Rangers take on a similar form of organisation. The star close-ups here are of the Zords, the dinosaur-machines which look like grossly oversized toys (the limitations of the effects-work actually evoking this toy-like quality). When the teenagers don their masked outfits they are reduced to colour-coded components of a team and cannot themselves sustain that kind of hook. The machine toys can and do, in precisely repeated ways in every episode – which raises a tricky question about the visual pleasure of the male look, the second form of hook, habitually centralised and directed at women in the classic realist text. The look directed at these machines is similarly employed as the organising line around which the visual space is structured, but here the libidinal energy would seem to be directed at the machine imagery rather than at women (although there are plenty of other *anime* and *manga* examples that do follow the familiar pattern).

In *Speed Tribes*, Greenfield describes the *Otaku*, as the Japanese media call them: the kids whose only real relationships are with machines (*otaku* meaning 'you' in the most rigid, formal and impersonal style of address). He quotes one: 'I get along with objects and data better than people. If it were possible to have sex with machines, then that would be more interesting.'[23] That is the alternative scopophilic hook which Power Rangers offers to its predominantly prepubescent viewers. The question of whether it is any longer a male look, in some fundamental sense, is an interesting one. The ambiguous costumes of the Rangers (allowing a Japanese male to become an American female in the adaptation) suggest some ambiguity here too.

24

The third kind of hook is the main form of aural and visual organisation in the stylised battle scenes in Power Rangers. The theme song
'Go, Go Power Rangers' orchestrates repeated pairings of musical and
visual motifs.

The most repeated elements are shots of martial-arts high-kicking
leaps, filmed from below so that the figures spin through the air;
karate-type arm movements reduced to a set of even more stylised
gestures; effects shots of the dinosaur-machines (often the same shots
repeated in different contexts) as they rise up against a lurid sky, speed
along in a trail of dust or shower electric sparks; a distinctive sound
effect, an air-slicing sound that gets repeated dozens of times per
episode (with karate movements, high kicks, sword swipes, etc.); rapid
short zooms, often outwards from Red Ranger to show the whole group;
and the 'Go, Go Power Rangers' theme in a synthesised pseudo-heavy-
metal style (more contained and without the harsher, less smoothly
integrated sound of separate instruments of the typical heavy metal
performance).

These elements are not consecutively deployed within an audiovisual
space organised around conventional narrative development and its
supporting spatial continuities. Instead they are piled on top of each
other, the space is fragmented (it is hard to know where people and
objects actually are in relation to each other except in very general
terms) and the organisation of elements is much more a choreography
of visual and aural 'hooks'. Typically the command 'dinosaur power!'
from Red Ranger initiates an extended choreography of this kind at the
climactic scenes in each episode (usually two or three per episode). With
each added cluster of motifs, from among the range listed above, the
orchestration of the 'Go, Go Power Rangers' theme becomes more
layered, building to a plateau of sustained percussive energy on top of
which the synthesiser motif ('Go, Go') continues to rise and fall in
synchronisation with the other hooks.

The layering is highly organised: individual karate-like arm movements are often choreographed across the group in conjunction with
their battle cries, the musical 'Go, Go' motif is usually synchronised with
major transformations or 'morphs', such as the combining of separate
machines into Megazord ('Bring 'em together', shouts Red Ranger), and
identically repeated shots of the group poised for action or running
towards the camera get used time and again. The overall effect is to
construct moments of predictable but exciting (however unresponsive

one might want to be, it is difficult to look away at these moments) visual and aural stimulation. Stylistically, this could be traced back to the experiments of producer–director Bob Rafelson in *The Monkees* (1966–73), which in its day took great liberties with the dominant form of US primetime television, but the specific contemporary reference points are undoubtedly MTV and *anime*.

These moments build into rapidly intercut layers, through which the entirely predictable narrative resolution is always reached; but the latter seems only minimally attractive in comparison with the rhythmic accumulation of these moments, each a little epiphany. Goodwin says of music video that its formal arrangements, 'defy certain conventions of classic realism, yet the form may still contrive to forge reading positions of great stability and coherence'.[24] It is my view that the Power Rangers videos function similarly in their most important sequences, those involving the climactic confrontations around the machines (while the contextual high-school scenes are entirely 'classic realist' in form). It is the strength of these 'reading positions' that binds children to the videos in such fascination.

Are these in fact reading positions though, or merely the positioning of a consumer in front of a demand-stimulating artefact, allowing the subsequent delivery of these consumers to Bandai, PolyGram, Grosset & Dunlap or Boxtree? This question takes us back, not only to the heart of the issues raised in the first half of this chapter, but to one of the core problematics of cultural theory during the past twenty years at least.

The textual thinness of Power Rangers, the rigid formula, the endlessly repeated visual and aural motifs, offer so little scope for anything but the most superficial of textual analyses that it would be easy to conclude there is really nothing here to be 'read', beyond the most basic and minimal forms of recognition and narrative sense. These are just advertisements, for toys and other merchandise. Anything else is mere academic over-cleverness at finding things in texts that are not there.

If the text itself cannot beef up the reading positions in this instance, what is it that holds them in place as 'reading' rather than mere 'consumption' positions? This is where we need the notion of effects, expounded above in highly abstract terms.

There are seven clusters of effects in which *Mighty Morphin' Power Rangers* is deeply implicated. The intersection or overlap among these clusters creates the stable and coherent reading positions through which children hold themselves enthralled. The seven are these.

1 *Identity effects.* There are questions here about American teenagers giving up their individuality to become Japanese-style superheroes, about the absorption of self into a team, controlled by a central male figure, and ultimately about absorption into a technology.

2 *Harmonising effects.* Those identity problems are smoothed out in the music-video-style climaxes when people and machines are finally one. But the kids can still go back to being 'typical' teenagers at high school, to suffering adult interference (the school principal) and to having to be 'good' all the time – like cleaning up litter in the corridor. This is a harmonising balancing act if ever there was one, since in their Ranger guise their battles make something of a cosmic mess!

3 *Relational effects.* What it means to be a child or an adult gets turned topsy-turvy here. In an everyday sense it is the adults who have the power, whether school principal or Zordon (who is the principal's *alter ego* in a way, issuing instructions as a disembodied head). But in the fantasy realm of the superheroes it is the kids who do all the work to save the world.

4 *Totemic effects.* The machines, suited figures and monstrous creatures are totems of power. The 'hooks' constructed around them serve to emphasise the link with the toy versions, particularly as the special effects here do not work too hard to disguise the toy-like appearance of these objects on screen.

5 *Narrative effects.* Each individual story is so minimalist and so formulaic that the weight of narrative interest is carried by the more complex meta-narrative (picked up in a repeated prologue and developed in bits and pieces within particular episodes). This grand narrative is then transportable as the context for playing with the toys, rather than simply re-enacting individual stories.

6 *Commodification effects.* The condensation of each formulaic episode around what advertisers would call the 'pack shots', the objects available as toys, reinforces the sense that these objects are being packaged for easy and pleasurable consumption. There is no getting away from that.

7 *Semiotic effects.* Here the whole world of dislocation and desperate images described by Raymond Williams as our contemporary cultural context comes into view: human inadequacy, role-playing, confusion and substitution of individuals, habitual competitive violence and destructive inevitabilities, mediated by the distinctive

hybrid American–Japanese form. Williams might have been writing the scenario outline for *Mighty Morphin' Power Rangers*.

The following chapters explore each of these effects in turn, in relation
to toys and popular culture generally. As children, toys and popular
culture have been much written about, it is important also to signpost
how the perspective being developed here might lead us to handle and
re-use in different ways some of the existing ideas about these matters.

Related research

Stephen Kline's compendious *Out of the Garden*[25] is an inescapable point
of reference; one outcome from a three-year project funded by the
Humanities Research Council of Canada, during which the research
team undertook 'quite a varied and unusual research programme
exploring separately the trends in toy-marketing, children's advertisements, television programming and play'.[26]

Kline takes as his starting-point the entirely accurate complaint that
'academic and journalistic commentaries on childhood seldom acknowledge the marketplace as a part of the matrix of contemporary
socialization or devote serious attention to how children learn those
roles, attitudes and sentiments that reinforce the consumer culture'.[27]
By exhaustively redressing the balance, Kline offers others a major
advantage – they can take as proven the role of the marketplace in this
respect. In other words, the marketplace, as one major component of
the 'formation', can be seen to have been fairly comprehensively
explored. The bulk of that work does not have to be updated or re-done
for the time being, freeing us to concentrate on other aspects of how
the 'formation' as a whole functions – the interplay among clusters of
effects, the structure of feeling, etc.

In fact the combination of detailed research into the marketplace and
the interviewing of several hundred children effectively realised for Kline
and his colleagues what direct encounters with children *can* usefully
reveal – how children learn to be consumers from the marketplace itself.
Taking this as given, it is then possible to move beyond the fact of the
linkage between the television and toy industries, what Kline refers to
as the 'direct link between the merchants and imaginative play'.[28] Kline
evokes this moving beyond in the term 'synergy':

> Television permeates children's daily activities and conversations: when we observe them arguing about GI Joe's firepower, or simulating World Wrestling Federation bouts, or staging mock battles based on Ninja Turtle heroics, or even when they tell us that they can't fall asleep without their Care Bears or that they want to grow up to be as beautiful as Barbie, synergy between television and children's wants and play fantasies is abundantly evident.[29]

There is, however, a risk of reducing the 'synergy' to the status of a mere epiphenomenon of that 'direct link'. In one sense, to discover that children ask Santa for more media-marketed toys when they are exposed to heavy doses of such marketing is only to say that children have to find objects of want from somewhere: asking Santa for a wooden truck rather than a Transformer is not to express some organic, inner-oriented need as distinct from the outer-directed response to TV marketing. The child will still have seen such a truck somewhere. TV, in part, just extends the size of the shop window. That is a link but not a 'synergy'.

Of course where the link is especially strong, as in the US, where less regulated television has led to more pervasive and undisguised TV character-marketing and licensing than in many parts of Europe, it is understandable if the link between marketing and playing seems to be all that is left. If licensed toys make up nearly three-quarters of toys purchased as opposed to, say, a third (which is close to the relative balance in the US and Britain at the moment), it is important not to dismiss fears about the consequences. Where, as is often the case, the toys are associated with narratives and imagery based on aggression and male-supremacist perspectives, it does not seem unreasonable to assume that aggression and male-dominance have found yet another way of propagating themselves. Such fears are not without foundation, and have been extensively discussed, not only by Kline (see also Miedzian and Provenzo, for example).[30]

Again, however, that is a possible set of socially-located characteristics of the _link_ between marketing and children: debating the fears that arise around those characteristics does not directly further our understanding of what Kline calls the 'synergy': 'The synergy created between television and toys through their merger within a single narrative universe . . .'.[31] Understanding the latter should be a prerequisite for debating its supposed effects (in the conventional sense of influences, as distinct from the more specialised use of the term elsewhere in this chapter). Kline asks, therefore, who or what the child is identifying with when playing with media-marketed toys, and what opportunities for exploring specific problems and related emotions those particular contexts allow? The proffered 'narrative universe[s]' are thus understood to be made up of such identifications and opportunities.

That is a good starting-point. Respondents to Kline's question about identifications and opportunities tend to fall into two camps. The extreme pessimists reply that identification is constrained either to simplistic, male-dominated perspectives, reliant on violence to solve problems, or to glamour-doll objectification, primping and posing for the invisible watcher who is always assumed to be there – whether Daddy, boyfriend or envious other girls. Thus GI Joe and Barbie. The pessimists view the opportunities to explore problems and to experience emotions as too tightly scripted in advance to allow any genuine imaginative activity; all that the child can do is copy the formulae. Extreme optimists say that play has the inherent capacity to transcend such pre-imposed limitations, to use given identifications and opportunities merely as starting points, as resources to be imaginatively reworked. They tell us not to worry so much.

Often, though, both kinds of response are offered only in the context of what Kline calls the specific 'narrative universe'. So playing with GI Joe toys is understood within that particular 'narrative universe', whether one then argues that the children are either constrained by it or transcend it. Kline himself seeks something of a sensible compromise position between the pessimist and the optimist but does so largely within this notion of an operative 'universe' around each character-licensed toy. The argument which will be pursued here is that this is only one of our seven clusters of effects. This is an important difference.

Kline's research with children revealed a looseness about both identifications and emotional experiences: seldom do children seem in any sense to be 'experiencing' the horrors they enact with war toys, for example, and having a 'favourite' character seems a better description for their loose attachments than 'identification'. This looseness allows Kline's compromise position – the conclusion that 'having fun' is sometimes not as complicated a phenomenon for children as either our hopes or fears would lead us to believe, but that none the less the pervasive influence of 'action drama and fashion pretension',[32] through GI Joe, Barbie and the like, prevents having fun from leading to the best kinds of learning that play is, in theory, capable of supporting. (Whether such potential has *ever* been widely realised is a question worth pondering.)

Once diminished in this way, play then becomes a fertile ground for the shallow and the meretricious. The link between the toy and television industries cannot bear all the blame for things that are shallow and meretricious; but it can be blamed for the diminishment that encourages them to take hold in this particular context.

Inherent in this diminishment is the disposability of the particular toy. The marketing cycle moves on, today's 'must have' is replaced and loses its appeal. Children's lives and domestic spaces are littered with abandoned toys. Many parents evidently feel a real unease, a kind of disappointed pathos, about this – but it is hard for anybody to see precisely what it means, precisely why their child's enthusiasm for play needs new material so often, why their child should be so sensitive a pick-up device for marketing pressures. Parents often detect the cues in the culture around them much later than do children and, therefore, tend to be confronted by 'I want' before they are aware of where it might be coming from, if not from their own child. When it is there, the enthusiasm seems 'real' and thus hard to resist. The great value of Kline's study is that it demonstrates so clearly what is happening here – children are being trained for consumerism. As possessions, toys have a function that may be relatively independent of how they are (or are not) played with: they naturalise acquisitiveness, they make it normal to say 'I want' and then 'this is mine'. And at that point, one part of their work is done.

And so finally, Kline's comment: 'It is not a question of "harm done" but, rather, of our failure to find ways to make the marketplace a positive cultural force in contemporary society'.[33] What has happened here is that the marketplace has been found to have filled up entirely the space of those 'narrative universes' where children and toys interact. And then it has been found wanting; a choking off of potential. If, however, we understand that space to have been marked out by only one set of effects among several, there is still room for a different form of analysis. The 'narrative universe' (of thin identifications and opportunities that merely disguise the proffered identity – that of consumer) is just another object, set up to bear the brunt of attention where the form of attention being applied can only deal with such objects. We can re-think it in terms of effects, as sketched in the opening paragraphs of this chapter. With what consequences remains to be seen.

Superficially this approach may seem similar to Brian Sutton-Smith's in *Toys as Culture*, where the marketplace is taken to be one of four relevant contexts, the others being the family, technology and education (with history lurking in the background as a fifth).[34] Valuable as Sutton-Smith's work is in all sorts of practical ways, its method is to extract the 'complexities' at work in each of these contexts and then to identify the contradictions or 'paradoxes' that result: this leads to the different social contexts in which toys appear being treated as the determining factors in the meanings that toys have. Where these meanings appear to be contradictory it is because they have their origins in different contexts. Toys are rich resources, then, because they can be used to invoke so many different meanings at different times and in different ways.

This is fine as far as it goes. But by taking these contexts as separate realms of significance (rather like the 'narrative universe' for Kline) Sutton-Smith runs the very real risk of not giving himself the methodological wherewithal to deal with their interpenetration, except in the form of contradictions. It will be useful, however, to summarise his main points about each context.

Of the marketplace, Sutton-Smith notes that a training for consumer society may be taking place through the mass marketing of toys, but leaves open the question of whether this is a training in 'distractibility' or in coping with that form of society. Of the family, he notes a socially ritualised gift relationship, but one which often seems to carry the obligation of solitary play for children – their side of the deal, as it were. Of technology, he notes that toys are 'ideoglyphs of modern object reality':[35] tools through which children indirectly handle objects in the world. Of education, he notes that when children work at understanding the world around them, it may be adults who see 'play'.

This last is worth holding on to: it may be that some of the narrow 're-enactment' play encouraged by spin-off toys, with their preformed stories to tell, is a very particular form of playing, perceived by children themselves as playing at something else, an 'original', and therefore different from the *work* which Sutton-Smith tells us we often mistake for play. And perhaps one form of 'play' can be converted into the other?

In general, Sutton-Smith's analysis throws up several resulting contradictions: are toys part of the social development of children or 'solitarizing objects'?;[36] are toys tools for learning about the world or mechanisms of escape from it?; is play something which adults see rather than something that children do? (which is not to say that children do not do something playful but rather that play is what adults see when they look at what children are doing, and it may be a misrecognition); and finally do toys incite consumerism or prepare children to deal with it as a social fact? For Sutton-Smith, where all of these contradictions intersect there is a tantalising undecidability: 'Will the plastic doll be used for mothering or to make mock of mothers?'[37] That is an immensely powerful question, and should not be underestimated. The potential for going either way is always there for Sutton-Smith (so he's on the side of the optimists, in a guarded way).

The difficulty, however, is that the always-poised-on-the-cusp place for toys within each of those sets of contradictions seems finally to be more in the eye of the critic–analyst than in the reality and materiality of a culture which appears rather more ruthless than this at deciding how things are. Sutton-Smith's analysis is invaluable, but as a statement of how things were, abstractly in a sense, before the culture pushed them one way or the other. That is another way of saying that in their actual interpenetration, the cultural contexts deployed here actually resolve many of the paradoxes which arise when they are considered separately. What is missing is the structure of feeling that runs through these sorts of context and forms the basis, in part, for their interpenetration.

Cedric Cullingford's remarkable *Children and Society*[38] demonstrates the empirical reality of a structure of feeling. It is an interpretative overview of what emerged from some two hundred interviews with British 8–11-year-olds. Cullingford has for long been among the very best of educational researchers at listening to children and at refusing to play safe with what he finds (for example by only focusing microscopically on isolable hypotheses). The result here is a resonant description of what Cullingford calls a 'mood', which is in fact very precisely a structure of feeling as Raymond Williams proposed the term.

> Children demonstrate that they have little belief in the perfectibility of human nature. In this respect they are very conservative. They witness too many examples of natural depravity to believe that society will improve . . . They see powerful arguments for competition, for distinctions between people, for choice, and know that they must look after themselves. They are aware of the larger future into which they will enter.[39] . . .
>
> Mood is especially important for children because of the ways in which they view television and overhear remarks . . . A series of images and statements cohere into a very general blur . . . There is no framework of understanding into which their reflections can be placed. It is as if children's education were dominated by the overheard remark . . . It is

not as if they see the adult world as separate and of no interest to them. On the contrary, they show such interest that they struggle hard to make sense of it in their own way.[40] . . .

Children are neither initiated into adulthood, nor kept within the 'ignorance' of childhood. They observe until the time when they are suddenly responsible for their own actions.[41] . . .

They are taught early to observe the worst forms of human behaviour, and to form the view that people are naturally bad, some in small ways and some in ways that are wholly unacceptable. But children also grow into the belief that people are unreformable. Bad behaviour warrants the threat of punishment as the only effective deterrent.[42] . . .

The sense that people should behave well to others because it is their moral duty to do so is replaced by the belief that if people did not behave well they would be punished. The pervading sense of society is that it is run through a sense of fear rather than guilt. This is the essential conservatism of these children.[43] . . .

Children's views do not consist of unrelieved gloom. They are caught up in private pleasures as well as private griefs. They are as much entertained by all their favourite programmes on television as they are reminded of the news. They know about all the acts of kindness that people do for each other and they can share their pleasures at school. But their analysis of society is a bleak one. They are not so much cynical as pragmatic. This is how the world is presented to them, not deliberately but by accident. All the previously hidden aspects of human nature, like child abuse, are now publicly shared. Children grow up in a context of awareness of what disasters take place all over the world. Those events which take place far away might not have as much salience as something that happens in the neighbourhood, but they are part of the mosaic of society. Children have to accept that it is so and make sense of their own part in society as best they can.[44]

What is especially important about Cullingford's description of evidence for such a structure of feeling is that it is not doom-mongering speculation, it is grounded in what a large number of children actually said to researchers. The interpretation is a powerful one: children making sense of the endless chatter of 'overheard remarks' that spill out to them through the now permanently open door to the adult world; doing so using the only means available, the decontextualised messages about law and order, about horror and blame, about competitiveness and pragmatism that circulate endlessly through media, home and school via channels largely established and sustained now by the media. Clearly toys are caught up in this somewhere. To the wealth of children's remarks repeated by Cullingford – 'There's the polar bear that's learned to do tricks and the Government is having rows' or 'I think all the fighting in South Africa is horrible and the cricketer who walked to Land's End raising money for leukaemia' – one is tempted to add, 'And I pulled Barbie's head off and my Power Ranger saved the world yesterday.'

If the new mode of adult–child relations, historically, is this observational one, sitting by the open door to adulthood trying to make sense of what is overheard, then the image which comes to mind is of the child absentmindedly playing with toys while keeping an eye on what's happening through that door. The threat of cognitive disintegration is inherent: of it all being just fragments without connection, of the available stories being too weak to hold the fragments together. Cullingford's book is full of examples of children repeating fragments without any semblance of order – 'The vicar's daughter that was raped . . . the swans being cleaned', girl aged 9 – except perhaps some sense that the original ordering held things apart that *feel* as if they are related.

It seems not at all unlikely that toys function in some way in relation to this disintegration and attempted reintegration. With the Lego set as a kind of pure form or paradigm, is it possible that toys are a kind of cultural construction kit – with the 'overheard remarks' gathering to this or that toy at a particular moment as children abstractedly fiddle with making sense while the chatter continues to spill over them from the adult world?

As we have seen with Williams's description of how popular culture has become caught up in a structure of feeling through its dominant images (precarious and desperate images which place it squarely into the same territory as Cullingford's), and with *Mighty Morphin' Power Rangers'* MTV-style selection from among those images, it is going to be necessary to undertake a lot of connective work before that question can be answered. Where toys might sit at any one moment within such connections is precisely the problem.

While drawing on previous insights, such as those of Kline and Sutton-Smith, their monadic analytical 'objects', whether narrative universes or cultural contexts, will have to be put back into play as clusters of effects which take up various positions at different moments in relation to those other effects – the toy, the child and the texts of popular culture which do most of the business here. The following chapter concentrates initially on identity effects, the first of seven sets in all that will be examined.

2

Toys today and the playing child

Despite the impact of computer games, the word 'tradition' hangs around toys like a ghost. Behind the excesses of consumerism there is still the idea that toys are about Christmas, about parcels under the tree on a snowy morning. The frenzied buying of toys at that time of year says something about how desperately this image is pursued. The imagery on the Christmas toy catalogues usually links this explicitly with a notion of family. There they are, spread out on the floor amidst opened parcels: father clutching the controller of a racing car set like it's a gun, mother trying to interest her daughter in the educational value of some worthy toy while the little girl instead hangs on to her toy pony with its brushable mane, and the little boy who can't decide whether to play with his new truck or his 'Terminator 2 Bio-Flesh Regenerator'. A few days later, if it lasts that long, the image undoubtedly fragments and each of these players returns to his or her relatively separate world until the next socially constructed 'family day', remembered no doubt in snapshots.[1] Or if the image becomes too badly fractured there is always Disneyland or Euro Disney to be planned for – the ultimate therapy for an ailing family self-image. To say as much is not, one hopes, undue pessimism but rather an acknowledgement of the trouble the family is in as an idea – and the toy along with it.

The roots of the 'traditional' image go deep. A Father Christmas decorative figure mass-produced in China for export to Europe and the United States in 1992 could in fact be taken for a German itinerant toy-seller of the eighteenth or nineteenth centuries, carrying a jumble of toys on his *kraxe* or backpack to sell in the mountain villages, or collecting toys made there to sell on to a wholesaler in one of the big towns.[2] We have forgotten that the toy industry began in this way, and the Christmas catalogues and greeting cards show us the North Pole instead, relocating the historical figure into a land of pure imagination to counteract its sometimes rather grubby commercialisation.

2 Christmas 1992 catalogue imagery from Beatties and Toys 'R' Us.

3 The idea of 'traditional' toys is linked to the imagery of 'small town' capitalism. Within the Disney 'tradition' nature is always cutely humanised, the beast tamed by the princess, and the social misfit reinvented as the endearing dwarf.

The 'toyshop' from this imaginary place only really exists in idealised form on Christmas cards – its nineteenth-century simplicity (before mass-produced imports) and Dickensian glow now cleverly shade over into the Disneyland notion of Main Street USA, where a turn-of-the-century bustle is of a supposedly friendly capitalism before it all went transnational and grossly impersonal. Disney toys manage symbolically to bridge the gap between the 'traditional' and the newer mass culture, despite in fact being themselves absolutely typical of the latter in terms of global marketing and profitability.

On a more up-beat note, it is worth reminding ourselves of the sheer imaginative energy which children invest in the playthings of their mass culture; and it is very much *their* culture. Whether it is Bugs Bunny flying his biplane, a toy car from some briefly popular television show, or a futuristic machine steeped in sci-fi mythology, children are playing a necessarily complex game with these objects because the meanings and other 'effects' that attach to them are culturally complex. That has always been so to a degree with toys, but contemporary popular culture increases the complexity many times over by linking toys into its networks of cinematic, televisual and print media. The purpose of this book is to unravel some of that complexity.

Even within a mass culture that is so much more fragmentary than the 'traditional' image of a family circle held together by sharing the simple meaning of toys at Christmas, there are still strong signs of the adult wanting to connect with the child through toys. The revival of *Thunderbirds* toys along with the old British puppet series on television in the 1990s is the construction of a point of contact between children on the one hand and, on the other, parents who were *Thunderbirds* fans themselves thirty years earlier – and who may even still be able to find

4 Small objects of desire, their meanings inseparable from their referents. The highly stylised figure of the *Thunderbirds* pilot from Imai of Japan predates the more recent Matchbox toy range which coincided with the revival of the TV series. The Bugs Bunny toy was made in 1988 by Ertl. The car dates from 1981 and featured in a briefly popular TV series from Warner Bros.

5 Popular culture has many byways. Doctor Who and the Dalek from English firm Dapol are immediately recognisable, but the Marvel Comics character Hulk is best known from the TV version, while a popular comic character such as the Punisher (middle), who only exists in comic-book form, is meaningful to a much narrower audience. Hulk and Punisher were made by US company Toy Biz in 1990.

some of the original toys in the attic.[3] But in general that kind of contact is more difficult to achieve. Many toys now only really have meaning for the children who read the relevant comic or have time to follow the convolutions of the relevant animated series on TV. So a toy figure of Doctor Who may be clearly enough understood by parents; but stand him beside the Punisher and we are into a murky world where the child is more adept at making meaning than most adults.[4]

A few typical examples will demonstrate how the relationship between toys and a popular culture sustained by the media evolved since the 1920s.[5] In London at that time a toyshop run by S. G. Hulme Beaman specialised in small wooden toys from which a whole stylised town could be made up. In 1925 he published the first in a series of 'Toytown' stories based on the toys. The stories were subsequently adapted for radio by the BBC to be broadcast in their *Children's Hour* slot. They were frequently re-broadcast on radio over a thirty-year period, sustaining interest in the toys, and a version was even made by Thames Television as late as 1972. Annette Mills and her puppet Muffin the Mule were even more popular on BBC television in the 1940s and in the early 1950s the toy firm Moko made 'Muffin Junior', a jointed metal puppet, for which the box art announced 'a small Muffin for you to work yourself, modelled on your favourite Television Star'.

In the United States, the Ideal Novelty and Toy Company of New York launched a Shirley Temple doll in 1934 and were overwhelmed by its success, having to increase their factory workforce by 50 per cent to cope with the instant demand. The same toy company, thirty years later, struck a deal with animation specialists Hanna-Barbera to produce a children's television series, *The Magilla Gorilla Show*, as a vehicle for promoting their toys, which then became cartoon characters. The January 1964 première saw trade advertising announce that the show 'is on the air 52 weeks a year in 150 cities advertising Ideal Toys exclusively!' In the early 1960s the Aurora toy company began manufacturing plastic construction kits of movie monsters, under licence from Universal Studios, and these proved to be enormously popular from their very first releases: Frankenstein's creature (1961), Dracula and the Wolfman (both 1962) and the Mummy (1963). Thirty years later the same licensed movie characters are still appearing as toys, such as the range of small plastic monster heads from Kidworks that can be filled with water and will then spit and squirt when squeezed! It was from 1964 onwards, though, that the number of media-related toys seemed to explode exponentially, centred on film and television 'character licensing' and TV advertising of toys. In 1964 the New York International Film and Television Festival gave its 'Best TV Commercial' award to the advertisement for the GI Joe soldier doll (called Action Man in Britain). The commercial intercut shots of the doll with documentary footage from the Second World War, just as a Hollywood war movie like *Sands of Iwo Jima* had done with shots of John Wayne. Over six million of the toys were sold that year, thanks in no small measure to the 'aura' of meanings which television evoked around the doll.

Those few representative examples could be multiplied a thousand-fold. Today it seems impossible to conceive of the toy industry as being anything other than dependent on a popular culture which shapes and structures the meanings carried by toys.[6] But behind these often superficial meanings there exist some deeply embedded and more generalised themes. Even a cursory glance at today's toys will suggest four dominant themes. There is of course the inescapable Barbie – the theme of young womanhood embodied by a doll. (We will take Barbie

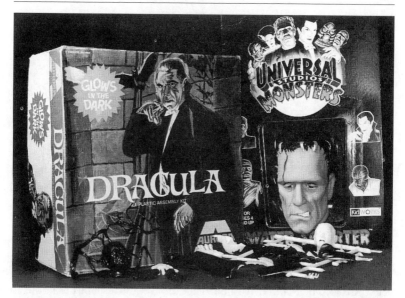

6 A 1969 re-issue of a 1962 Dracula kit with luminescent parts. Universal continue to license their classic monster characters, the 'water squirters' in the form of monster heads being a recent example.

to be representative of the type, of which there are of course other examples such as Sindy, her main rival.) There are the 'animals' – which is to say the theme of animality realised in hard plastic or soft fabric and in a million different forms. There are the toy cars and trucks, the construction sets and model spacecraft – in short, the theme of the machine. And there is the imaginary play space inside the computer's video-chip (precise thematisation of which we are perhaps not yet ready for). These will later be identified as four divergent semiotic dimensions expanding outwards from a central point – but that idea, and probably that vocabulary, may be inappropriate at this early stage.[7] So we will start with some less forbidding reflections on each of those themes.

From Barbie to Aliens

What can one say about Barbie that has not already been said? One of the most commercially successful toy lines the world has ever

7 Mattel's 1992 catalogue was full of images of Barbie's independent lifestyle. For poor Ken things don't look quite so exciting.

seen, Barbie is a plastic paradox.[8] In Italy, in 1992, girls between three and ten years old each owned seven Barbie dolls on average, in the United States it was six each, in France five, in Germany four and in the UK two. The popularity of Barbie in the 1970s (escapist glamour in a time of recession?) has translated twenty years later into young mothers wanting Barbies galore for their own daughters.[9] Yet this has occurred against a social tide questioning the plasticity and objectification of images of women in advertising and magazines. Evidently very many women who would angrily reject the notion that they, or their daughters, should be living, breathing Barbies none the less find the toy acceptable. In fact the imagery of Barbie offers much more than the stereotypical bimbo she is often made out to be by her detractors. Whether taking to the hills on her mountain bike, screeching off in her red Ferrari, wrestling her jeep off-road, scuba-diving or just camping with her friends, Barbie's vitality and independence are astonishing. Poor Ken, her 'boyfriend', can only hang around wimpishly in the background for years hoping that she can spare him a few moments (manufacturer Mattel's 1992 catalogue even shows him as a mere supermarket checkout boy past whom Barbie cheerfully breezes!).

The point, of course, is that Barbie is neither an insultingly pacified and plasticised image of woman nor an emancipated and progressive one, but rather a site of unresolved tension between these two possibilities. There is considerable merit in the criticism that dolls 'stimulate a rehearsal of women's traditional role'[10] and Barbie's kitchen and bedroom certainly seem rather blameworthy in that respect, but how 'traditional' are jeep-driving and scuba-diving for women (given all the associations of independence and mobility that go with both activities)? On the other hand, are those only signs of the glitzy escapist 'independence' of *Dallas* or *Dynasty*, television's soap-opera incarnations of woman's independence as problem, as narrative disruption, and perhaps the point of Ken hanging around in the background is precisely that Barbie is doomed to be re-claimed by him eventually? Of course the very activity of playing with a doll may be where girls rehearse the traditional domestic, mothering role, irrespective of the doll's own imagery. These are open-ended questions, not because we shouldn't try to answer them but because Barbie seems cleverly to slip out of their grasp most of the time.

What Barbie undoubtedly is, however, can be readily enough admitted: as an image of a human being she is distinctly ascetic. Whatever the external vitality of lifestyle imagery or the vibrancy of her clothes, as a body Barbie is the 'perfect' child – passionless, always smiling (with baby eyes that, strictly, are too big for her face) and with a sort of symbolic as well as actual rigidity that says this body knows its place, holds no surprises. Most hard dolls are like that, of course. Whether they represent children or adults, they offer an image of childhood rendered ascetic – little people as empty vessels, nothing troublesome within, unruly flesh mortified in plastic but smiling back at us and being good. Barbie is nothing if not good.

The next image, the next toy, presents the body encased in a machine. A plastic model kit based on a scene from the Hollywood film *Aliens*,[11] it shows us the female protagonist 'wearing' a huge mechanical–industrial robot version of the lowly fork-lift truck. The toy's nature as a construction kit to be pieced together with glue and effort, until it is more than the sum of its parts, is apt enough – in coming into existence it rehearses the nature of the machine in general. Each of these images – Barbie, and now the anthropomorphised fork-lift truck – is something like the kind of fragment Fredric Jameson identifies as so typical of contemporary culture: 'an image shard marked as narrative'.[12] In this case the original film provides a story but, in all these cases, narrativisation will be something more important and general than that local instance. For the moment, it will suffice to suggest that the body imagery here tells a story of the human subsumed by the machine. The new, extended body has the power without the expressiveness. It too displays

8 Licensed from Twentieth Century Fox Film Corporation and made in Japan for English firm Halcyon, these construction kits based on the films *Aliens* and *Alien 3* are mainstream examples of a style of model increasingly appearing as 'garage kits' – unlicensed and expensive kits catering to a near-obsessive interest in horror and science-fiction films.

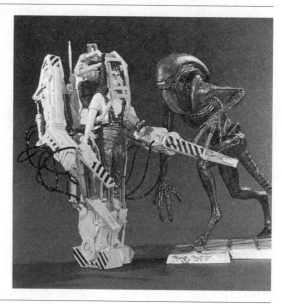

a rigidity, binding the human body to its exoskeleton, bending it to the visual rhythms of a hydraulic system.

The third example, and a further theme, follows the cinematic *Alien* trilogy into yet another medium – the video game based on *Alien 3*. Running on the Sega games console which, along with rival Nintendo, irrevocably displaced so many conventional toys from the Christmas lists between 1989 and 1993, the *Alien* game offers a murky multi-levelled world of tunnels and chambers, a penal colony in space where the female hero must rescue human prisoners from the nightmarish, slime-dripping, skeletal, eponymous aliens. These are all rendered as small but detailed figures ('sprites' in computer parlance) who move about with frantic energy. What is interesting about games like this is their illusion of an energetic 'soft' space within the rigid machine, inside the computer. There is a delicate balance between the overarching sense of a programmed world and, down at sprite level, an insubstantiality and flexibility about these little mobile characters that says they somehow flit around freely amidst the programming. It is an illusion of course, despite the apparent freedom offered by the games console (by definition, all is programmed here); but it is a powerful and oddly memorable one, of a secret life in the machine.

Toys today and the playing child

That a fearful monster with dripping jaws can be conjured up from a video-chip takes us one step towards a final theme: representation in toys of animality at its most extreme, of the beast, of the orgiastic that stands as a polar opposite to the asceticism of Barbie and in contradiction to the imagery of the machine. We need look no farther than the toy version of Mongor, the evil animal mutant from the animated television series *Thundercats*.[13] There we have in fact the extraordinary situation of the devil being given to children to play with. What a striking reversal we have here of Goya's painting in which children are given to the goat-like devil.[14] The same devil figure now becomes a mere plaything, but with connotations intact. The suggestion of animal passions unleashed is unmistakable. In fact Mongor stands at the end of a scale of animality which, in the representational universe of *Thundercats*, stretches outwards from the very human figure of Lion-O, who is something like an Arnold Schwarzenegger or a theatrical wrestler of the sort popularised by television's World Wrestling Federation – a bulging muscle-man with lion's mane. The other cat-humans include a Barbie-

9 Goya's *El Aquelarre* shows children being offered to a devil who could have been the model for Mongor, a principal villain from Lorimar Telepictures' *Thundercats*, simultaneously launched as TV series and toy range in 1986, after sophisticated market research using a six-minute test video, focus groups and telephone surveys of cable TV viewers.

lookalike called Cheetara, except that her cheetah's spots and narrowed eyes are supposed to tell us that this body is something more exciting.

What we have in the *Thundercats* toys is an especially clear set of images arrayed along the dimension of animality, with something fairly human at one end and the gorging monster, Mongor, the orgiastic animal–devil at the other. Less extreme images of the animal had multiplied along this scale long before *Thundercats* arrived of course, giving children everything from cuddly bears to little plastic pigs. In fact both Cheetara and Mongor offer children far less intimacy than toy animals typically do. It is as if in part they mark out the scale, and the *Thundercats* range then carefully fills in other toys which draw children more intimately into their imagery: so there are the good and evil 'companions', like Snarf and Ma-Mutt, who condense the imagery of Cheetara and Mongor into more playful bodies, cute and fierce respectively, but with a sort of domesticated acceptability.

Going back to the other three themes, we can see that each too is a scale of sorts. So the newly elaborate, representationally sophisticated and flexible video games, of which the marvellous *Super Mario Bros.* and notorious *Street Fighter* have been perhaps the paradigmatic examples, represent a movement away from the geometric flatness of early overtly-programmed games like *Breakout* and towards an illusion of spatial and bodily freedom in which somehow the asceticism of the doll is avoided by these jerky little minimalist electronic figures, but the orgiastic connotations of the most excessive animal toys are only fleetingly captured by an electronic excess that remains none the less encapsulated in the machine. The construction kit of the anthropomorphised 'power loader' machine from *Aliens*, which also encases the human, is perhaps only an extreme vision of a machine dimension which additionally and more comfortingly contains toy cars and trains, construction sets and plastic power tools. And Barbie's asceticism is relative to a world of dolls, some of which cry and wet their nappies. Barbie herself has some room for manoeuvre. While the pallor of the 'Plantation Belle' (a 1992 recreation of the 1959 original) is Barbie at her most rigid and contained, the 'Sun Sensation' range (including a 'shimmering golden bikini') seems more conventionally passionate, although the body now exposed looks even more as if it has rigor mortis and the only real hint of feeling remains in those 'love me' baby eyes.

Indeed it is only fully in relation to each other that these four themes settle into the positions allocated to them here.[15] Barbie is an ascetic

10 The evocative and richly symbolic imagery of *Thundercats* included more domesticated versions of the main characters.

image in so far as she is not the orgiastic Mongor. The machine from *Aliens* is monstrous but not orgiastic, being essentially rigid rather than organic. The computer game character has a machine-transcending non-rigidity and flexibility and, even though constituted by merely a few hard screen pixels, can hardly be thought of as ascetic. If we think of each of these as contributing to mapping out a space, as marking its outer limits in a sense, then a lot of other toys and their cultural associations fall into place.

From wrestlers to dinosaurs

Three further examples will suffice, particularly as they also demonstrate clearly what toys now have to do with popular culture. Each sits somewhere closer to the centre of this space than the previous examples (a semiotic space we will call it in Chapter 4) but gets pulled in various ways along one or other of those four dimensions already mapped in outline. The first example is the range of toy wrestlers based on the popular success of the World Wrestling Federation. The second is the range of little 'action figures' based on the children's animated television series *Captain Planet*, favoured by Ted Turner who, as captain of a global television news network (CNN), may have patronised a toy version of his own self-image! The final example is the dinosaur toy, a perennial favourite as they say – but especially so since the success of Spielberg's movie *Jurassic Park* in the summer of 1993.[16]

Powerplay: toys as popular culture

The US-based World Wrestling Federation revitalised the 'sport' of wrestling in the early 1990s by reorganising it as television show-business, with larger-than-life characters in extravagant costumes and a network of licensing deals embracing clothes, magazines, comics and toys. The toys reproduce in miniature characters such as Ultimate Warrior and Sgt. Slaughter, and even provide a ring for them to play in. Such characters are steeped in popular culture imagery – so, for example, Ultimate Warrior is a version of He-Man from *Masters of the Universe* (TV series and toy range) and Sgt. Slaughter of war comic characters like Sgt. Fury (themselves an influence on the famous GI Joe/Action Man toy).[17] WWF celebrity Bret 'Hitman' Hart, for instance, is a gangster in a leotard, and reappears as a five-inch plastic toy figure with a wind-up punching arm. The stylisation of violence, indeed its virtual scripting, has led indirectly to related developments such as the television programme *Gladiators*, in which male and female combatants fight ritualised battles in a public arena.[18] Inevitably too there are *Gladiators* toys and other merchandise. The imagery focused by the wrestling toys in particular gets pulled in two directions. There is a clear quality of animality in the bared teeth, the crouching postures and many of the names (such as 'Bulldog') that typify the WWF celebrities' collective image. But the ritualised and repetitive nature of what these characters do has more than a little of the video game about it. Inevitably, therefore, there are computerised versions of both WWF and *Gladiators*, replacing their animality with that other kind of energy, a programmed electronic freneticism.

Very differently, *Captain Planet* is about a group of young people recruited from various countries by Gaia, the spirit of the Earth, to be her defenders.[19] By acting together they can summon up the superhero Captain Planet; but he can also redistribute his abilities among them. 'The power is yours' is the theme of the animated television series. The influence of Japanese TV's *sentai* or superhero team shows is evident (see also Chapter 1), but the 'green' awareness is a very American variation. Of course the planet is constantly under threat from various eco-villains. The toy range consists of small plastic figures of the heroes and villains, with the vehicles they use. Looking distinctly like one of Mattel's black companions for Barbie, Gaia is not included in the toy range, but in the animated series she takes human form and has the ascetic quality to set against the excesses of the villains (and against the old 'earth mama' stereotype of the motherly black woman, one of

11 Toys based on TV wrestling and competitive spectaculars such as the *Gladiators* series revived the basic idea of the Marx company's 1930s *Popeye* boxing toy. Popeye had a proper wind-up mechanism, while the modern versions typically only have a spring-loaded arm. Unfortunately one of the few black figures among mass-produced toys in the mid-1990s is this bulging muscleman, reinforcing an old stereotype.

the few female figures whom many white male American writers seemed able to allow to be a woman in, for them, an unproblematic way – the conspicuous unreality of the 'supermodel' appears to have taken over this position, here cleverly combined with earth-spirit connotations). Among the villains, the toy incarnation of one in particular, Sly Sludge, very clearly demonstrates the pull of what we have termed the orgiastic on the meanings deployed around these little plastic figures.

Sludge runs a 'disposal' service for toxic waste but instead dumps it wherever he can. The toy is of a grossly overweight, drooping-jowled man in industrial overalls, with a huge drum of 'sludge' (which can be mixed up from a packet provided!). All the connotations of excess are there: the corpulent figure who uncontrollably and gleefully leaves his excremental sludge all over the place. Gaia's asceticism throughout is contrasted with belching chimneys and oozing pipes, and Sly Sludge

12 Barbie's friend Maoni is a near-perfect match of TBS Production's character Gaia from the animation series *Captain Planet*: an ascetic image of the black 'supermodel' as an icon of 'nature' and 'roots', without any substance that might be threatening to the white point of view.

seems a clear example of this orgiastic threat to proper self-restraint. The animality of this dimension is reinforced by a second villain, Verminous Skumm, who is half man, half giant sewer-rat. The clean-living young heroes, however, rely a good deal on high-tech machines to effect their global duties, such as their submarine with huge robotic arms or their 'geo-cruiser' (solar-powered flying car), both available in toy form. They sail above the messier world where the supermodel is surrounded by Skumm and Sludge, and just manage to remain untouched by the sexual anxieties that seem barely disguised there. So, more generally, the meanings that cluster around these toys are pulled in various directions by the overarching themes we have already identified.

If we place a male figure at the central point and imagine those four themes or dimensions extending outwards like the diagonals of a quad-rat, then what we have is a notable structure of meanings within which toys appear to 'test' the nature of male identity by pulling it first in one direction, then in another, in relation to animality or the machine, in

13 The Sly Sludge figure, made by Tiger Toys of the United States, comes with packets of powder that make up into 'toxic sludge' to ooze out of his oil can.

relation to the asceticised female or the orgiastic beast. These all represent, given the male at the centre, a difference in relation to which that maleness is defined. Perhaps the perfect representation of more generalised otherness, to the child's mind, is the dinosaur (before the dimensions of difference introduce their male/female, human/animal, organic/machine distinctions and anxieties). As a real creature but somehow so remote as to be mythical, the dinosaur can and does take on whatever shape one's dreams or nightmares of otherness require. Although inaccurate by millennia, the image of primitive man somehow walks among the dinosaurs – they are the monstrous otherness from which he emerges into history. As toys 'dinosaurs' are an appropriately malleable category. In addition to models of actual dinosaurs in seemingly endless variants there are dinosaur-shaped robots, mechanical dinosaurs that transform into military tanks, or the example of an ordinary plastic dinosaur from a toy manufacturer in Southeast Asia who, finding sales flagging, cut off its head and replaced it with that of a two-headed monster painted bright red. And in the toys based on the Walt Disney Company's television series *Dinosaurs* they even take on the personalities of an American family.

14 Dinomania or Dinojunk? Amidst a merchandising bonanza that embraces everything from dinosaur biscuits to hundreds of cheap plastic toys, the more interesting items include holograms, robotic dinosaurs that transform into armoured vehicles, a radio-controlled dinosaur capable of walking on two legs and Disney's satirical dinosaur family who suffer the tribulations of suburban life. The archetypal dinosaur toy remains the gaping-jawed carnivore as all-purpose embodiment of a child's best/worst fantasies of power.

Male identity as organising principle

Dinosaur toys are only the most adaptable and re-usable forms of otherness. The more closely defined examples of toy imagery already discussed here each pins down the meaning of otherness, repositioning it within dimensions of difference, more precisely than the dinosaur allows. That it is a male body at the centre, and not a female, now seems an inescapable fact. It is Captain Planet at the centre, not Gaia (she doesn't even get to be a toy), although she nevertheless pulls his identity a little towards her own asceticism; but then there are also the likes of Sly Sludge advertising a gorging, careless excess. So male identity can have it both ways.

Similarly, in donning the anthropomorphic machine, the female figure inside that toy (representing Ripley in *Aliens*) is remaking her body into that of a male machine (or a machine for males) in so far as all these toy machines, from cars to construction sets, have been identified as icons of an essentially male world (it being unlikely that any girls will have bought or been given the plastic construction kit of Ripley in the machine). The video arcade is a miniature version of that male world – relatively few girls venture into its shadows and when they do they know they are on boys' territory (which can have its own very real transgressive pleasures, of course).[20] So a game like *Alien 3*, for home use, takes the male at the control console as the norm; its mode of address locates him out there. It is the male figure Lion-O at the centre in *Thundercats*, the toys then arraying themselves outwards along the dimension of animality until Mongor the devil stands as its very essence. Finally, the little plastic wrestlers and their real counterparts (not that there's much 'real' about them) perfectly symbolise the game of male identity that we are seeing in all these other examples too.

Is Barbie, then, part of a game of male identity? Leafing through Mattel's catalogue it seems as though Barbie lives entirely in her own enclosed world, but in the life of the child Barbie has to live in what is very much an intertextual universe. It is in that intertextuality that we have to look for an answer. This becomes clear if we place Barbie alongside a couple of representative figures from other texts, the Danny doll from New Kids on the Block and the Dylan doll from *Beverly Hills, 90210*. The New Kids were, of course, a pop group on whom an animated television series was based, along with all the other merchandising spin-offs, from books to toys. *Beverly Hills, 90210* was a successful television series integrating soap-opera elements concerning a group of Californian teenagers and their families into an episodic series format, and has spawned an equal quantity of material in other forms, most notably a popular series of paperback novelisations, a cosmetics range and the set of dolls.[21] The importance of the meanings attached by textual association to dolls like these is attested by the fact that Christmas 1992 saw the Dylan doll selling for four times the price of the Danny doll: the New Kids were a declining phenomenon and *Beverly Hills, 90210* very much on the rise at the time. You don't get anything more for your money than these meanings, in that the dolls themselves are strikingly similar as objects.

Barbie's Benetton 'look' was also very much an image of the moment.

15 Intertextual Barbie: even in her sexiest clothes Barbie is unconvincing as an erotic body; but, in the play of meanings around her, teenage sexuality finds other points of contact. The smouldering Luke Perry doll (Mattel) is counterposed by the wholesome fun of the New Kids (Hasbro). Can Barbie make up her own mind about which she prefers? The Luke Perry doll is made from a soft, warm, pliable plastic rather than the more usual hard shell.

A controversial advertising campaign had brought the company notoriety, and the success of the Formula 1 motor racing team they sponsored had given flesh to 'Ken' in the form of the young star of the Grand Prix circuits Michael Schumacher, whom Benetton heavily promoted. Mattel joined in by providing Ken with an appropriate motor racing outfit, complete with Benetton sponsorship patches. It is not difficult to see how this dense cluster of meanings begins to take shape according to the themes already identified.

The motor racing connotations give us the machine as an appallingly easy sign of masculinity. The New Kids' imagery is archetypally playful: they are represented as fun-loving and visually exciting but entirely safe. Danny's motto of 'Eat healthy, stay healthy', according to their official 1992 Annual, is anything but orgiastic and, in similar fashion, the band is represented visually as 'sprites', little dancing spinning figures, all physical dynamism and sparkling primary colours in their

16 Intertextual Ken: Barbie's friend has a Grand Prix racing outfit with Benetton logo to match her Benetton clothes. Benetton have their own successful racing team and a real-life 'Ken' in Michael Schumacher, heavily promoted in the company's fashion and lifestyle magazine *Colors* until his move to Ferrari in 1996.

videos. The television animation sparks and crackles with energy, blends live action seamlessly with cartoons, and often has a video game quality of electronic freneticism about it. Dylan from *Beverly Hills, 90210,* on the other hand, is something else entirely. The undercurrent of sexuality on the prowl, which has always defined this ex-alcoholic character in the TV series, began to be more explicitly reinforced by other media. Perhaps the clearest example is the 1992 issue of the supposedly sexuality-celebrating magazine *For Women,* with its cover picture of actor Luke Perry as Dylan and the caption 'The New Sex God'.[22] When the character persuaded the series' resident good-girl Brenda to 'go all the way' with him in a hotel bedroom, moral-majority protestors in the United States were outraged.

Barbie becomes, in short, rather like the female protagonist from *Aliens* in this one crucial respect: she too becomes a body encased in a male machine – a meaning machine. An enclosing structure of intertextuality such as is outlined here defines her place. A key issue pursued by this book is whether the child is similarly positioned by the toy industry as a whole, through its now habitual participation in the meanings of popular culture more generally. That question is inescapably overshadowed by the single most pressing fact about toys today – the dominance of the video game console.

The video game

In 1992 Japanese video game giant Nintendo for the first time made profits that exceeded the earnings of Hollywood movies in total for that year; a phenomenally sudden reorientation of what we think we mean by the term 'popular culture'. Sega, the other major company in the field, earned in that period a third as much as Nintendo but has been catching up fast. Atari, US originator of the video game, began digging up old software it had stockpiled in the Nevada desert a decade earlier in the hope of capitalising on renewed interest. Atari had run into difficulty because its market became saturated with poor-quality games. The new companies have instead tightly controlled the flow of games for their consoles (licensing and packaging everything themselves), keeping both quality and prices high.[23]

Even more successfully, both Nintendo and Sega have marketed directly to children and young adults. Much previous video game marketing was based on selling them as fringe leisure benefits of fundamentally more 'useful' computer technology – an appeal to parents' better instincts – but the new game systems are unashamedly sold as toys. Sega's television advertisements revel in being barely intelligible to adults who do not understand the games. But as video-game-fixated teenagers turn into young adults, so the range of titles expands to include golf simulators, adult mystery games and the like. The move towards CD-ROM based systems (Sega 'Saturn', Sony 'PlayStation', Panasonic '3DO' and Apple/Bandai 'Pippin'), with their hugely increased capacity and audiovisual sophistication will undoubtedly sustain and extend this whole area of 'play', as video and computers inexorably converge in a unified multimedia technology.

Now the point I want to make about this (and will explore more fully in the final chapter) is that the video game as a cultural form can best be understood in relation to toys as a whole. We are dealing here with a more general system of meanings – sustained by the toy industry, by the history of toys and by our very concept of 'childhood' – of which the video game is now a part.[24] The concentrated 'mode of address', directly targeting in both the selling and design of games the 8–15-year-old male 'game boy' who constitutes some 60 per cent of the market, would appear to have led to the flattening of a potentially rich intertextual space into the basic routines of the 'zap and jump' game. Movies, television, history and sport have all been raided for themes and characters; but the results, while superficially vibrant and attractive, look to non-players in particular like so many endless variations on the same basic game format of beating the opponents and progressing through various stages or levels of complexity in terms of eye–brain coordination challenges.

What this remarkable technology could support is a much richer play space and with it a position for the player less rigidly tied to a simplistically projected male identity. In the final chapter I will suggest that, in fact, the whole system of meanings and other effects generated around toys today makes available some of the resources for such play and for more diverse, open and flexible identity effects – but that the video game simultaneously opens up this space and closes it down, reinforcing in the end the central identity effect, the configuring of dimensions of difference around male identity reductively defined. To understand the nature of the resources, the space that is temporarily opened up, entails understanding what toys are, where they have come from and how they are played with.

In the theoretical terms of the preceding chapter, the dimensions of difference which have been described are a set of identity effects – each toy is simultaneously located by one or other dimension and contributes in turn to the (re)production of those dimensions. In turning from this first set of effects to those that reside in play itself, it has to be said by way of qualification that this book is not exhaustively about play. As both a social discourse (i.e. almost as much written about and discussed as actually done) and a field of research, this is vast and complex, and even adequately summarising the main approaches to an understanding of play would take more space than is available here.[25] On the other hand it would hardly be sensible to write about toys without considering in some way the nature of play. So the following notes are trawled from the vast literature on the subject and offer ideas about play that will connect in productive ways with the other kinds of analysis pursued in subsequent chapters.

The developmental approach to the playing child

A recent collection of essays functions as a useful survey of research, principally by psychologists, into play and child development. All share the view that playing is, for children, 'a critically important feature of their development of cognitive and emotional skills'.[26] The developmental approach to play has always been much concerned with skills – at the possible cost, it could be suggested, of often not seeing the wood for the trees. Much of the psychological research tells us a great deal about the development of motor skills through the manipulation of toys, the development of interactional language skills through playing with others, the development of emotional skills through winning and losing (and cheating?) in games, and so on. These much-researched details, however valuable as such, do not add up to the totality of what is going on between children and toys. If they did, psychologists would not flounder quite as much as they do when confronted by the major 'issues', such as the relationship between toys and violence. Of course, the real problem lies with the social expectation that such research should provide answers to these (socially formulated and value-laden) 'issues'. Psychological researchers are not themselves to blame for this mismatch.

In the cited collection of essays based on such research, Goldstein offers the evocative description of play allowing the child 'to make sense of the large, the looming, and the loud in her world by forming manageable units'.[27] This notion of the manipulable 'units' (more abstract than actual toy objects), from which something can be constructed, will be carried forward here into consideration of the culturally-informed 'units' from which children make something. Pellegrini and Jones add the important point that 'children's interactions with specific toys, rather than being defined by the physical props themselves, are a result of the ways in which the participants themselves define the toys'.[28] So the 'units' are, at the very least, toys plus cultural associations plus context-bound definitions of the original objects. Where those definitions are largely derived from parental attitudes and other social sources (school, older children, etc.), it is important to note, as several of the contributors to the cited volume do, that perceived 'aggression' in play or 'gender-stereotyping' may tell us as much about the defining forces at work as about any inherent characteristics of particular toys: thus, for example, 'perceived differences between boys' and girls' play depend on who is doing the observing'.[29] There is then a socially convenient sleight of hand involved (convenient for those who want easy targets to blame) when the defining factors are dissolved and the toys themselves are accused of inherently generating the characteristics in question. They may carry or relay these characteristics, but that is not the same thing.

Another common theme in several of these essays is what Wegener-Spohring calls the 'sensible dramaturgy'[30] or organised and regulated structure which children themselves impose on what they do with toys, as a defining feature of their own awareness that they are playing. Goldstein notes the effect of this on apparently aggressive play: 'In fact, the most aggressive children appear *least* likely to engage in play fighting . . ., perhaps because highly aggressive children violate the shared, if unstated, rules of aggressive play, particularly the idea that one is not supposed to injure playmates.'[31]

This nuanced understanding of the dramaturgy through which 'manageable units' are staged and choreographed has much to offer. It puts clear frames around the toys themselves and relocates questions about stereotyping and aggression: we have to ask at which level of 'framing' such effects are actually at work. Thus Smith, for instance, notes the frequency of 'pretend aggression' accompanied by 'positive . . . or neutral facial expressions', the incidence of 'real aggression' directed at toys themselves (hitting teddy while saying 'ouch!'), and the (rarer in his study) cases of child–child real aggression during play.[32] These all represent different framing levels and have to be understood differently. So too with differences in boys' and girls' preferences for certain toys and types of play – as Pellegrini and Jones put it, 'children, as they interact with adults and each other around a specific toy, define the meaning of the toy for that particular situation'.[33] This framing and reframing of toys relocates them inevitably within the larger social construction of gender (and, incidentally, raises the possibility of reframing interventions designed to challenge the dominant constructions).

How parents behave as men and women, how boys' and girls' rooms are decorated, how perceptions of gender in the world outside the home infiltrate that environment – all of these things contribute to the framing of specific situations in play. Of course, those defining factors will also include the deliberate marketing and selling of toys complete with preformed meanings about aggression and gender. Advertisements show girls caring for their dolls and toy ponies, boys acting out a superhero adventure – and, as Goldstein points out, the very distinction between, on the one hand, adopting a role in relation to a toy person or creature, and, on the other, *being* that person or creature in play, is itself a socially constructed gendered distinction. In this way of understanding toys, however, the toys themselves are not made to carry the blame for everything that is held to be wrong with the forces that define those toys.

More generally, what emerges from Goldstein's editorial overview of this set of useful essays, is the 'metarepresentational ability' which develops as the child itself moves out through these framing levels. Not only do the surrounding frames or horizons (derived from other children, parents, home, school, media, society) define what is happening in every instance of play, but they define at the same moment the possibility for the child itself of reframing the act of play in order to grasp, in some indirect way, pertinent aspects of the defining frames. Goldstein does not quite claim as much, limiting himself to the view that children discover 'different ways of manipulating mentally the representations of objects and situations'.[34] But he is drawing on Leslie's work[35] which does suggest that a 'decoupling' from the primary object occurs, enabling 'fuzzy' representations of that object to pull in what Leslie calls 'possibilities'. My suggestion is that, where such possibilities are in fact features of the various available frames, it is the frames themselves which the child is exploring 'metarepresentationally'. I will try to demonstrate how this might occur in subsequent chapters, and we will return to Leslie's theory in the final chapter. First, it is necessary to look at the underlying assumptions of the developmental approach itself, from which these insights have been gleaned.

Conformity or coping?

An inescapable fact strikes anyone who contrasts research into play with theories of culture generally: much more than the latter, the former is dominated by a notion of the self striving to achieve wholeness and balance. A humanistic psychology has found itself very much at home in the field of play research. The child is discovered to be using play in order to explore adaptively his or her relations with the world, to heal emotional wounds, to try out in safety some of the things that go on in the adult world and to reconcile him/herself to them. When things go wrong, 'play therapy' can intensify in a more directed way these 'natural' functions of play. The goal of play, whether therapeutically assisted or not, is then satisfactorily to adjust and stabilise the child's relationship with the world that surrounds him or her, to help build a self that is in harmony with its surroundings. Cultural theorists more generally have tended to view such harmony as merely conformity to the given reality of a particular society at a particular moment in time, however unkind, unfair or unpromising that reality might be to those who accept it. So a 'harmonising' notion of culture generally as the symbolic resolution of social tensions and the securing of conformity has been challenged by many cultural theorists who celebrate the disruptions, the nonconformity, the faultlines that to them can energise culture and offer people the resources for imagining better ways of being and of doing things. Where there are such faultlines in the culture is play then instead, inevitably and necessarily, only about building psychic earthquake defences?[36]

It is important briefly to juxtapose these two fields of inquiry because it is easy to take it for granted that a happy, conforming, balanced self is indeed a worthy goal to have identified within childhood play. It seems nonsensical to suggest that we might value instead processes by which the child comes to be 'out of synch' with or estranged from the reality of its social surroundings. What is confused here is perhaps our very way of posing the question. Erik Erikson has written informatively about the child as earthquake, gleefully knocking down some toy edifice: 'The almost manic pleasure with which children watch the collapse in a second of the product of long play labour has puzzled many, especially since the child does not appreciate it at all if his [sic] tower falls by accident or by a helpful uncle's hand.'[37] By making himself or herself the source of disruption the child's apparently destructive play achieves an effect 'which counteracts in childhood as it alleviates in later life the human readiness for bewildered reaction and rage'.[38]

In other words, it is not destructiveness that is being denied here, but rather bewilderment as an adequate reaction; not the collapse of the tower but the sense of its happening outside one's influence that is being dealt with. Leaving the construction intact for father to see when he comes home would only be to value its positive features, the fact of its creative existence, and would not achieve the deeper goal which is to admit the seeming inevitability of a destructiveness waiting in the wings. For the child, getting in first with his or her own destructiveness compensates for having it happen outside one's control – that lack of control being the real source of rage and bewilderment rather than the loss of the constructed object.

Rather than defending against or denying the earthquake the child wants, temporarily and safely, to be the earthquake! Forgoing the simple happiness of showing off its construction, in the interests instead of dealing in its own way with its destruction, the playing child may be accepting a certain unhappiness ('there then, it's gone!') in order to avoid the uncontrollable feelings that might arise when someone else topples the construction or it just falls down all by itself.[39] If the outside world, to which the child is supposedly conforming through play, should be full of destructiveness and threat, then by dealing with it 'unhappily' (though with a kind of gleeful *savoir-faire*) the child is not necessarily conforming but rather avoiding that ultimate bewilderment which makes the psychoanalyst's patients sick. It may then be that play is one way of avoiding a later 'sick' relationship with one's social surroundings, while the degree of 'harmonising' of self and surroundings remains relative to the extent that the world perceived by the child may be more or less occupied by bad things that cannot happily be drawn into such a 'harmony'.

The harmonising object (from steamboat to Mr Atomic)

One argument posed by this book is that the bad things out there, as perceived by children, are now so numerous that toys are increasingly impelled to take on forms capable of drawing those things into childhood play, in order to satisfy the child's determination to deal with them (such 'determination' being a structural feature of play rather than a conscious aim). In other words, childhood requires objects that are flexible enough to bring into some kind of balance a variety of feelings and meanings which might otherwise have remained disturbingly at odds with each other. An image of play relatively undisturbed by bad objects is evoked by Erikson when he recalls Mark Twain's character Ben Rogers (from *Tom Sawyer*). As Tom paints the fence, Ben chugs up the street pretending to be a steamboat, complete with sound effects and shouted instructions to the crew, stopping only to offer mock sympathy for Tom's plight:

> My clinical impression of Ben Rogers is a most favourable one, and this on all three counts: organism, ego and society. For he takes care of the body by munching an apple; he simultaneously enjoys imaginary control over a number of highly conflicting items (being a steamboat and parts thereof, as well as being the captain of said steamboat, and the crew obeying said captain); while he loses not a moment in sizing up social reality when, on navigating a corner, he sees Tom at work. By no means reacting as a steamboat would, he knows immediately how to pretend

sympathy though he undoubtedly finds his own freedom enhanced by Tom's predicament. Flexible lad, we would say.[40]

As always with Twain, the 'harmonising' potential of the available cultural resources – the imagery and reassuring connotations of the steamboat – involves us in a kind of nostalgic reading, not because we recall some such world but because we want to recall that easy reconciliation of self and world. For today's Ben, however, the equivalent would be Captain Jean-Luc Picard at the helm of a starship (from television's *Star Trek: the Next Generation*).[41] The culturally available imagery for playing with now far outstrips any present reality, except that it suggests something of the unbounded forces loose in that world, from hugely powerful technologies to the uncanny abilities of those who understand and direct them. Picard seems like a disembodied brain in the machine, his authority somewhat monstrous when compared with a Mississippi steamboat skipper. The point is this: the modern version of such play-acting could barely hope to 'harmonise' around the image

17 Illustration of Tom and Ben by True Williams from the Collins edition of *The Adventures of Tom Sawyer*. The nineteenth-century engraving of a steamboat pilot-house evokes a very different sense of mastery from that carried by the Captain Picard toy from Playmates of Hong Kong, based on the character from *Star Trek: The Next Generation* (1992). The American tinplate steamboat from the 1880s is typical of a popular genre of toys of that period.

of that starship captain all the complex meanings evoked by such an image. Too much is going on there for this to be achieved, so play must have some other 'aim'. This is not an unsupported assertion. In part, the present book will develop an argument about a consequent 'opening' through play on to a complex field of cultural resources.

The notion of play having to deal with bad, unharmonious things perceived by the child is a colloquial restatement of a position developed by psychoanalysts interested in object relations, an interest which takes its original bearings from the work of Melanie Klein, who analysed playing children extensively (although Klein herself remained very close to Freud's not very helpful psychobiology, a tendency to root everything in instincts and drives).[42] Previously taken to mean only people as perceived by the child, the term 'object' was extended by the Kleinian approach: 'Not just people, but all experiences and situations are internalized.'[43] Toys become something of a half-way point in this, mediating between the internal world of the child and the more remote objects of the outer world. Toys are, therefore, deeply implicated in what Greenberg and Mitchell, principal contemporary synthesisers of the object relations approach, very promisingly call 'blending': 'Early internal objects of a harsh and phantastic nature are constantly being projected onto the external world. Perceptions of real objects in the external world blend with the projected images. In subsequent reinternalization the resulting internal objects are partially transformed by the perceptions of real objects.'[44] (The spelling 'phantasy' conventionally refers to Klein's extension of the escapist or substitutive notion of fantasy to embrace an inescapable and essentially positive creation of mental objects, from the nightmarish to the comforting.) For Klein, everything a child feels is attributed to good or bad objects. Some will be internal, like monsters in the night, while others will be external, like the parents (or for very young children merely parts of the parents); but many will be a 'blending' of the two. Without excavating back as far as the first internal objects (the Freudian ground) we can enter the spiral of object relations at a higher level where 'blending' is most fully achieved.

Erikson rather humorously recounts the efforts of a class of psychiatric social-work students to interpret Ben Rogers's steamboat game. Various traumas and frustrations are invented to account for the satisfactions of play-acting the steamboat (including the possible connection between bedwetting and the river!), but Erikson's point is only that, whatever the inner phantasy that impels Ben (such as the harshness of adolescent self-perception, of being 'different parts which move at different rates'), Ben has in fact found for himself an object that blends what might otherwise have remained fragmentary and unsynchronised. The 'machine god of his day', the steamboat captain, allows that harmonious blending, and the fictional image of Ben is something we still find deeply attractive, as he chugs his untroubled way down the dusty street of nostalgia (nostalgia for a harmony perhaps increasingly difficult, if not impossible, to attain).

The fictionally achieved reinternalisation of a harmonious external object (the steamboat) then pulls together the fragmentary internal 'objects' (the self-image of a gangling body, a dilemma about whether one is captain or merely crew of one's own progress, an awe of the things of a new machine age, etc.). This is a fictional example, perhaps because it is only in fiction that such a smooth and felicitous blending is possible. But of course that is precisely the point which we can carry forward into a consideration of how toys are now inextricably linked to the fictions of a popular culture: the new fictionality of toys makes them more powerful objects in reconciling for the child inner and outer worlds that are so much harder to bring into balance than they were for a fictional Ben Rogers.

To take only one eerie example of an object that appears to have blended those worlds against the odds, we might consider the case of 'Mr Atomic'. This toy of the 1950s is unnervingly reminiscent in shape and connotations of 'Fat Man', the nuclear bomb dropped on Nagasaki on 9 August 1945. It is an even more striking example when we know that 'Mr Atomic' was manufactured in Japan for export to the United States (the Cragstan company identified on the toy's body being the US distributor). The monstrousness of 'Fat Man' takes on a more thinkable scale as a fat little robot called 'Mr Atomic' that might have been labelled 'return to sender'.

It will finally be argued in this chapter that the dominant mode of adult–child relations in this century has tended largely to deny children access in their mental lives to inner reflections of what are perceived to be 'bad' objects in the outer world, often breaking the spiral of projection and reinternalisation described above: the child cannot, without guilt, think of him- or herself as lazy, dirty or aggressive; but of course the toy soldier can engage in the most awful trench warfare in the back yard and Barbie can lie in bed all day. They can also be punished by

18 Mr Atomic, made in Japan for export to the United States, shown here with a diagram of the Fat Man bomb: the apocalyptic connotations are now very much part of Japanese popular culture. Robot toys have been one location for a sense of technological displacement of the human. The Japanese robot figure on Mr Atomic's left represents the armoured suits worn by people as protection in the 'Gundam' saga of animation videos. Hollywood's *Terminator* films, with toys from Kenner (right), develop these themes into cyborg figures, half human and half machine, with bodies that go molten. The Kenner toys even include 'debris accessories' such as melted girders.

the child for doing so, just as a child might chastise a doll for being frightened of an imaginary lion in the night.

Characteristics of play

Meanwhile, there are some other things that we can usefully glean from the great deal of research which has been undertaken into the nature of play. Six key observations can be derived from one important source. Unlike more narrowly academic researchers, John and Elizabeth Newson have written about toys on the basis of their long and detailed experiences of working with children and are therefore especially reliable guides to the principles and practices of play (although a moralising tone is their own contribution, which one can take or leave – it has led Elizabeth Newson recently to adopt a narrowly censorious stance, to which we will come back in Chapter 4).[45] They make the useful point, for example, that although play may be intended to achieve something it will typically be pursued rather 'aimlessly' in the sense that it will have a superficially free-wheeling, improvisational quality. (Playing a rule-governed board game is, therefore, not playing in this fuller sense.) Indeed, goals may only emerge as a result of such improvisation, leading to a progressive narrowing down or focusing of activity. Playing with a doll in a loosely structured way may evolve into a very definite ritual of washing and dressing, etc. As part of this process, objects may take on temporary but very specific meanings. Thus, toys are infinitely adaptable and can take on meanings other than those they originally came with, and indeed any object can temporarily become a toy.

As a result, what we might call the 'modality' of the toy, its degree of representational accuracy and realism, is itself highly adaptable: 'Replica cars and animals mix in happily with pipe-cleaner dolls, and all are made to inhabit a fantasy city in which wooden bricks, cotton reels, match-boxes and old cardboard tubes are eked out by the scale-model steel bridges borrowed from an older brother's electric railway.'[46] Indeed this jumbled effect is distinctively appealing to most children, even if it offends adult aestheticism: as the Newsons say, 'sometimes perhaps we overdo the "plain polished wood" philosophy'.

The Newsons have distinguished a category of what they call 'hypnotic' playthings within toys more generally. Swings, spinning tops, so-called 'snowstorm' glass spheres and similar playthings exert a sensory attraction that seems to precede the assignment of much meaning to the activity, achieving a withdrawal for the child from the demands for attention made by the everyday environment. It seems likely, therefore, that most toys have to achieve something of this effect even if less noticeably – effectively displacing the child's attention from his or her immediate reality.

There is also the important fact of ownership itself. Children want to be able to say 'this is mine'. Dealing with homeless or institutionalised children, John and Elizabeth Newson offer a poignant reflection on 'what terrible destruction we do to their sense of identity if we deprive them of the experience of possession'.[47] We might add, however, that the other extreme will be marked by consumerist excesses – another kind of 'terrible destruction'.

Analysing the behaviours of infancy in particular has led the Newsons to identify what they term the child's 'happening-hunger'. Children need things to happen and are impatient of the adult temper which, from time to time, simply wants things to stop happening. Many things can count as happenings, and in fact playing becomes a way of generating happenings when none are forthcoming from other sources. Happenings feed the growing mind and have to display numerous characteristics to achieve this properly, but one stands out. With babies, mothers will often intuitively steer happenings to achieve a 'we got it right!' effect, such as building up through tone of voice and timing to the moment when a wooden block fits into the right hole. Subsequently, happenings generated by play seem often to have an underlying 'right' scenario, even if there is a good deal of surface improvisation, and children can get irritated by attempts to deviate too far, as if the happening has then degenerated into random events.

Although they do not identify it as explicitly as this, the Newsons' work is full of accounts of what we might call an 'Escher' effect in play, referring to the artist's preoccupation with a reality that endlessly chases its own tail, that reproduces itself within itself. Two examples will make this clear. In a doll's house a child carefully arranges a doll in the miniature bed and then uses a matchbox to make a smaller bed for a smaller doll to set beside the first one. Whether this is intended to be a baby in bed or a doll for the doll, the effect is the same – to set up a moment of potentially infinite regress with the real world as the outer frame and then a series of worlds within worlds. The key thing about this is that it allows the child to occupy at any one moment a world that is more real than the next one in, as it were, without having to occupy the 'real' real world. A child talking about what frightens her doll makes this effect even clearer. As the Newsons say, who is talking about whom in the following example?

'Er – yes – when she's in bed, she says "I'm frightened of a lion coming in the night!" – and that's not true. It won't, will it? She puts her head under the blanket so the lion can't get her; and I say "It's not true, there isn't a lion." And she really knows there aren't a lion, truly, and she's making a joke and thinking it is. So I try to tell her, there's no wolf and there's no animals, and they're not anywhere, and I know there perfectly aren't. I know very well, don't I?'[48]

Play's characteristics modified

Now what is intriguing about the proliferation of toys based on popular culture, and supported by television, comics, etc., is that such toys interfere with all six of those important observations about how play functions. This has led Elizabeth Newson ultimately to condemn contemporary culture's impact on children's play, but there may be another way of understanding the following 'interference'.

1 The aimlessness of play and the discovery of goals is now subject to a more readily available sense of direction – to re-enact with toys what one has read in a comic or seen on television, for instance.
2 The 'realism' or otherwise of the toys has now to do with the accuracy with which they reproduce the appearances familiar from other media; a plastic bottle that might once have served as a spaceship won't do as a representation of the starship 'Enterprise'.
3 The subtle effect of having one's attention displaced from reality is now achieved by the aura of meaning which a particular toy derives from its cultural references. Try looking at a little plastic doll of Captain Picard from *Star Trek: the Next Generation*: there is an irresistible wandering of attention into one's memories of the character from the series. Indeed without those meanings, the functionality of the doll as a toy would be seriously in question – a small plastic figure of a balding man!
4 Ownership has become a more complex issue. The Picard doll is one of a series and there is huge pressure on a child to own them all. This is more than the familiar compulsion to collect – the meanings that surround the Picard figure are only fully realisable if one has the other key figures from his crew and a few of the familiar villains. Conceivably, the Picard toy could be played with separately, perhaps having him chased by a large plastic dinosaur, but the child is likely to feel that this isn't what is 'meant' to happen.
5 In fact the 'happenings' which such toys facilitate have a new but largely given complexity – it is the narrative complexity derived from other media (explored in Chapter 4). Getting these happenings right has become a matter of judging their narrative appropriateness, given a knowledge of characters, plots, and so on.
6 So the 'Escher' effect of levels of reality across which the child moves has now been structured around a given level of fictional

narratives which may, through intimate familiarity, seem very 'real' to a child.

In considering these six key points of 'interference' in play, we should bear in mind the argument posed above that the fictional can allow a more felicitous blending of internal and external objects than may be attainable more directly.[49] May it be the case that these apparent interferences, disturbing how play would otherwise function, are ways of making play more efficient, given its increasing difficulty in grasping what is going on out there? To recapitulate briefly on a plausible understanding of how toys can function within object relations generally: experiencing feelings that are difficult to deal with and/or sensing that all is not well 'out there', the child generates his or her own internal objects capable of giving shape to a more generalised anxiety; in turn these inner friendly or threatening monsters are projected on to objects in the world which remain then only partly themselves and are partly understood by the child in their monstrous guise; where appropriate toys are available they will tend to carry a significant load in terms of those internalisations and projections; as this process continues the inner and outer objects are gradually reorientated in relation to each other until some satisfactory balance is achieved. 'Satisfactory' may mean only a state in which the child is not bewildered by the things that make him or her unhappy – not necessarily the same as a conformist adaptation in which those things are now happily accepted. Toys embedded in and opening onto the massive resources of a popular culture seem to be important props in achieving such a satisfactory state.

The pretence of being good

If we are in any doubt about the anxiety, perhaps even the dread, which the looming outside world and the reciprocal inner world of feelings persistently occasion in children, we need look no farther for confirmation than Alice Miller's writing, particularly *The Drama of Being a Child*.[50] There we are shown the child of the mid-twentieth century having great difficulty in forming internal 'objects' of things in the world that cause him or her anxiety – because, in doing so, things would have to be admitted that adults forbid as badness in the child. Miller offers us the voice of that child: 'What would have happened if I had appeared before you, bad, ugly, angry, jealous, lazy, dirty, smelly? Where would your love have been then? And I was all these things as well. Does this mean that it was not really me whom you loved, but only what I pretended to be?'[51] It is difficult to overestimate the importance of that question. Consequently, it is worth entertaining the hypothesis that the children of the late twentieth century are relocating the problem identified there into the playthings of a powerful popular culture where messier and uglier kinds of pretence are possible.

The contemporary nurturing mode of adult–child relations is based on a notion of the good child which the actual child can be helped to become.[52] This is not quite the same thing as simply dealing with the actual child. However well behaved a child might be there is an inevitable gap between the child's sense of self and that ideal condition of expected goodness: the former is all too aware of, and perhaps confused by, conflicting impulses and feelings, while the condition of being 'good' is going to be experienced often as a set of moving goalposts. So in a period of parental tolerance and automatic washing machines, Miller's invocation is less the voice of a child speaking literally and more an inner voice troubled by a sense of pretence (in describing which the vocabulary of object relations, Miller remarks, 'seems to me emotionally more true').[53]

What Alice Miller reminds us, drawing on her depth of experience in exploring childhood, is that the child's is primarily a 'lost world of feelings', and that society acting through parents will not allow the child safely to experience impulses such as aggression or selfishness as 'ordinary' or a very mundane physicality as 'natural'. However much 'tolerated', these things are almost always experienced as a slippage from an ideal condition of being the 'good' child. Such things in the outside world then have the potential of failing to connect with any allowable part of a child's mental life, leaving the child largely bewildered and helpless to understand them. From the very beginning children have to learn to pretend, which does not mean merely to play but rather to be other than themselves; not to be smelly or selfish, not to rage or defy (and these are not so much literally understood behaviours, it bears repeating, as potential transgressions in the inner life of the child). Quite understandably, given the way family life is currently organised, there are few ways children can be those things without causing genuine distress and real inconvenience to adults. Of course all those things do emerge; but Miller suggests that their expression often lags well behind what the child might actually be needing to feel (and we should remember that this is not some release of the 'true' self, but a complex transaction between inner and outer, mediated by objects). Children inevitably feel less 'good' than they are perceived to be. Some give in and embrace the 'bad' for their sense of self, often on the streets where the family seems an irrelevance. The irony, according to Miller's clinical observations, is that the pretence demanded of children, by adults who believe they are helping the child, does not teach them to be good adults. Rather it is the child more genuinely able to feel all these 'bad' things (as a child or later in a therapeutic situation) who is equipped to reject them consciously as an adult: 'they will no longer need to ward off their helplessness, in turn, with exercise of power over others'.[54] The exercise of such power in an angry, jealous, selfish, often dreadful, adult world creates the outer world of bad objects perceived by the child but seldom understood because the spiral of internalisation and projection, which leads to understanding rather than bewilderment, has been cut short. It is important to note, however, that the 'spiral' identified by analysts of object relations is a definite structure of psychological coping – something very different from any simple notion of giving 'cathartic' free rein to any and all feelings.

Play exceeds the pretence (from Struwwelpeter to Freddy)

In contrast to the required pretence, play begins to look like the best that a child can do in order to find some space where the 'bad' can be explored and lost feelings temporarily re-established. Toys can sometimes become usable objects or props in attaining that brief respite from pretence – an escape to the reality of feelings. It should be noted, however, that this is not the same as simplistically advocating a *laissez-faire* attitude to toys and what children do with them – that supposedly enlightened adults should necessarily look on tolerantly while children enact the most racist, sexist or mindlessly violent fantasies, because they should 'get it out of their systems'. The point is not to advocate some phoney notion of 'catharsis' but to identify the structure of object relations in which toys become implicated. If, as Alice Miller suggests, adult dealings with children too often block that structure and the spiral process of coming to know which operates through it, then proposing that we understand play as having the potential to exceed such blockage is not at all the same thing as actively advocating a deliberately and singlemindedly orgiastic kind of play in which anything goes. A child playing with 'Mr Atomic' in the 1950s was grasping an object that made some small part of the ungraspable accessible. Recognising the usefulness of that object for that reason is not the same as sanctioning a game in which the child announces, 'Now Mr Atomic is going to kill 100,000 Japanese people!'

Nevertheless, were we to settle on a word which encapsulates everything that Alice Miller tells us childhood should not be, then that word could well be 'asceticism' – in short, the child as Barbie doll, as 'convenient' in Miller's damning terminology. The rigid denial of feelings which the Protestant Reformation allowed to be generalised outwards from monk's cell to nursery, school, prison and hospital (and which Weber, contentiously, saw in the very origins of capitalism), is regularly and self-evidently exceeded in childhood play. But it is equally self-evident that this is not any easy or total evasion – Miller suggests that 'probably everybody has a more or less concealed inner chamber', a reversal of the monk's cell as it were, where such an evasion is attempted, resulting in latent perversions and delusions because no such escape is possible.[55] Play is where the pretence of asceticism, rather than trying to find some opposite extreme (such as the dungeon *mise en scène* of kinky adult escapism) encounters the challenge of feelings that won't go away and relocates the ascetic pretence within a structure of other possible meanings – a structure capable of allowing more scope to those feelings. Logically, then, the ascetic pretence now demanded of children by the adult world can be supplemented or even challenged through three interrelated alternatives: its opposite or contrary, the orgiastic; but also the contradiction in turn of those first two terms – i.e. the non-ascetic and the non-orgiastic (in the sense that a contradictory term need not be an opposite). That is to mark out a system of possibilities rather than to suggest that all play should itself be orgiastic in some supposedly cathartic sense. Indeed it is possible to suggest that play is that system of possibilities. As such, it renders visible a principal structuring model for this study as a whole, one already hinted at in the first half of this chapter and more fully detailed in Chapter 4.

The special significance of this line of thought for our present purpose is that it marks the moment when conventional accounts of play can give way to the concerns of cultural studies proper – in particular, a concern with that spread of effects (as described abstractly in Chapter 1), with the way in which a set of meanings embedded in those effects draws together far more than just a child and a few toys. But before getting to that more fully, it is still possible to find those potential meanings located in play as conventionally described.

The orgiastic is there in the account of play given by a teacher of 3-year-olds: 'One boy got red paint on his hands and went around threatening the other children with "blood from where he was shot". Another child, with no warning, started crashing into children [who were] playing ball, saying he was "Rambo". In the house area recently, three children tore the head off of the teddy bear. All they could tell me was that the bear was the "bad guy".'[56]

The not-ascetic is there in David Sudnow's account of watching his son playing a video game in an arcade. There is a lot going on and yet the scene is static, the feeling intensely present but wholly contained:

> I stood off and watched him play, or whatever you could say he was doing. If 'doing' was the right word . . . Each body rivals the other as perfect specimens of the strangest human conduct I've witnessed in a public place. I see right hands putting epileptic seizures to shame, while the rest of them just stares and cares, standing up, watching TV . . . Yet from where I stood it looked like he was having a tough go at it, for his overall stance had tightened as though the fingers were getting through to him. And in about five minutes he missed whatever it was that finally matters, hit the machine, and said 'Damn'.[57]

The not-orgiastic is there in Elizabeth Matterson's account of a child allowed to get himself thoroughly dirty in a sandpit where he becomes the very machines of the construction site, all the feeling and energy satisfyingly disciplined and directed into explicitly constructive activity approved of by the watching adult: '. . . for a whole morning, making an elaborate road system with tunnels, overpasses, hills and hairpin bends. He dampens and mixes the sand to get the right consistency and comes in several times to find something to use as a tool for a particular operation. The work goes through several phases as more ideas occur to him . . . He chatters to himself as he works.'[58]

The ascetic itself is simply and terrifyingly there in Alice Miller's brief but telling account of a moment which at first seems extreme, until we realise how representative it is: 'When a six-year old's mother died, his aunt told him: "You must be brave, don't cry; now go to your room and play nicely".'[59]

In the examples above we begin to sense what is at stake in each of the themes or 'semiotic dimensions' described in the first half of this chapter. It remains, of course, to consider more fully the very idea of the child, however limited the feasible scale of ambition for doing so might be in the present context. In Frankfurt in 1845, Heinrich Hoffmann appears to have sensed an impending change in the social construction of the child and in his infamous *Struwwelpeter* picture-book offered harsh cautionary tales to children while simultaneously satirising the adult world's growing determination to sanitise its view of childhood. Translated into English three years later, the *Struwwelpeter* book eventually went through scores of versions. In 'Shock-headed Peter' we see a child with huge fingernails and an enormous shock of uncombed hair. The admonitory verse says 'Anything to me is sweeter, Than to see Shock-headed Peter' but of course it is Peter as he is that we find fascinating. And in the 'Story of Little Suck-a-Thumb' we see

19 From Hoffmann's Peter to Hollywood's Freddy and Edward, children have feared but also identified with the monster who doesn't fit in. The Freddy doll on the left was forced off the market by moral protestors.

the 'scissor-man' cutting off the child's thumbs ('Snip! Snap! Snip! They go so fast.'). There is a striking echo of these images in 1989 when the Matchbox toy company introduced a doll based on the character Freddy Krueger from the Hollywood film *Nightmare on Elm Street*.[60]

With talon-like knives for fingers, Freddy haunted and slashed the children of American suburbia. Capitalising on the film's popularity, other toy companies produced finger-knife gloves with plastic blades, etc. But religious groups, citizen action groups, parents' associations and the press in the United States mounted a campaign against the Matchbox doll, and production stopped after 50,000 of them had been sold. In 1990 a more escapist version of the same imagery appeared in the form of *Edward Scissorhands* in the film of that name, but no attempts were made to base toys on that character.[61] Without Hoffmann's earlier versions of such things, we might pass by these contemporary examples as merely the routine merchandising that goes on around many successful films; but *Struwwelpeter* serves to remind us that something with deeper roots is visible here. The fate of the Freddy Krueger doll dramatises the very intersection of child's phantasy and adult admonition that we have been describing here in terms of object relations.

The child itself has to be an implicit or explicit presence throughout any discussion of toys and play. But in a book of this nature it is impossible to give thorough consideration to the concept of 'child'; such a concept will remain largely implicit. It is important, however, to be clear that it is a concept, not a simply given fact, and that 'childhood' is something actively constructed and reconstructed by societies to fit with what we might term the social totality – the sum of the parts, cultural, political, legal, etc., that make up that society at any historical moment. This leads into two further points. Those social 'parts' are seldom uncontradictory. Different values and practices interweave in tension to make up the social fabric and, where fissures open up, any concept, but particularly one as complex as the 'child', can find itself pushed and pulled in different directions.[62] Further, the biological and developmental basis of what we think of as childhood will always be in a kind of dialogue with its social construction.

The 'nature–nurture' controversy is well documented.[63] For our purposes, it will be enough to take from it the idea that human 'nature', our capacity to develop into a particular kind of feeling, thinking, acting organism, has evolved in order to support our adaptation to changing environments. As the social and cultural environment supplants in significance the raw encounter with the natural world, so too our adaptive processes become more geared to coping with social and cultural factors. 'Nature' simply is that adaptability. Under the microscope it appears fairly stable. Taking the long view reveals that it changes with the times, historically speaking. 'Nurture', the social and cultural construction of child-rearing, is, seen from this angle, merely the vehicle for those changes to realise themselves.

It is important then not to be too complacent about our own culture of intensive 'nurturing'. What Lloyd deMause calls the 'helping mode' of parent–child relations only really appeared in the twentieth century and in a few societies.[64] It was based on the notion that a child could be helped to realise his or her fundamentally good nature and to reject the bad. It has been almost entirely lacking in the more dialectical understanding of 'good' and 'bad' objects that object relations theory offers. The massive quantity of available information, advising enlightened parental involvement as caring nurturers in the inner and outer lives of children in order to realise them as essentially 'good', is an epiphenomenon of a welfare state, a reading public, the extension of paediatrics to embrace the 'whole' child, and parents with both leisure time to devote to their children and money to spend on them. Outside the Western societies in which similar variants of such things have appeared, three-quarters of the world's children are born into contexts in which perhaps a fifth of them will die within a year, and of the survivors something close to three-quarters will have no modern medical care throughout their childhood. Not much more than half of them, predominantly boys, will sit in a classroom; and of those less than half again will be schooled for more than a year or two.[65]

That litany of what seem to us to be harsh terms for living is not meant to elicit despair or condemnation. We should first of all recognise that for most children in the world our concept of 'child' simply doesn't apply. We may well be right to decide that our own concept is worth exporting, and with it will go charitable aid and international welfare programmes. But we have to be careful to recognise that with the 'helping mode' we will be re-inventing the child in many of those societies. It isn't too far-fetched to suppose, in fact, that our 'discovery' of a seemingly dependent Third World (often, in the media, wearing the face of a hungry child) is an extension of our domestic helping mode on a global scale, an imperialism of nurture suited to changes in our own societies since their more militaristic imperial days. Its value, in human terms, is in a sense a different question; but Alice Miller's doubts about the pretence around which the helping mode is based should be enough to make us wary.

Turning this line of thought back on itself has some striking consequences. If our concept of the child, within a helping mode of adult–child relations, is a relatively recent historical invention, sustained by local conditions in which parents have time to consider their own role in this, and access to information about how to fulfil it (actually an industry in itself since the 1950s), then there is no reason to suppose that the concept will remain unchanged as the societies change or indeed that all aspects of those societies necessarily partake of the particular invention.

Historical versions of childhood

Lloyd de Mause identifies a 'socialisation' mode as the phase prior to the 'helping' one, and indeed this has a longer history, spanning at least the nineteenth century and the first half of the twentieth. Here the child had to be moulded, not to realise its own potential to be 'good', but simply to fit its social niche. This objective, of course, still informs much schooling and some child-rearing, in an often uneasy balance with the newer mode. And as we excavate deeper we find other modes, no longer dominant but still interwoven in often contradictory and troublesome ways with what most of us now say we believe about children. So, the eighteenth century's 'intrusive' mode, in which the child had to be turned inside out and its rawness conquered, its secrets delivered for judgement, still lurks within moralising about childhood sexuality and in Christian fundamentalism generally. That explicit battle was very different from the pretence which Alice Miller now sees as characteristic of a helping mode, informed in turn by a residue of the socialisation mode. And the earlier 'ambivalent' mode, in which the child lived very much in the adult world as a kind of amusing curiosity or an exploitable resource, is perhaps not so far away after all from the minds (or at least deeds) of those who make and market a consumer culture for children and who refuse to worry about the children they manipulate. Parental surrendering of the child to the modern media, and the fragmenting of family life, even seem to recall the 'abandonment' mode of the fourth to thirteenth centuries, in which children were left to get on with it as best they could – where thirteenth-century paintings showed Mary holding the infant Jesus awkwardly at arm's length, she might now have parked him in front of the television.

These subterranean traces of earlier relational modes remain largely overgrown, of course, by the comfortable if sometimes rather thin rhetoric of the now (temporarily?) dominant helping mode. And that mode, as Alice Miller has shown us, often comes down to helping the child participate in an elaborate pretence, denying everything that is 'bad' and blocking the process by which the child could otherwise come to deal more adequately with the threatening, a process now increasingly displaced, we will suggest, into the world of toys. There we have identified our second and third sets of effects, the harmonising and relational effects. The important thing about Hoffmann's *Struwwelpeter* was that its vivid illustrations of bad children undoubtedly functioned as significant and usable objects in the mental lives of the many children who dwelt on them with a mixture of fascination and fear. Many toys may now function similarly, even if the Hoffmannesque Freddy Krueger doll is no longer among them.

Figure 1 does two things to deMause's original periodisation of adult–child relations. The vertical axis of the original is unlabelled. It isn't a scale but, presumably, a sort of axis of conceptual dominance, allowing him to depict the relationships among child-rearing modes. In fact it maps quite neatly on to an axis of information growth, as here. The second alteration is to extend the evolutionary line beyond the helping mode. If microprocessor-driven information growth is a convenient index of late modern social and cultural transformation, then intensified transformation (and further compression of the time-scale for change) seems inevitable.

It is important to notice with deMause's time-line that, as with so much else linked to the exponential growth of information, and to late-modern temporal compression, it gets steeper all the time – as a consequence, the changes tend to pile up on each other. There seems no reason to suppose that the process ends with the helping mode (and, therefore, deMause's tendency to view it as the 'end of history' in this respect is suspect, even without Miller's scepticism about its satisfactoriness), so we can speculate at least about the next 'branch' and its relationship to the others. Here the graph extends beyond 1974, when de Mause published the original, and continues the branching as well as the steepening process. Logically, one would expect to find another branch, one rising almost on the vertical. While this is merely

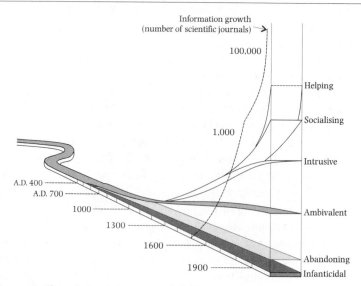

Figure 1 The relative importance of child-rearing modes, correlated with information growth (after de Mause).[66]

speculation, it raises some provocative and apt enough questions, which unmistakably have something of the postmodern about them.

What are the salient features of the next mode? Is it perhaps a condition of 'verticality' that the underlying modes become visible in some sense, so that rather than living unquestioningly within only one mode we recognise, though perhaps in coded forms, the historicity of the whole process and the provisionality or contingency of the prevailing mode (part of a more general contemporary anti-foundationalism tending towards relativism)?[67] Instead of pursuing such issues directly, the present study aims to find evidence one way or another in the realm of toys. So implicit throughout will be the concept of 'childhood' as informed by this graph of modes, but the study of toys will be used to test the concept rather than vice versa: have children already discovered the new mode through their new kinds of toy? And, in doing so, have they found a way of supplementing to some extent the less-than-helpful pretence identified by Alice Miller? Before any sort of answer becomes possible we will have to be clearer about the toys themselves, particularly about that very notion of a 'new kind' of toy.

3

The history and
narrativisation of toys

In the Moravian Museum in Brno there is a miniature mammoth made from fired clay some 25,000 years ago. About 5 cm. long and 4 cm. high, it was found at Dolni Vestonice in Moravia. It could happily join a collection of little animals called 'Whimsies', made by Wade in England in the twentieth century for children to collect. The Piette Collection of archaeological finds at St Germain-en-Laye includes a similar-sized object from Brassempouy in France. About the same age as the little mammoth, it is a human head carved in mammoth ivory. A slender neck, long fine nose and flowing hair give the female face a stylised delicacy that we might call doll-like. There is a Mesopotamian model of a sheep dating from 2300 BC, and an Egyptian miniature tiger from about 1000 BC, both in the British Museum. Examples abound, in other words, of miniature replica animals, people and objects from many cultures and across thousands of years of history. Many clearly had ritual significance for adults; some were funerary offerings, as in the Egyptian tombs filled with models of daily life to give comfort to the journeying dead; while others were merely decorative. Some were play-things. The three-thousand-year old Egyptian wooden tiger had a hinged jaw that could be operated by pulling a string. Probably most of the playthings have been lost because they were in robust daily use, while ritual objects were carefully kept.[1]

The arrival of the toy

The blurred line between playthings for children and miniatures for adult amusement or other use, extends from prehistory to at least the late eighteenth century. This is perhaps unsurprising, since the concept of childhood as a distinct phase is a relatively recent one, as we have seen. In the eighteenth century in English, the word 'toy' tended to mean small accurate reproductions of everyday objects, often in luxury materials such as gilded copper, ivory or silver. While domestic items began to proliferate, as with the novel idea of distinct table settings offering utensils for each person, so wealthy adults were delighted by tiny plates, cutlery or furniture, icons of the new domestic taste. It was only manufacturing innovation and cheaper production techniques using pewter or tin that gradually extended the availability of such 'toys' and made them accessible to children.

The eighteenth century refined the idea of the precise miniature replica, admired for its accuracy, essentially without function except to replicate, and added it to the much longer established tradition of pre-dominantly wooden objects for actively playing with – tops, hobby-horses, puppets, little stylised figures, rag dolls, etc. – which extends back through the Middle Ages to Greek and Roman times and beyond. In the nineteenth century other elements converge to make up the complex concept which we now mean when we use the word 'toy', such as an element of spectacle derived from the toy theatre and an element of mechanisation derived from automata. There also appears a growing contrast between mass production and the notion of a craft tradition, rooted in German wood-carving. The latter still colours our sense of what a 'traditional' toy is, although tinplate offers just as interesting a tradition.

A few key features of these convergent histories will help us to understand better the contemporary concept of the toy. A number of persistent themes were inherited by the twentieth-century toy industry from these earlier features. The eighteenth-century fashion for miniature replicas, for example, seems still to dog twentieth-century toy makers, who often assume that a small accurate replica must necessarily be an acceptable plaything. In fact from the 1980s onwards many toy designers have rediscovered the attractiveness to children of a more deliberately stylised form, such as the popular 'Playmobil' range from the German company Geobra Brandstatter of Zirndorf. So the general elements defining the toy are clearly not fixed, but shift dynamically in relation to each other and to the times. The notion of the miniature replica remains strong, however. So too does a generalised element of spectacle that probably has its roots in the toy theatre.

The element of narrativised spectacle

Originating with William West, whose haberdashery shop was close to several London theatres in the early nineteenth century, the English toy theatre or 'juvenile drama' was initially a business sideline of West's. In 1811 he had the idea of printing and selling a sheet of character illustrations based on the pantomime *Mother Goose*, then playing nearby. Setting up toy theatres based on such cut-out characters seemed instantly to appeal to children of the time, especially those whose parents attended the theatre. For middle-class English children of the nineteenth century, evenings were often spent consigned to an austere 'playroom' by absent parents. Making and enacting miniature dramas of the kind the adults attended must have seemed a very appropriate way of spending the long evenings. With elaborate stage fronts, back scenes and cut-out characters, the toy theatres and accessories proliferated from numerous London manufacturers. Simultaneous developments in a number of German cities and then Austria, France and Denmark consolidated this form of amusement. Many European examples were soon being exported to the United States.[2]

What is particularly worth noting about the toy theatre is that it introduced to the concept of 'toy' strong elements of spectacle and

20 Nineteenth-century toy theatre. The front and two characters are by Hodgson and Company of London, dating from the early 1820s. The backdrop is by Winckelmann of Berlin, a little later. The orchestra strip is by John Redington, date unknown.

narrative. The visual pleasure of setting up miniature scenes, with colourful backdrops and characters, must have shaded over into the story-telling pleasure of enacting the popular dramas of the day.[3] This would have been especially so with exotic stories such as *The Forty Thieves*, character sheets for which West published in 1824, or *Ali Pacha* published by Bernard and William Hodgson a couple of years earlier. Seductive dancing-girls in vibrant red dresses, scimitar-wielding Arabs, mysterious palaces and unspeakable villainy combine with the secrecy of the peepshow (and conspire with the whole discourse of Orientalism)[4] – tiny enticing dramas are enacted for the private fantasy of the child. Certainly in Germany the paper theatre sheets developed directly out of the peepshow dioramas, spectacle and intimacy going intriguingly hand in hand.

The peepshow man was a familiar aspect of European eighteenth-century popular culture. He carried or wheeled his peepshow boxes from town to town, fairground to fairground, and for a penny a time people could peer through an aperture at dramatically perspectivised scenes made from several planes of printed card. These purported to show famous places or events, and sometimes depictions of recent occurrences for which the peepshow man would offer a spoken commentary in a basic but dramatic kind of news service. A striking example was a diorama by Martin Engelbrecht of the Thames Tunnel. The French peepshow version of the technological wonder appeared in 1845, only two years after the original opened. The box front shows a printed scene of the river and city beyond. Peeping in reveals an initial series of receding arches and then a marvellous sense of deep perspective as tiny carriages and people disappear into or emerge from the tunnel. There is an odd prickly sense of visual pleasure and secrecy to be derived from these peepshows, and it undoubtedly carried over into the toy theatre, with its additional element of active personal involvement for the child.

The atmosphere and vividness of many toy theatre scenes are remarkable, particularly those from German manufacturers. A back-drop for *Hamlet* from Joseph Scholz of Mainz in the 1830s shows a shadowy graveyard overhung by glowering trees and shrouded in mist. A mid-century example from Winckelmann of Berlin shows a scene of Eastern exoticism, with a glowing orange sky pierced by shimmering minarets. The Danish firm of Carl Allers continued this tradition of artistry into the 1940s, with for example a marvellous galleon as a setting for piracy and adventure on the high seas. It is not difficult to recognise, however, that a Hollywood swashbuckler such as *The Sea Hawk* in 1940 marks the cinematic experience's ascendancy over the tamer peepshow-like pleasures of the little cardboard proscenium arch.

Totems of power

The basic idea of cut-out paper or card figures, which West adapted to the toy theatre, was derived from a Strasburg printer called Seyfried who, in 1744, produced sheets of such figures showing a regiment of Louis XV's cavalry, then visiting the city with the king. French 'flats' of this kind from manufacturers like Pellerin were popular throughout the Napoleonic Wars, although the term 'flat' is now more often taken to refer to the metal versions from German tinsmiths, which flourished throughout the nineteenth century, overwhelming in numbers a longer-established tradition of carved wooden soldiers. Those flats or *Zinnfiguren*, and the three-dimensional lead soldiers which developed from them, joined miniature and often stylised animals in wood or metal as the epitome of the simple toy.

The hugely popular Noah's Arks of the nineteenth century – large wooden 'arks' providing convenient storage for a carnival of little animals – mark the clearest relay point linking the 25,000-year-old miniature mammoth to sixteenth century German wood-carvers and the Britains plastic 'Zoo' range of the twentieth century (now renamed the 'Wildlife' range for a greener 1990s). The small plaything, typically an animal, a soldier or a miniature version of adult transportation (from ancient Mesopotamian boats to Dinky cars), represents the staple toy across the centuries – a kind of childhood totem. These small and relatively simple playthings, hoarded by children and frequently the object of deep attachments, have subdivided into distinct categories as the societies producing them have grown more complex and the available materials of manufacture more varied.

Toy animals and then, especially after the Thirty Years War in Europe, toy soldiers, together seem to have had the deepest totemic appeal. Perhaps the power of nature and the power of men are captured for children in these simple objects; as later the power of technology is embodied in tinplate cars and aircraft. Whatever the explanation, the quantities of these objects produced and played with have been enormous.

Given, in *Emile* (1762), Jean-Jacques Rousseau's imaginative empathy as evidence of a general reinvention of childhood at that time, it is not difficult to understand why the contemporary atmosphere of technological advance and manufacturing growth (for example the machines of Hargreaves and Arkwright) converged with that social invention to generate a renewed interest in the mass manufacture of playthings for children. The roots of an emerging interest in the child's difference from adults lie in the contest for the souls of succeeding generations initiated by Luther, in the growth of nation states which intervened more actively to define social identities (for example through orphanages), and in a fashion for giving children distinctive names, instead of re-using the handful that ran in the family. Naming something can often generate an increased sense of its specialness. And satire such as Swift's suggestion that a year-old child makes a 'most delicious, nourishing and wholesome food' of course depends on the very recognition of childhood's specialness that will be outraged by the suggestion.[5]

This opening of a cultural space for children and their increasingly manufactured playthings culminates in the nineteenth-century nursery of the wealthy, with its clutter of objects that would have been unimaginable three centuries earlier. Several of the by then clearly defined categories are worth commenting briefly on. The animal-filled arks and distinctive oval wooden boxes of tin soldiers were especially common. But the previous century's fad for miniature replicas of domestic objects had also established the dolls' house as a playroom commonplace for the relatively wealthy family. Evolving from the cabinets in which adults had kept their own valuable miniature collections, the dolls' house may often have been strictly supervised and provided more amusement for the ladies of the household than for the children, but it won its place as an established category of toy. Dolls themselves, of course, have their own complex history as totems of adult power over children.

Dolls as adult visions of childhood: the Million Dollar Baby

Wood and rag dolls of the simplest kinds have provided centuries of children with moments of intimacy and security, of contact without risk or unpredictability. The massive elaboration of the basic form, through materials such as papier mâché, wax, and bisque (unglazed china), the variations in size and style, and the complex traditions of costume and facial appearance, all represent essentially an adult fascination with dolls rather than childrens' interests or preferences. What we have here is undoubtedly a reflection of the adult world's discovery and re-invention of the child itself. From early miniature adults to Kathe Kruse's sad-faced children of the First World War years, dolls have been a revealing sign of how adults have viewed children. Picking out key moments when the child has had something to say in all of this is not easy.

A two-thousand-year-old Peruvian doll, which had been buried with its child owner, is a fine example of the cross-culturally ubiquitous style of doll: its soft responsive body, warm colours and appealingly stylised face offered the tactile pleasure and reassurance that children have always sought from dolls. Parents, if they had the time and inclination, have undoubtedly always made such dolls for their own children from whatever materials were handy – until mass manufacturing offered convenient alternatives. In Europe, nineteenth-century manufacturing innovation led to materials capable of replacing the stylised face with a sort of mirror image for the child. A typical papier mâché doll of the nineteenth century may have had something of the same tactile fullness to its soft cotton and horsehair body as the Peruvian doll, but a realistic small, pink, wide-eyed face looked back at the child who played with it, beginning the process by which children were encouraged to recognise themselves in their dolls.

Those two tendencies – tactile attachment and a harder repre-sentationality – then took themselves off in essentially different directions. The first diverged into the soft or 'plush' toy, emerging into mass production in Germany from pin-cushions which were given in-creasingly playful shapes, and culminating with the Teddy Bear in 1903, from which a whole self-contained category of cuddliness has developed up to the present day. The representational impulse mean-while led to the increasingly adult-oriented market for realistic costume dolls, creating an expensive collectors' market. The French firm Jumeau was at the centre of the fashion doll industry, but in the 1880s their complementary range of baby-like dolls started to sell phenomenally well: by 1889 they claimed to be selling 300,000 dolls per week. The 'bébés' clearly appealed to both children and adults, for whom the image of the child was becoming an object of culturally-supported sentiment (for instance in painting).[6] With features such as a couple of prominent baby teeth, loosely jointed bodies and remarkably open, playful and endearing faces, these dolls managed to stay in touch with what children themselves would respond to. The approach was successfully repeated in the United States in the 1920s when Grace Storey Putnam, a Californian art school teacher, designed the 'Bye-Lo Baby' head for the company of George Borgfeldt: attached to various bodies over the years, it became known as the 'Million Dollar Baby', so consistently did it sell. It had the sleepy, flat-nosed look of a baby a few days old, and again readily appealed to children.

We have, then, a subtle mirroring process in which the adult world imagines the child in the form of the doll while the child is simultaneously encouraged to recognise itself in that form. The representational tendency in dolls culminates in the 1990s, for example, in the collectors' items created by Annette Himstedt of Germany. Her 'Fiene', a little girl of curly-haired, pouting, dark-eyed provocativeness is unforgettable in a slightly disturbing way: except for enthusiasts immune to the thought, it is somewhat unnerving to find such a 'realistic' child frozen for our gaze. So dolls are a fascinating category of toy in which a complex dialogue has worked itself out, between, on the one hand, the child's tactile, playful interests and feelings and, on the other, the adult's visualisation of the child itself.

The coming of the machine

Of the other elements that the history of toys bequeaths to our modern concept, the most important is a cluster of developments around tinplate and mechanisation. The Egyptian tiger miniature with its string-operated jaw from 1000 BC is an early example of the mechanically operable toy, the plaything that will actually do something. There is a Greek pull-along wheeled horse made from clay about a thousand years later. In the second century BC Hero of Alexandria designed models to demonstrate various physical principles, such as pneumatically operated singing birds and hydraulically operated human figures with moving arms, and stimulated centuries of interest in automata.[7] With associated developments, like mechanical figures on medieval clocks, and influences from elsewhere, such as the rich tradition of Japanese *karakuri* (fortune-telling or writing machines, etc.), the automaton reached a peak of complexity and popularity in the public entertainments of the eighteenth and nineteenth centuries. Large automata were toured by showmen, offering such wonders as a life-sized mechanical musician and an excreting duck. Cheats abounded, such as an infamous chess-playing machine, which was actually operated by a hidden accomplice. While Victorian fairground audiences continued to be amused by such elaborate contraptions, playthings began to mimic their simpler mechanical principles. These reflected in particular the developing transportation of the day.

Spring-operated cycling dolls appeared in the second half of the nineteenth century and steam-driven boats, wheeled engines, etc. were common by the end. When the brothers Montgolfier took to the air in a balloon, toy versions quickly followed, and in the 1870s flying toys driven by rubber bands anticipated, and probably influenced, the experiments of the Wright brothers. Small clockwork toys were, however, the most popular and readily available of the newly mechanised playthings. Ernst Paul Lehmann introduced to toys in the 1880s the principle of the coiled wire spring that could be wound tight, its stored energy ready later to be released. Babies that could crawl, monkeys that could climb and cats that could knit all embodied simple clockwork motors; but the appearance of the automobile sparked a proliferation of toys for which clockwork was even more suited – tinplate cars that could propel themselves around the floor, simple enough in design to be standardised for mass production.

Tin toys in general from 1850 onwards most clearly show the effects of increasingly prevalent factory production methods, supplanting small family workshops and loosely organised domestic outworking. Steam-powered metal-tooling machinery encouraged new mass production techniques, and the brief proliferation of tin playthings of every conceivable kind began to give way to more standardised forms. Chromolithography, patented by Engelmann in 1837, developed in the 1860s an 'offset' technique for transferring printed coloured designs from paper to tinplate (by fixing the paper carrying the printed design to the metal and dissolving away the paper base, leaving the coloured inks on the tin). This effectively ended the need for expensive and time-consuming hand painting, and consolidated the mass production of small, cheap, highly coloured metal toys. By the turn of the century, 'penny toys' of this kind were beginning to dominate the European and North American markets, ensuring the fortunes of firms such as Marklin of Germany, Martin of France and Marx of the United States.

Mass production and industrial growth

The toy car is the supreme paradigmatic instance of these new tin playthings. As the toy car developed in parallel with the real automobile, representational accuracy began to take over from mechanical activity. While clockwork cars remained popular for many years, the market gradually shifted towards detailed replicas. The simpler inertia motor (a friction-driven flywheel good for a few yards of travel) has been used from time to time, but in general the toy car became less of a mechanical plaything and more a celebration in static detail of the real thing. Around 1910 a 'die-casting' technique (casting thin metal in moulds rather than fabricating objects from sheet metal) produced increased detail on a smaller scale and confirmed the accurately representational direction the toy car was going in. Appropriately the first mass-produced toy car to be accurately based on a real prototype was the 'Model T' Ford in 1915, made by Tootsietoy of Chicago.

The impulse towards mechanisation, while gradually abandoned in the case of toy cars (until the electrified race track appeared in 1958), none the less continued to inform the toy business. The clockwork railway was home to that impulse from the 1890s, having largely supplanted the older and briefly popular steam-driven 'Piddlers' – large engines that leaked water on to the floor. Electric toy trains, such as those from the Hornby company in England, remained popular until largely appropriated by adult hobbyists in the 1950s. But the chief manifestation of the mechanical impulse is to be found in the 'constructional' toys, among which Meccano has been perhaps the most famous.[8] Its English inventor Frank Hornby had devised a constructional toy for his own children around the turn of the century. Patented in 1901 as 'Mechanics Made Easy', the more familiar name was registered in England in 1907. The earliest version used perforated copper 'girders' that could be bolted together in various ways; then manufacturing shifted into varnished tin strips along with gears, cogs and wheels used to make all sorts of machines. Eventually the sets were made from nickel-plated steel in the familiar red, blue and green colours. From 1916 a Meccano magazine was published to encourage children further in building 'the world's mechanical wonders in every home', as the early box artwork put it. American manufacturer A. C. Gilbert, probably influenced by Frank Hornby's design, introduced his own version in 1913. Called the Erector Set, it included a simple electric motor and was hugely popular.

21 Meccano and its imitators captured the excitement of industrial expansion, capitalist growth and unproblematic technological progress, celebrated by *Meccano Magazine* which successfully interested a generation of boys, and some girls, in engineering.

In 1964 Meccano Ltd. was taken over by Lines Brothers, after which the monthly magazine disappeared and the toy line declined, finally being sold to an American buyer in 1981, at which time the Meccano name itself was taken over by a French company, the latter eventually reviving the concept in the 1990s in a redesigned up-market version. There is no doubt, however, that the heyday of such constructional toys was during the first half of the century.

Meccano and the Erector Set were deeply symbolic products of the period 1894–1913, identified by Ernest Mandel as a 'long wave' within capitalist development – characterised by rapid expansion, a second industrial revolution, a steep rise in the productivity of labour and a vigorous extension of the world market.[9] That wave launched those two construction toys, with all their connotations of industrial excitement, into the twentieth century, throughout the first half of which they spawned many imitators. Meccano's dominance was challenged by the more adaptable and less mechanical plastic Lego system, which appeared in 1955 and would eventually fill the gap left by Meccano in the European market in the 1980s by including electronic components. But what is especially noteworthy about the rise and fall of a toy such as Meccano is that its simple constructional theme was energised by that capitalist wave early in the century, held steady for some forty years, and then straightforwardly if very gradually lost momentum, clinging on for its last four decades on habit and 'tradition' alone. (The current French version is probably buoyed by parental nostalgia as much as anything.)

It is not too fanciful to suppose that what happened in part was a process in which toys in general became 'constructional'. Instead of referring emulatively to the once exciting but now mundane realities of the building site or factory assembly line, toys found new referents within a burgeoning popular culture. The meanings deployed by that culture became the new constructional materials, as it were. At the same time the meanings of the entire history of toys seem to have converged, to have explicitly informed the new conception of the toy. In the light of the last chapter's argument about underpinning modes becoming visible since the late 1960s and early 1970s, it is possible to

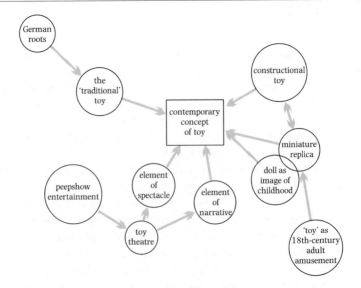

Figure 2 Historical characteristics converging on the contemporary toy.

suggest that the convergence might better be understood as the history of toys suddenly becoming visible to itself in the very contemporary concept of the toy.[10] That history delivers our fourth set of effects – the totemic effects by which toys symbolically take on the powers that children perceive in the world.

Media merchandising

If one were to select a group of people who constitute the symbolic centre of today's popular culture of toys, prime candidates until very recently would have been the team at LucasArts Licensing in California. Set up to control the merchandising spin-offs from the *Star Wars* series of films, the most popular sequence of movies ever and therefore a pivotal phenomenon of late-twentieth-century culture, LucasArts Licensing has managed its own massive commercial empire on behalf of film maker George Lucas. The spin-off products became too numerous to list and the licensing deals quite byzantine in their interconnections.

A few examples will make the point. Made in Korea for the Coca-Cola Co., the 'Cobot' toy was modelled on the tin-can-shaped robot from *Star Wars*, but with a Coke can for the body. The resulting object looked utterly meaningless unless one could 'read' it in terms of its popular cultural references. The Burger King chain of fast-food outlets ran a promotion in which buying a glass of Coke entitled the customer to keep the glass – with a *Star Wars* scene printed on it. Hundreds of small companies, as well as the transnationals, got in on the act. Bridge Farm Dairies in the UK made a line of *Star Wars* yoghurts with character designs on the pots and flavours to match – the hero was raspberry and the villain black cherry. In Japan rice snacks came in *Star Wars* packaging. A Mexican circus introduced a *Star Wars* act with costumed performers. The spin-offs got increasingly bizarre, and nobody thought it especially odd. Around the world, you could eat, drink and wear *Star Wars*. Clarks Shoes introduced a line of *Star Wars* sneakers with the film's logo emblazoned across the heel. Wallpaper with matching bedlinen appeared, so that children's rooms could be literally filled with pictures from the films. That kind of merchandising proliferated globally, infiltrating everybody's consciousness with *Star Wars* imagery. But toys were at its heart, at least until 1985, when the overall momentum slowed. *Star Wars* toys and children's merchandise produced in the previous eight years were so numerous that whole books are needed to catalogue them.[11]

In today's terms, the three films in the series have earned something over US$6 billion, including cinema releases, video earnings, television rights and spin-off merchandising. The merchandising is responsible for about a third of that, original cinema box-office takings for only a sixth. The success of licensed *Star Wars* products set a trend: international merchandising of this kind is a ten-times more lucrative business now than it was before *Star Wars*, and is currently worth at least an annual US$66 billion worldwide.[12] May 1977, when the original *Star Wars* film was released, marks an unmistakable watershed in terms of a much more densely interconnected and interdependent global popular culture of imagery and artifacts. And *Star Wars* itself was already a pastiche of such elements, drawing together imagery from earlier swashbucklers and war films, comics and pulp adventure fiction.

The merchandising is not an indiscriminate process, blitzing consumers with stuff that they will inevitably accept. Along the way fine details are agonised over in order to ensure a 'fit' with public taste that remains intriguingly difficult to define. Lucas's original name for the villain's spaceship was 'Executor'. Toy-maker Kenner (part of the Tonka conglomerate) had to hire US agency Grey Advertising to come up with 153 alternative names until they found one that they were confident about putting on their boxes of toys ('Star Destroyer' as it happens, something of an anti-climax perhaps). Multiply that kind of strategic background planning a thousandfold and the term 'merchandising campaign' takes on a new precision of meaning.

Now, there are two ways of looking at all of this. Either big businesses and sophisticated marketing techniques conjured it all up from nowhere, or something deeper was going on which the merchandising was able to amplify and take advantage of. A clue that the second option should be taken seriously comes from the experience of Kenner Products, the major manufacturer of *Star Wars* toys. Under their then president Bernie Loomis, the Cincinnati-based toy company analysed the *Star Wars* concept in detail in 1977 when they applied for worldwide rights. Loomis found it 'toyetic', a function of Lucas's deliberate pastiche. The imaginary universe was in many ways comfortably familiar: there were spaceships like fighter aircraft, animals that were either monsters or cuddly friends, robots which were perennially popular toys, and a clear thematic core which kept it all organised. That core can

22 *Star Wars* toys represent a diversity of alien cultures in over a hundred little figures of endlessly varying appearance, surrounded by quirkily varied technology. The large figures here are Kenner originals from the late 1970s in their Cantina Playset. Kenner sold over twenty-six million of these figures in 1978 alone. The smaller figures and base are from Airfix's Jabba the Hut Throne Room playset. The spacecraft is from Denys Fisher Toys, the land-walker vehicle in the background from Kenner. The influence of these toys went well beyond licensed *Star Wars* products: the inset shows two toys that would be very much at home in the *Star Wars* universe; but, along with many others, these were sold without mention of the film.

be described, somewhat clumsily perhaps, as the theme of context-bound self-realisation against the odds, the contexts being a 'rainbow coalition' of diverse interests (human and non-human) and an environment of useful but subservient technology (elements that would not be so successfully tapped again by the genre until the TV series *Babylon 5* in the 1990s). Not much there, apparently, to affect putting successful toys on the shelves, but in fact there were implications for

Kenner's success, whether or not the toy makers were fully conscious of them at the time.

Metonymic elaboration

Luke Skywalker, the young hero of the film trilogy, is actually a rather softly defined character. His filmic identity and self-realisation are defined by the two contexts in which he operates: the loose coalition of misfits, adventurers, political idealists, robots and aliens marshalled against the evil Empire; and the ever-present technologies on which survival depends in that hostile galaxy. (The dense elaboration of such contexts can be called 'metonymic' in rhetorical terms.) The character's interactions within these two contexts give substance to his identity, rather than any more conventionally individualistic representation of character traits or private compulsions. Identifying with Luke, especially for a child, will consequently depend on imagining oneself in those contexts rather than isolating Luke or actor Mark Hamill from them as an object of reified identification.

Why *Star Wars* turned on such a context-defined character is a complex issue. Critics Ryan and Kellner see in the film a symbolic reconciliation of libertarian individualist motifs with a conservative message about traditional values being defended against an intrusive State by loosely organised right-thinking, gun-toting, freedom-lovers.[13] 'Freedom' encoded in this way then supports the notion that 'natural' forces operating in a free market society offer the best way of doing things, and that people should remain meekly obedient to those forces while resisting any 'unnatural' attempts to impose more order on society. The image of a farm boy like Luke leaving home to defend this 'freedom', driven by some mystical inner 'force', is certainly deeply evocative of the United States' own myth of origin, and the ordered society offered by the Empire is representationally straight out of Hitler's storm troopers and Stalin's Gulags; but Luke remains rather less than full-blooded as an image of possessive individualism. Certainly Luke discovers how to trust his own instincts rather than accept social conditioning. And the 'rainbow coalition' he joins depends on every-body's doing their own thing in contrast to the sameness offered by the Empire; but the dependence on contextual factors remains unusually strong.

Nobody achieves anything worthwhile on their own in these films. They are always coming to each other's rescue or depending on technology to get things done. There is a skin-of-the-teeth aspect to this though: rescues are near-run things, dependent not on brute force but on an individual's special skills or odd characteristics, and the good guys' technology is often rusty and patched together. It is as if the films are saying that quirky, patched-up, temporary arrangements, alliances and reconciliations are better than gleaming, efficient, 'imperial' ways of doing things, and will achieve success where individualism on its own might have ended in heroic failure but failure none the less.

This is a subtle message, residing somewhere between the USA's older myths of its own supposed frontier individualism and a contrasting Soviet totalitarianism. It depended on embedding Luke as hero very much within the loose communitarian image of a coalition that runs the full gamut of skin appearances, from white through black to green or furry and from flesh to metal. And it depended also on surrounding him with technologies which, thanks to his intuitive control over them, become a construction kit of resources rather than dehumanising machines (at one point Luke switches off the computer and flies his spacecraft on gut instinct and mystical communion between man and machine). Ryan and Kellner, who offer the most convincing interpretation of *Star Wars* to date, still miss this aspect of the trilogy; unsurprisingly perhaps, because it is most clearly visible in the distillation of the message achieved by Kenner's toy range rather than in the films themselves which fill it out, as often happens in popular narratives, with contradictions and ambiguities. The next section explores the underlying 'message' in more detail.

From GI Joe to Star Wars toys

It is important to put the first 'action figure' toy range, the *Star Wars* toys, in context. Since 1964 one of the most popular toys in the United States and Europe had been GI Joe, or Action Man as the licensed British version was known. Conventional-doll-sized (the same scale as girls' doll Barbie, introduced six years earlier), the military figure was resolutely individualistic. Large and expensive for the time, the soldier doll tended to be owned in ones or twos, with separate costumes then being collected instead of more figures. Its promotion drew quite clearly on imagery already tested for popularity in comics. Sgt. Rock had been created in 1959 as the first continuing character in DC Comics' war series. The comic *Our Army at War*, especially when drawn by Joe Kubert, perpetuated a memorable image of the tough heroic loner as the essence of that army. Renamed *Sgt. Rock* in 1977, the comic ran until 1988. It spawned successful imitators, such as *Sgt. Fury* from Marvel Comics in 1963, the year before GI Joe's launch by Hasbro. The soldier doll was, in spirit, very much a toy version of that comic-book stereotype of rugged individualism. Indeed Hasbro's competitor, the Ideal Toy Company, produced a *Sgt. Fury* costume for their superhero doll in 1966. These large character figures proliferated during the next decade. In 1977, when confronted by the potential of *Star Wars*, Kenner already had on the market a twelve-inch doll of the Six Million Dollar Man, a successful television character,[14] but Bernie Loomis at Kenner decided that the heroes in *Star Wars* did not comfortably stand alone in that way.

Practical considerations came first. Large play figures could not be put in toy spacecraft without the latter becoming ridiculously large and

23 An original GI Joe, who seemed to have stepped straight off the pages of American war comics. On the right is a record of marching music and battle sounds to accompany him, in his British version.

impractical. Hasbro were having difficulty with GI Joe's equipment for this reason, trying to sell a helicopter that was scaled down too much to be convincing. Kenner settled on a range of Star Wars figures based on an average height of three-and-three-quarter inches, allowing them to make all sorts of vehicles into which the figures could actually fit. In so doing they created a new category of toy – what has come to be known as 'action figures', to which even Hasbro had to convert when they abandoned the large GI Joe between 1982 and 1984, phasing in a new team of small toy figures to replace him. This would look like no more than the vagaries of the market, except that when Kenner attempted to build on their success of 250 million little action figures by going back to the concept of large *Star Wars* dolls, extensive design and prototyping work came to nothing when the market seemed resolutely uninterested, and an extensive line was cancelled after only a few items. The large Luke Skywalker doll just didn't work.

Perhaps unwittingly, what Kenner had tapped into with their original range of ninety-two small *Star Wars* figures (with more for the succeeding films) was precisely those contexts in which the original character of Luke Skywalker had been meaningful. The little plastic version of Luke seems very much at home surrounded by his menagerie of odd associates. And fitting him neatly into a plastic spacecraft with lots of opening panels, movable bits and quirky shapes was precisely the point – the technological environment was being adapted to offer a human 'fit' and qualities of human variety.

To be clear about what this example tells us: for the marketing of *Star Wars* toys to be successful on the scale that it was, there had to be a dovetailing of what the toys offered to children with what the films offered to audiences. The relative failure of a spate of films copying *Star Wars'* superficial elements suggests that the dovetailing went deeper, connecting distinctive features of the *Star Wars* trilogy with significant social and cultural factors which determined the audience's favourable response. Just as superficially emulative films which failed to connect with those factors then failed with audiences, so toys which Kenner expected to be successful were not, because they too missed the connection. It is difficult in a book of this limited scope to pursue those underpinning factors in detail. For the moment, a summary of the most relevant clues will have to suffice.

Firstly, the nature of identity does seem to be an issue that is put into play in the *Star Wars* films and even more clearly in the toys. A child looking at GI Joe in the 1960s was being offered a self-sufficient and fixed metaphor of individualism, backed up by that image's proliferation in comics of the time. A child looking at a crazily diverse collection of small toy figures from the *Star Wars* universe in the late 1970s was being offered a set of questions about the white male hero's relationships with furry dwarfs, hairy giants, intelligent machines, and a human community of various colours and creeds. Unlike what happens in traditional fairy tales, those others do not constitute a supporting menagerie compliant to the hero's will but rather a complex imaginary 'culture' to which the hero has to accommodate in order to achieve anything. Making sense of the dozens of varied figures in the toy range demands a developing knowledge from the child that is virtually anthropological, while it all tends to look like a rather meaningless multiplicity to the uninformed adult.[15] Secondly, the *Star Wars* spacecraft and robot toys are not a technology of sleekly efficient standardisation and impersonality, but a jumble of mechanical parts, opening hatches and secret compartments into which the little figures fit. Indeed, the people very distinctly appear to 'wear' this technology like over-sized mechanised costumes. These features opened out what *Star Wars* meant in interesting ways – and such narratively-sustained 'opening' may be a clue to the toys' huge success.

To defeat others now entailed unleashing inhuman cosmic powers against them – the war against Japan had 'proved' this for the post-war generation of George Lucas. The older narratives of frontiersmen, the 7th Cavalry, or GI Joe types hand-fighting their way through the jungle of Pacific islands no longer worked – not even in the form of President Kennedy's 'limited war'. Vietnam's defeat of the US destroyed them, except as tales of nostalgia, and the 'limited' Vietnam narrative was never itself going to end with the nuclear destruction of Hanoi. This dilemma, between older ineffective narratives and the newly available but 'impossible' narrative of nuclear victory, combined with the 'enemy within' thematics of Cold War paranoia to generate a representational crisis into which *Star Wars* finally came. There was almost a sense of cultural relief around *Star Wars* – relief that there was a story to be told with all the old mythic resonance.

It was as if the diminished figure of the *Incredible Shrinking Man* (1957), reduced in significance in his own home by the forces from the fractured atom, is relocated into a galaxy far away. It is the cosmic scale that now makes him seem small (in the figure of Luke Skywalker) – so the symbolic diminishment suddenly seems inevitable rather than a loss of confidence. And suddenly too the enemies are not alien others – they are the young hero's father and white armour-suited 'Imperial' troops who are clearly human. The many aliens are mostly a bemused audience, onlookers at the spectacle of two sides of the human (i.e. white, male) 'identity' locked in perpetual conflict. That conflict dramatises (and therefore holds in a new balance) the very dilemma evoked above in the contrast between total cosmic destructiveness and 'limited war'. Luke's father has sold his soul to the former. By dramatising the dilemma, *Star Wars* does not have to opt for one or the other, and cleverly evades the problem of finding a resonant, mythically trustable narrative by making the problem into the story.

The fact that the *Star Wars* enemy is not finally some monstrous alien other breaks the link which is sometimes supposed to exist between this fictional return of confidence and the science-fiction representations of the war in the Gulf against the Arab-as-alien. In fact, interestingly, the pursuit of Saddam Hussein stopped short of total destruction – as if in fear of crossing that line and becoming the Imperial other rather than the farm boy out to prove that he has escaped his father's pact with the devil of total, cosmically destructive war. The other here is the perpetrator of that awful pact, and *Star Wars* exorcised him. Luke had to be both the white American male, sorting out other people's problems while achieving supposed moral authority over them (including the princess), and a questioner of the logic that had linked that role to a complete and terrible destructiveness as the price of victory. By re-staging this as a (heavily coded) father–son conflict, *Star Wars* makes the problem which destroyed the old myths into the new myth.

In achieving that, *Star Wars* could not hinge on the GI Joe, John Wayne figure who had been the centre of the old myth (although Luke's friend Solo is a knowing caricature of him). That figure was too implicated in the problem itself. So Luke is a diminished figure (perfect for a toy) who exists in a much more complex relationship with others and with the otherness of high technology (his new tools on the new frontier). The technology is no longer simply an extension of identity (like GI Joe's gun) but rather furnishes resources with which identity sorts out its problems – so too the hero's relationships with others of all shapes, sizes and colours. They are now more necessary, more inevitable as providing the context of relationships within which the central identity sorts out who he (*sic*) is. Those relationships underpinned a narrative

opening out, soap-opera fashion, through which the mythic reconcep-
tualisation of the problem endlessly ripples (the original cycle of three
films established narrative links with other films, yet to be made, and a
series of novels and comics developed new plot lines). That opening out
and deliberate generation of complexity, the proliferation of characters
and ultimate refusal of narrative closure, transferred perfectly into the
world of toys. Where the films resettled all of this around the triumphal-
ism of the white farm boy who saves the day, reducing otherness to
difference-from-him, the toys perhaps sustain the opening out as part
of the very condition of being toys rather than narratives looking for
how to end.

Narrative and total marketing

Instead of speculating further at this stage about what all this means,
it is important simply to note that deep synchronisations are detectable,
of the kinds indicated. Films, toys and the culture generally appear to
be offering us at specific moments certain patterns of meaning that are
sustainable where others are not: these patterns will be further clarified
in Chapter 4. The implication of toys in this has a lot to do with what
we might term their 'narrativisation'. Throughout the 1960s the toy
industry became increasingly dependent on cinema and, especially, on
television for play-worthy objects that could borrow the popularity of
a screen character or story. Such objects then came with a narrative
attached. Instead of being a Native American or 'Red Indian' in some
general sense, a small plastic toy might represent Tonto from *The Lone
Ranger*, and consequently a familiar set of story ideas and character
relationships informed playing with the toy. By the time of the Star
Wars toy boom, this narrative dimension was all-pervasive. Mark Bou-
dreaux, one of the key designers at Kenner, made certain that the likely
narrative elements could be played out with the toys, right down to fine
detail such as ensuring that the spaces inside particular vehicles were
large enough for these two characters to play their chess game or for
that one to do whatever it does in the story.[16] Again, deviating from
this narrative principle caused more problems for Kenner. In 1982 they
tried a *Star Wars* 'Micro Collection' of very small, detailed playsets which
could interlock to make up larger scenes; but the static results ran
counter to the open-ended narrative principle, and it became clear that

24 The 1960s saw a massive expansion of TV-related toys. This pile includes the *Wagon Train* playset of little plastic Cowboys and Indians, a model kit of John Lennon and the famous Corgi diecast James Bond Aston Martin with ejector seat.

the toys were not going to sell. Try as they might, Kenner could not escape from a set of principles for the toys that seemed to have been dictated by something fundamental about the *Star Wars* films themselves, and beyond them the culture more generally. Clever marketing could make the most of those principles, but not escape them.

The narrativisation of toys developed along with the increasingly important concept of 'total' or multi-media marketing aimed at children. In this marketing assault on all fronts the toys are typically related also to a television animation series, videos, a comic-book (with hardback 'annuals'), conventional books and occasionally a cinema film. Any one of these forms can come first, its success triggering the others; or sometimes success depends on the mutually reinforcing effect of simultaneous appearance in several or all of the forms. Under the influence of the successful *Star Wars* toy range, Hasbro altered their GI Joe, discontinuing the large soldier dolls and replacing them with an extensive range of small 'action figure' Joes and adversaries who also appeared, through a series of licensing deals, in a comic from Marvel and a series of television animations subsequently released on video. The new toy range had a narrative idea incorporated from the start, allowing easy spin-offs into those other media. The learning curve for the toy industry, in terms of narrativisation and multi-media merchandising, continued from the success of the new GI Joe/Action Force through the Transformers and Teenage Mutant Ninja Turtles into the proliferation of lines in the 1990s such as Thundercats, Bucky O'Hare, Captain Planet, Toxic Crusaders, James Bond Jnr., and the hugely successful Mighty Morphin' Power Rangers.

The narrative elements, or derived 'play scenarios' as Kenner's *Star Wars* toy designers thought of them, marked a substantially new development in the way children were being encouraged to interact with toys. While previous TV- or cinema-related toys encouraged children to play out scenes and stories from the originals, these new narrative contexts had multiple narrative possibilities deliberately built into them from the beginning. With clearly established teams of characters and basic story structures that would generate endless plots around those characters, children could certainly watch and read plenty of given examples, but were also being encouraged to extend those with their own variations. Adults unfamiliar with the often extremely complex details of these imaginary contexts tend to see a haphazard and worryingly 'meaningless' accumulation of elements. In the GI Joe/Action Force range of toys, for example, the proliferating character figures all have their own carefully developed identities which can be followed through the comics and videos. To the untutored eye the toys look confusingly varied. To the knowledgeable child it all makes a great deal of sense.

Once Upon a Joe

In fact, without the background knowledge, the meaning that can be most easily taken from the GI Joe/Action Force range is of course simply that of militaristic aggressiveness. Fully kitted out, the little plastic figures bristle with weaponry, and their vehicles are tank-like military leviathans, sprouting missiles all over and communicating a glorification of destructive power. In the television series and videos all of this comes alive in flashing roaring battle scenes. But on closer inspection the point of the thing is often found elsewhere.

For instance, it is worth considering a 1986 episode called 'Once Upon a Joe' from the animated television series (Sunbow Productions) based on the GI Joe/Action Force toys. The *GI Joe* animated episodes are re-dubbed for UK release, to substitute one name for the other, and typically two or three minutes of footage are cut to remove shots in which the GI Joe or US insignia are visible. Written by Buzz Dixon, one of the story editors for the whole series, this particular twenty-minute episode develops a complex story within a story. Even a predominantly action-oriented series like *GI Joe/Action Force*, for all its predictability, tends to contradict those who claim that children's television of this kind panders to short attention spans and superficial understandings: these stories are often narratively sophisticated and demanding.

In 'Once Upon a Joe' the Action Force team (referring to the UK version) are pitted against their terrorist adversaries, an organisation called Cobra. As the story begins, Cobra are raiding a secret laboratory in order to steal the 'MacGuffin Device' (with a sly nod to Hitchcock, for whom a 'MacGuffin' was any element that a plot could be hung on).[17] As Action Force arrives to thwart the attempt, an orphanage near the laboratory gets destroyed in their crossfire. Action Force, of course, has to save the orphans; and in the confusion the MacGuffin Device gets lost in the nearby woods. After the battle, Action Force rebuilds the orphanage and some of the team befriend the children. Most of the plot centres on a character called Shipwreck, a naval member of the team (talking parrot on shoulder), who tells the orphan children a story.

An animated version of Shipwreck's story is shown as he narrates it. In this story within a story, characters from Action Force and Cobra reappear as fairy-tale caricatures of themselves. For example, Cobra Commander is a huge snake. During a break in the story-telling, Zartan, one of Cobra's terrorist leaders and a master of disguise, infiltrates Action Force by impersonating Shipwreck. But when the children demand that he continues the story, he resumes with a nightmarish version in which evil triumphs. 'Please Shipwreck, it couldn't happen that way,' pleads a child. 'Well I say it did', insists the disguised Zartan, 'That's what always happens. The strong always win. Don't blame me. Facts of life, kids!' However, one of the children finds the real Shipwreck tied up in the woods. Released just as Cobra forces are summoned by Zartan to recover the MacGuffin Device, Shipwreck discovers it first and switches it on to see what it will do.

In a blinding blue light, emanating from the device, the characters

25 Frame stills from the 'Once Upon a Joe' episode of the *GI Joe/Action Force* TV series (Sunbow Productions). Having accidentally destroyed an orphanage with a misplaced missile, Shipwreck tells the orphans a story in which he and the other characters reappear as stylised cartoon versions – a cartoon within a cartoon – playfully maintaining a concern with questions of identity that would culminate in 1992–3 with the character Snake-Eyes.

from Shipwreck's fairy story appear in front of the Cobra attackers, causing confusion and a hasty retreat. 'It alters the fabric of reality', the Action Force commander explains to a bewildered Shipwreck, 'It draws out the innermost nature of the user.' Shipwreck finishes telling his story to the orphans. 'Don't you wish every story could end so happily?' says a little girl.

On this slender evidence, it is not immediately possible to surmise that the appeal of *GI Joe/Action Force* is located anywhere else but in its militaristic imagery. However, it isn't difficult to recognise that, for this episode's writer, the orphanage children in relation to Shipwreck's story parallel the relationship between real children and the Action Force master-narrative. Just as, for protection against the terrorists, the orphan children need the violent intrusion of Action Force into what is portrayed as their quietly routine tedium, so in some sense this writer presents the notion that real children need Action Force, the product. But Action Force also threatens the orphans's world, destroying their home by the indiscriminate use of force. The story within a story encapsulates this ambiguity in a highly significant and unmistakable way. The story is continuous but differs in its effects according to the teller.

When Shipwreck tells his part, the story tilts towards the reassuring. When Zartan takes over the narration, it tilts towards the frightening. It is as if the force needed to fulfil the child's desires (for security and freedom) and allay fears (of organised terror loose in the world) cannot completely achieve this, but rather can only perpetually re-enact the attempt. In doing so, the anxieties are regenerated and temporarily allayed in a continuing cycle of interdependence.

If this is what happens, it is so because the childish desires and anxieties which are addressed in the fiction are actually already the product of the very forces used to address them – the forces of organised violence. So the writer of 'Once Upon a Joe' cannot win. What he has exposed is the spiral of cause and effect that makes playing with the toys meaningful. This meaning is certainly reached, in part, by enacting the kind of narrative, or 'play scenario', encouraged by familiarity with the animated television stories (and/or the comics). Supported by 'biographical' information printed on the packaging, the toys (such as the little plastic figure of Shipwreck) are intended to intersect very clearly with the narrative knowledge created by the other forms. This narrative context sustains an object relation, through the toys, of the 'spiral' kind described in Chapter 2: aggression is shifted to and fro as cause and 'solution'. But by moralistically revealing this in 'Once Upon a Joe', the makers strip it of its actual resonance. They see what is happening so clearly that they make it too visible to work in this instance. The animated episodes can only be a part of the spiral of cause and effect: they cannot represent it without showing the strain.

According to one way of looking at this, the 'solution', the end of the spiral, is always finally a military one: unpack an 'Avalanche' toy vehicle and bury the enemy with missiles. But it could also be argued that this 'solution' is seriously weakened by, in fact, never being final, and that a real child's version of the question, 'Don't you wish every story could end so happily?' will be sufficiently aware of the solution's inadequacy as to suggest a more complex relationship between a child and the proferred representations (toys, TV series, narratives). Indeed what perpetuates the whole line, in all its interrelated forms, is perhaps the child's endless pursuit of the story within the story, of what is really going on while the aggression rages. This inner story may mostly be in the child's head while he or she plays with the toys; and if it is too explicitly represented, to be 'read off' as a message, its effectiveness dissipates.

Powerplay: toys as popular culture

Among the many narrative details that have been developed around the GI Joe/Action Force toys a few stand out: the Cobra terrorist organization is financed by a couple of city slickers, blue-suited twins who ooze city sophistication and stock-market unscrupulousness; their business, Extensive Enterprises, is based in a downtown skyscraper, connecting the terrorists to an image of capitalist 'respectability'. And Cobra Commander, the terrorist leader, wears a hood under which his 'face' is a blank metal plate – a kind of empty identity on to which a child can project whatever identity his or her own fears conjure up. In a 1986 episode from the animated series called 'In the Presence of Mine Enemy' (written by Chris Weber and Karen Willson), this fear embraces a monster unleashed when a biotechnology experiment goes wrong (anticipating the theme of *Jurassic Park* by seven years). Interestingly, this episode's sub-plot has an Action Force pilot and his Cobra foe forcing each other to crash-land near a deserted research station in a remote part of Africa, where our hero discovers that the Cobra pilot is a woman. When they find out that Cobra was behind the attempt to create a biological weapon, and that the knowledge will cost the woman her life, the two team up to escape. In doing so the woman turns out to be every bit as resourceful as her male counterpart. Under director of production Jim Graziano, many of the animated stories had this kind of depth to them. In 'Pit of Vipers', for example, a computer-controlled global surveillance and communication system is naively trusted by the Action Force team until they discover that Cobra has been secretly manipulating it. In 'Cold Slither' three female members of Action Force have to disguise themselves as groupies because the terrorists have been implanting subliminal messages in heavy metal music! For children a lot of difficult issues become representable in even those few examples.

Here then is our fifth set of effects – narrative effects which generate a spiral of endless disruption and restabilisation through each little toy object. There are themes here which will appear again as we trace the further development of this type of narrativised toy, beyond the continuing success of GI Joe/Action Force. Before doing so, however, we have raised issues about the toy industry generally that need to be addressed.

Production (from Sonneberg to Guangdong)

From the sixteenth to the eighteenth centuries the greatest concentration of organised toy making in the world grew up around five areas in Germany. Extensive forest supported an indigenous wood-carving tradition, water power was readily available to drive lathes, and topographically scattered clusters of workers, having few alternatives, were willing to work for low wages. A long-established tradition of religious carving began to diversify and expand into the world's first toy industry, as the idea of the child's special nature and needs took hold more generally: according to Luther 'the young must leap or jump, or have something to do, because they have a natural desire for it which should not be restrained (for it is not well to check them in everything)'.[18] In place of medieval Catholicism's repression of the child, as potentially evil until cleansed, there emerges a new interest in giving children 'something to do' that acknowledges their need to discover the world through a natural playfulness, however much that might then be checked by Protestant moral strictures and repression of feeling as the child grew. With a rapidly declining demand for religious carvings in Germany, the available skills were turned to this new outlet. Around Sonneberg, Seiffen, Oberammergau, Berchtesgaden and in the Groden valley (now in Italy), people worked in their own homes or in small community workshops, selling their wooden toys to wholesalers who took them to newly expanding markets such as Nuremberg or Leipzig.

With eighteenth-century growth came a need to 'mass' produce, in so far as this was possible for an essentially cottage industry to achieve. The 'ring method' was commonly used. A ring of wood, usually pine, was cut from a tree trunk and turned on a lathe to produce in section the basic outline of, for example, an animal, along the length of the ring. The ring was then sliced into individual figures, each of which could be hand carved to a more precise shape before being painted. Stylisation was encouraged by this method, and the staple of the German toy industry was the small stylised animal or peg-like human figure, typically a soldier, since parading regiments of identical figures suited the manufacturing technique. Unsurprisingly, as new manufacturing methods and materials became available, the German toy makers seized on them to make more of the same, efficiently and cheaply, and there is a direct line of continuity linking the products of sixteenth-century wood carvers with the tinplate 'penny' toys of the late nineteenth

Figure 3 The most significant areas in the history of toy manufacturing, showing the historic centres of toy-making in South-Central Europe and (inset) the site of today's concentration of the toy industry in southern China.

century, by which time manufacturing had moved closer to the markets, as in the case of Nuremberg, where the largest factories were located. Indeed the German industry's virtual invention of the modern 'toy', the small mass-produced plaything, may be thought of as culminating in the mid-twentieth-century in the hugely successful 'Playmobil' range from the Brandstatter factory in Zirndorf. The little plastic stylised people and animals in many cases look much like their wooden ancestors of four centuries earlier.

The 'Playmobil' toys no longer represent output from the world's major centre of toy making, however. In the second half of the twentieth century, that is to be found in South-east Asia.[19] The Youli Toys factory in Guangzhou, China, for example, is to the toy industry today what the workshops of Sonneberg or Seiffen were in the eighteenth century. Cheap labour there and in scores of similar factories produces toys that are packaged in Hong Kong for re-export to Europe and the United States, in a chain that links the crowded factory on Huan Cheng West Road to the airy headquarters of a corporate giant like Tonka in the United States. Sixty per cent of Hong Kong's total annual toy exports, worth well over three billion US dollars, originate in China, and those exports constitute some 80 per cent of the world's trade in toys (excluding computer games).[20]

China's Guangdong province, with its two enterprise zones set up in part to collaborate with Hong Kong businesses, is now home to two million people dependent on manufacturing, much of it of toys (for which the Chinese government's official figure is a conservative estimate of 30,000 directly involved workers). Only ten of the many Hong Kong toy makers have workforces of more than 500 people in the city itself. Injection and extrusion machines for moulding plastic goods are made in Hong Kong for sale to China. Most of the capital and the management are based in Hong Kong, where wage increases (and US trade tariffs which don't apply to Chinese manufactures) motivated the move across the border into mainland China. In 1990 Hong Kong's domestic toy exports fell by some 27 per cent but its re-exports of Chinese-made toys grew by the same amount. One company has indicated that its manufacturing costs in China are a sixth of what they would have been in Hong Kong. And in Hong Kong most of the toy companies have been, in turn, sub-contractors of transnationals based in the US or Europe, passing on the benefits of cheap Chinese labour.

Reliance on that chain of connections has real dangers for those at the manufacturing end. Apart from not seeing much share of the eventual profits, their jobs are as insecure as it is possible to be. When Worlds of Wonder, a huge US-based toy company, went bankrupt in 1987, dozens of manufacturers in South-east Asia either suffered enormous losses or disappeared. Meanwhile Worlds of Wonder, with its debts (over US$40 million) to Hong Kong and elsewhere written off, relaunched in the United States with a new product line of electronic toys based on technology from weapons guidance systems. Nevertheless, in 1989 half a billion US dollars were earned by Chinese toy makers, and two years later Ren Xingbang, president of the Chinese Toy Association, predicted a turnover of at least twice that by the year 2000.[21] The image of the 'sweatshop' and Western capitalist exploitation does not square too well with China's eagerness to engage in what the Ministry of Light Industries terms 'joint ventures'. In 1991 China had 1,700 toy-related businesses, many perhaps over-reliant on transnationals operating through Hong Kong subsidiaries and few seeing what we might consider a fair share of the profits which the toys are earning worldwide; but there remains an analogy here with what happened to the original industry begun by German wood carvers of the sixteenth century.

'America has been Turtled!'

Just as the cheap labour of poor rural communities in the Thuringian forest or Erzgebirge mountains led eventually in Germany to a successful national industry in the nineteenth and twentieth centuries, offering in the end a fairly good living to many thousands of workers, so it might be argued that the toy industry of South-east Asia is learning how to fend for itself. While the workers of Shanghai, Shenzhen or Guangzhou are not currently faring well compared with their equivalents in Europe or the United States, the companies for which they work are beginning to challenge the power of the transnationals from whom they have learnt the business. At Christmas 1992, most toyshops in the UK stocked a colourful, chubbily exaggerated, diecast metal toy Jumbo jet on wheels. It originated from the Shanghai Toys Import and Export Corporation, set up in 1979 and now the largest organisation of its kind in China. The corporation has thirty-one production subsidiaries with 12,000 employees and its own toy research centre and training school. According to deputy manager He Guan-Shan, by organising themselves in this way the Shanghai toy manufacturers have substantially freed their businesses from dependence and exploitation and now export directly into over a hundred countries, with toys which they have designed and manufactured themselves.[22]

In a further example, the Youli Toys factory in Guangzhou was in fact where many of the successful plastic *Teenage Mutant Ninja Turtles* figures were manufactured for Playmates Toys Inc., a major operation with a Californian address. But the parent company, Playmates Holdings, is a Hong Kong business that had already successfully sold to the nationalistic Japanese an electronic talking doll, cleverly marketed as a language-learning aid. Fortified by having proved that such markets are not impregnable to outsiders, Playmates licensed the Turtles from the writers of a very minor US comic book, because they liked the martial-arts element, and then marketed the whole concept back into the United States so successfully that Playmates' executive Chu Big-fung could justifiably claim in 1990, 'America has been Turtled'.[23] The big US and European-based toy companies could only look on while the Turtles dominated the 1988 Christmas market and continued to achieve considerable worldwide success for the following three years. 'Turtling' one's former paymasters has perhaps become a deeply symbolic gesture for the South-east Asian toy makers, though unfortunately still based to a large degree on low-wage labour in China and elsewhere.

But in addition to cocking a snook at Western dominance, South-east Asia's toy makers are involved in a more complex relationship with the West. Where, in a sense, the content of the original German toy industry was an increasingly subtle and aware conception of the child itself, the content of the South-east Asian toy industry is instead Western popular culture. Since the only common frame of reference for a global market is that popular culture, Yat Ming Industrial Factory Ltd. has its Shen-shen and Bangkok factories turning out five-inch-long 'Tomcat' jet fighter toys because the Hollywood film *Top Gun* imprinted its image on the global popular imagination (the US taking 50 per cent of their output and Europe 40 per cent); Unimax's factories throughout South-east Asia churn out suntanned Caucasian dolls with beach accessories, looking as if they have just left the set of television's *Baywatch*; the Silverlit Toys Manufactory Ltd. have a 'Galaxy Series Construction Team' range of science-fiction toys that looks like a catalogue of images from every Hollywood sci-fi success of recent years (their promotional illustrations even using as a motif a strip of movie film carrying photographs of the toys). The examples could proliferate. Global culture all too clearly mirrors the reach of the multinationals.

Multinational capitalism and culture

Since the 1980s, for the first time, the toy industry has been completely dominated by multinational companies. Distinctively national markets and manufacturers have had to adapt or have disappeared. From the 1950s to the 1970s in the UK, for example, British brands had been dominant. The Lines Brothers' brand names were household words

26 South-east Asia's toy manufacturers, when they design their own ranges, persistently turn to the content of Western popular culture. Interestingly, the compressed timescale of the move through a building and constructional phase of development to a multinational consumer culture (in this case in Hong Kong) is reflected in Silverlit's science-fiction construction range, in which Meccano meets *Star Wars*.

(Hornby, Dinky, Meccano, Tri-ang, Scalextric). Chad Valley, Britains, Mettoy (with their Corgi brand name) and Lesney (Matchbox) completed the picture. Along with a few cheap imports from Hong Kong, these companies filled the toyshop shelves, and their products litter the childhood memories of those born in the 1950s or early 1960s. It was still a period of the family business: Richard Kohnstam is a good example, following his father and grandfather into the toy trade, licensing some of the first TV-related toys, including Muffin the Mule, before having the idea for little diecast metal cars that could fit in a matchbox – the rights for which he eventually sold to Lesney as the basis for what would become a world-famous range of toys. Kohnstam continued to run the family business in England until his death in 1985, by which time he was serving niche markets of adult hobbyists (for instance model railway enthusiasts), as the toy market had passed such small-scale operations

27 Despite a belated attempt to develop a range of 'Space Ranger' costumes (left), the original GI Joe/Action Man was very much rooted in Second World War imagery. The SAS costume (right) was prompted by television coverage of the Iranian embassy siege in London in 1980. In the new range of small action figures the Democratic Revolutionary Front for the Liberation of Arabistan has become the international terrorist organisation Cobra, there are female troops on both sides and the imagery of hero and villain is a good deal more confused.

by. A few intruders on the English scene since the late 1950s were signs of things to come. New York-based company Marx exported toys based on popular American television series, such as their Wagon Train Playset (1960) of little plastic Cowboys and Indians. But, most notably, in 1964 an American freelance toy designer, Stan Weston, created GI Joe for boys and sold the idea to the US company Hasbro. Licensed to the British company Palitoy as Action Man in 1966, the soldier doll was, as we have seen, a huge international success, and presaged the increasing dominance of companies like Hasbro, which were to grow into multinationals as a result of such successes. (Palitoy would eventually itself disappear into one of these, Kenner-Parker, in 1985.)

Although heavily advertised, GI Joe/Action Man did not appear in a television series or comic (in what would now be known as 'total marketing'); but the soldier doll undoubtedly benefited from loose association with specific features of a then burgeoning American popular culture. The original box art for the toy very explicitly evoked popular comics of the time (*Sgt. Rock* and *Sgt. Fury*), and its launch coincided with the successful television series *Combat* (1963–68), which achieved top-ten audience figures in the United States in 1965 and was extensively sold to other countries. The first range of uniforms and equipment for GI Joe/Action Man could have been lifted straight out of *Combat* – Second World War infantry, French resistance fighters, etc. The aura which American popular culture gave to GI Joe/Action Man distinguished it from the more homely pleasures of the Dinky car or the Meccano construction set. However, when popular culture moved on and a simpler Second World War imagery failed to survive television's delivery of Vietnam's horrors into the home, GI Joe/Action Man in his original form lost his appeal. The general point underscored by this example is that the cycles of taste and fashion so typical of popular culture generally had begun to infiltrate a toy industry that had tended previously to be much more stable.

Stability, the long-term appeal of the Hornby toy train or the Corgi diecast metal toy car, necessitated new tooling by manufacturers only infrequently, and fairly stable workforces could be maintained on production lines. Fashion-driven instability pushed up the frequency and therefore the cost of changes in both tooling and workforces, driving manufacturers to seek cheaper 'adjustable' labour and international markets capable of justifying heavy investment in new tooling. Multinational companies plugged themselves into a global popular culture, sustained by a whole range of media, and emerged as the predictable winners in this altered marketplace. Control the 'fashions' by total marketing, and manufacture the products using cheap, manipulable labour in South-east Asia: this is the formula for success in the toy industry in the 1990s. A clear cyclical pattern has emerged as a result.

Most toy ranges now have a two- to three-year lifespan. Seventy per cent of sales tend to be in the three months prior to Christmas. Comics, television series (usually animations), books and sometimes cinema films create a popular aura around a toy. The toy may have come first or, more usually, may arise out of one or more of these other forms. In either case the first nine months of the year will see a gradual consolidation of the total marketing strategy, with trade fairs in January and February for the industry to tell itself what it's doing that year; but the details will then vary depending on the balance among the different media being used or responded to. An obviously exploitable summer-released feature film, for example, may give a particular shape to the year. So in the spring of 1993 dinosaur toys, comics and children's magazines began to proliferate in anticipation of the summer's *Jurassic Park*, the heavily promoted film from Steven Spielberg, which in turn then focused the interest in dinosaurs on to specific licensed spin-off toys in time for the three-month pre-Christmas sales boom. This pattern may vary, but the cycle remains essentially the same: the momentum of the first year's marketing will usually carry the toys for another year. If interest is sufficient, the marketing effort will be sustained (as with the Transformers); but this will overlap with creation of some new fashion, and disappearance of any one toy range within three years or so is now considered almost inevitable.

The final stage is usually recognisable when boxes begin to get shifted around the international market to get rid of them – heavily discounted toys with packaging in Italian or Spanish will appear on the UK market, and so on. The last remnants of the *Ghostbusters* range were cleared in this way at Christmas 1992, for example, four years after their first appearance. Sometimes the lifespan of a toy is very much shorter: *ET* toys, based on the film of that name from Steven Spielberg, survived for only their initial three-month peak period. Set against the overall argument of this book, it can be suggested that such relative failures do not function adequately within some or all of the seven sets of effects and, therefore, have insufficient 'resonance' for children. (*ET* toys, for instance, were too remote and isolated in what they represented – a very distinctive lone alien visitor – to function well as harmonising or totemic objects, and did not fit into a sufficiently elaborated meta-narrative.)

Toy retailing

For the national manufacturers who had emerged from thirty years of stability, based on product lines that either stayed essentially the same or evolved slowly, the choice was to compete on the new terms or settle for a reduced background role.[24] Behind the hugely profitable fashion-driven, cyclically marketed toy ranges there remains a background of more modestly successful toys, usually relying on niches within the overall toy market: outdoor toys with a summer-based seasonality that protects them from the main cycle, technical construction toys like Lego with an educational element, toy car ranges that keep step with new models from the manufacturers of real cars, pre-school toys, etc. And some toys are deliberately marketed as alternatives to the popular culture tie-ins and hype – most notably the ranges carried by the Early Learning Centre shops in Britain. Generally, though, such toys are chosen by adults for their children, adults who are concerned that children should learn through play (Almqvist interestingly analyses the social phenomenon of 'educational toys' in its historical context),[25] adults who are themselves interested in cars, or whatever. The market among adults not directly influenced by what children say they want will continue to exist. Indeed, 'traditional' manufacturers may be able to appeal to these purchasers simply by virtue of the familiar brand names: Corgi or Lego may evoke memories of one's own childhood that seem more trustworthy than the brasher demands for our attention of Bandai or Nikko. But most toys are now either chosen by children themselves or result from persuasion by the child. Toy marketing gives children not only something to want but a vocabulary of persuasion to use on parents and on each other.[26]

A further factor has arisen from the cyclical, fashion-driven nature of the new toy market, a factor which now operates in turn to maintain the nature of that market – increasingly difficult stock management and prediction. Like other goods, individual toys or toy lines are grouped into stock keeping units or SKUs. To take Britain as an example, at any one time some 250,000 SKUs may be on offer from toy suppliers. Even the very largest toy shops will only have shelf space for perhaps a twelfth of these. With demand rapidly changing in step with the marketing cycle, it is crucial for retailers to have the right items on their shelves at the right time and in the right quantities. It is easier to play safe with a few heavily promoted lines than to risk others that may or may not sell at a particular moment. So the pattern of a few massively promoted toys in the foreground (literally, as they get the prime sites on the shelves) with the old reliables (the ones with parent appeal) in the background, is now the safest for retailers.

Since at any one moment the heavily promoted toys, the ones at the peak of the cycle, will be relatively few, retailing has shifted away from reliance on specialist toy shops with extensive lines, and those few select toys can be found in department stores, variety shops like Woolworth, gift shops, filling stations, etc. At the other end of the scale, toy supermarkets such as Toys 'R' Us are able to pick up the thousands of SKUs ignored by the smaller outlets and make a virtue out of stacking them high, even if some of them then gather dust.

A manufacturing case study: the UK

The current state of toy manufacturing in Britain reflects the situation described above.[27] The British Toy and Hobby Association represents 285 manufacturers (although there are estimated to be some 200 further toy makers, predominantly one-person businesses on the handbuilt, traditional craft fringe of the industry). However, most of the 'manufacturers' do not in fact make toys themselves but rather 'source' them: that is, they obtain toys manufactured overseas and badge them with their own names. Those that do maintain complete manufacturing operations are firmly established in narrowly defined niches – Casdon of Blackpool making doll's pushchairs, Waddingtons near Leeds making their board games, etc. The others are predominantly now in the business of marketing and selling. Even then, the concentration of effort remains often directed towards filling niches – train sets, jigsaws, pre-school items, and so on. The big toy success stories, from Barbie to Transformers, are firmly in the hands of the few multinational corporations which now dominate the market.

Bandai (UK) Ltd. is perhaps now more typical of how the industry works in the UK than any of the niche-providers mentioned above. With some 140 employees, the company is a wholly owned subsidiary of Bandai of Japan. It was the UK distributor for the Nintendo computer game system (until Nintendo took over its own distribution) and UK licensee, from Playmates of Hong Kong, for Teenage Mutant Ninja Turtles and for the toy figures based on the television series *Star Trek: The Next Generation.* Many of these toys are made in China by subcontractors controlled from Hong Kong, and the Bandai parent company has factories of its own in Hong Kong and Thailand. UK sales in 1990, even before the Nintendo boom, were £35 million. The UK sales force consists of six employees and eleven agents. A relatively small group of people, then, manages a huge commercial operation by forming a channel through which a multinational toy industry goes about its business. Bandai (UK) is successful by implementing the licensing and distribution deals made by its parent company in Japan, sticking its label on toys made elsewhere and supplying them to retailers in

Britain at the moment and in the quantities dictated by a marketing strategy that is largely coordinated from elsewhere (with the help of television programmes made in Hollywood, comics published in New York or computer games made in Japan). One further example confirms the trend: the 'traditional' British brand name 'Corgi' is now owned by the multinational Mattel, its metal vehicle toys are all made in the Far East, the UK company has less than thirty employees, and its 1990 sales in the UK were around £10 million. With no UK manufacturing, very few employees, but all the right connections, a few 'British' toy companies can make a lot of money. The rest can only hope to plug a few very small gaps in the market.

Of course a UK-based multinational can operate in the way Bandai or Mattel do. So the Hanson corporation owns Ertl Ltd. of Exeter, which, with only twenty-four employees, none the less handles some £5 million in UK sales annually by licensing and distributing toy lines from Hollywood, including the *Star Trek* and *Batman* series of motion pictures, with many of the toys being made in Mexico. But the Hanson group is something of an exception on the UK scene. A company like Fisher-Price in Berkshire is not in fact a separately registered company at all, but merely a division of the US-based multinational of that name. The list could go on. The point is simply that the UK toy industry, like that of most European countries, is now inextricably linked to and dominated by the handful of multinational companies, mostly US-based, responsible for integrating toys into a globally powerful popular culture. The actual selling of toys has to follow the dictates of that system.

The new consumer

The available ways of analysing the buying of toys are many and varied, with birthrate trends charted to correlate with gross domestic product, pocket money levels, seasonal factors, and so on.[28] There is some virtue, however, in attending to only a few key features of consumer behaviour and attitudes, including some that may not appear initially to have a direct bearing on toys.

First, a key fact in recent years has been the huge dominance over children's television viewing habits in the UK of the Australian-made soap operas, predominantly *Neighbours*. In the early 1990s various surveys put these top of the viewing preference lists for as many as a quarter of British children between five and twelve years old – that is, of prime toy-buying age. The sunny simplicity of these soaps seems shallow to some adults; but if we think of them as stories for children then the open-ended plot complexity, elaborate character interactions and refusal of conventional narrative closure (the hero's intervention, the happy ending) all combine into something quite challenging to a ten-year-old mind. That the subject-matter is the adult world and its tortuous complexities makes children's liking for these programmes all the more interesting (and makes the summery never-never land of stylised Australian suburbia a landscape of the young mind, a simplified version of the real world, displaced from everyday reality). What we have here is a growing and significant taste in general among children for the elaborately extended narratives so typical of soap opera.

As the earlier analysis of the 'Once Upon a Joe' episode from *Action Force* suggested, the explicit narrative realisation of this interest (in this case *Neighbours*) itself openly presents and contains the particular interest involved – in this case an interest in open-ended narrative elaboration. So toys based directly on *Neighbours* would be overwhelmed by the TV original. The latter occupies that particular space with too tight a fit to leave any more room for play. So, although there are few toys based directly on these soaps, the most successful toys in recent years have had hugely elaborate narratives constructed around them, narratives that in their open-endedness and their large evolving casts of characters in fact deeply resemble the basic principles of soap opera. The imaginary universes of *Star Wars* (as elaborated in comics and books) or Transformers consolidated this trend. Unlike a mundane TV soap, *Star Wars* thematically licensed its opening up in other ways; so too more recently with *Mighty Morphin' Power Rangers*, which cleverly combines soap-opera sub-plots (the high-school scenes) with its Japanese-TV-derived special effects scenes.

Secondly, books and video tapes feature just as prominently in children's Christmas present request lists as do toys. In 1991, for instance, books topped the lists along with clothes and bicycles, together making up almost half of the Christmas preferences for five- to twelve-year-olds. Video game systems shoved their way on to the top of these lists for the following Christmas, consigning conventional toys to an even lower position. So, although toys are a very important part of childhood, they do not dominate children's own behaviour as consumers. Given what was broadly characterised above as a significant narrative interest it is not difficult to see how toys associated with books and video tapes have come to be especially popular, representing a taste for particular narratives as much as a preference for a particular toy.

Lists of parents' intended or actual purchases tend to place toys higher than they are on the children's own lists (the desirability of dolls and toy cars, for example, being over-estimated by parents, perhaps mothers and fathers respectively).[29] Parents appear, by and large, not to recognise the narrative interconnections which endow toys that may be meaningless to them with a complementary role in relation to books and videos. Indeed the video game boom of 1992 simply drew these things more explicitly together: computerised versions of the Teenage Mutant Ninja Turtles, for example, could be manipulated like toys but still lived very much within the video world of the narrative already established for them – and the 1995 Power Rangers video game was similar. The appeal of these narratives (variously represented in different media, including toys) is what appears to matter most to children. In terms of regular weekly expenditure throughout the year, comics and magazines account for almost twice the expenditure on toys. Comics based on the Turtles, Transformers, or whatever happens to be popular at the time, appear to offer the regular narrative sustenance which underpins less frequent expenditure on associated books, videos, computer games or toys. Many mixed retailers have the advantage that they sell toys next to comics, magazines, books and videos. These are no longer, for the most part, separate goods to children, but different forms through which their preferred narratives seamlessly weave their way.

Interestingly, some of the heaviest spending on television advertising (apart from the video game companies) is to support brands like Hornby and Lego. These are the fairly stable background brands, highly familiar to parents, rather than the cyclical multi-media-promoted big-sellers. It is the former that benefit most from the 'reminder' function of television advertising, especially between October and December. In fact toy companies are increasingly concerned about the negative effects of what they term 'clutter and clashing' during peak toy advertising periods: that the proliferation of toy advertisements might have a numbing effect on viewers and that similar products advertised side by side may confuse rather than elicit interest. 'Building awareness', as it is called, is now increasingly achieved in other ways through other media. The multimedia narratives of total marketing achieve such 'awareness' as their basic principle, and so rely much less on television advertisements than on television series based on the narratives – which of course function implicitly as extended advertisements. We have described the contemporary context that generates the sixth set of effects – the commodification effects through which toys are caught up in the elaborate processes of 'building awareness' around the complex chains of multi-media marketing.

4

Toys and society

The *Star Wars* toys demonstrated that children would respond enthusiastically to an imaginary 'culture' inhabited by a diversity of characters
whose interactions are organised by a master-narrative, and that such
a narrative could be sustained through other media. The adaptation of
GI Joe/Action Man to fit these conditions proved successful for the
Hasbro multinational toy company. But it was their Transformers concept that pushed these trends to their limit, locating an extensive range
of toys in an amazingly complex imaginary universe, explored in a
television series, videos, comics and books. Many of the concerns of
late-twentieth-century life become representable here in ways accessible
to children.

The mechanical soap opera

The Transformers' master-narrative provided a soap-opera-like framework for endlessly complex ramifications. Four million years ago,
according to this story, in a distant part of the galaxy a terrible war was
waged between two races of highly advanced and intelligent machines,
the Autobots and the Decepticons. These robot-like machines could
transform their appearances in various ways. Spreading out into space
from their planet Cybertron, the warring factions were driven farther
afield as the planet's natural resources were exhausted. Two opposing
forces crash-landed on Earth, the machines burying themselves in an
area of volcanic activity. Millions of years later, the eruption of a dor-
mant volcano stirs the machines into life and their conflict continues
on Earth. Using their transformative powers they disguise themselves
as Earth objects, from trucks and caterpillar diggers to ghetto-blasters
and helicopters. The Autobots, aware of the tragedy that befell their
own home planet, attempt to protect the Earth's resources and inhabitants from a similar fate. But the Decepticons prove more ruthless and
the conflict escalates.

As the war between the machines is more openly waged on Earth, they begin to draw on the planet's animal forms for their transformations. Simpler machines known as 'primitives' take on mechanised animal shapes, a lion, a dog, a rhinoceros, while others even discover prehistoric forms and a class of Dinobots emerges. All the individual machines have dual identities (for instance Hound is a four-wheel-drive vehicle that transforms into a scouting and tracking robot!) and many have characters that gradually evolved through the animated series or the comics (for example Hound secretly wants to be human). In a complex mix of organic and mechanical imagery, a future world of post-industrial mayhem was created. From the dozens of characters and the proliferating plot lines a few further details stand out.

28 The Transformers heralded a new kind of machine imagery, a long way away from the tinplate replicas of turn-of-the-century cars and trains. At the centre is the basic figure of an intelligent humanoid robot who can reshape himself into some kind of machine. The toys were often very cleverly designed, like a sort of mechanical Rubik's cube, to allow these transformations.

The machine civilisations elsewhere in the galaxy discover their lost outposts on Earth and, the machines having mastered time travel, the conflict between Autobots and Decepticons on this small planet becomes embroiled again in a galactic struggle that spans both space and time. By the year 2000, the Decepticons have been largely defeated on Earth, and six years later they are faring so badly elsewhere that they retreat to a remote and devastated hulk of a planet to reconsider their position. The original leaders of the factions on Earth, Optimus Prime and Megatron, are upstaged by the galactic leaders Ultra Magnus and Galvatron, Autobot and Decepticon respectively. On Earth, the Autobots build a huge machine city called Metroplex, with modular components which make up one vast machine but can also function separately.

Machine sub-cultures were explored extensively. The Junkions, for example, were allies of the Autobots and perhaps epitomised this future vision. They lived in an environment of machine junk which they cannibalised, and their entire culture was based on Earth's popular culture, picked up from radio waves. They talked in lines taken out of context from Humphrey Bogart movies, TV commercials, situation comedies and game shows. The Junkions were only an extreme version of the basic Transformers principle: everything had become mechanised but remained inhabited in some way by the traces of a more organic culture. In addition to the imperialistic ambitions of the Decepticons, other recognisable sources of evil were identified: the Quintessons, for example, were a race of unscrupulous galactic capitalists whose arms dealing was carefully planned to fuel the machine wars that raged everywhere and from which they profiteered.

The infiltration of everyday life

During the Earth-bound stage of the Transformers narrative the infiltration of everyday life by machines with secret double identities, however far-fetched the idea may seem, was so convincingly handled that it must have had a powerful imaginative hold on the children who owned the toys in such large numbers. An Autobot called Blaster has played an important part in this. His disguise is as a ghetto-blaster tape deck and his cassettes are 'primitives' – simpler robots with animal-based identities. Blaster himself is a highly intelligent robot who acts as 'guardian' to these 'primitives'. Blaster took on this transformer identity

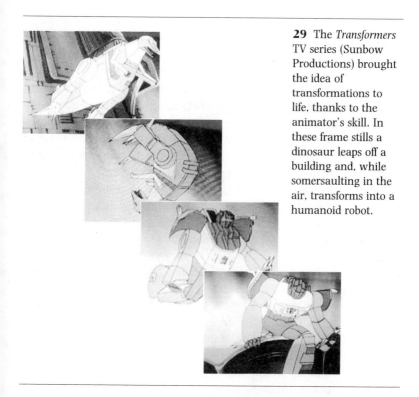

29 The *Transformers* TV series (Sunbow Productions) brought the idea of transformations to life, thanks to the animator's skill. In these frame stills a dinosaur leaps off a building and, while somersaulting in the air, transforms into a humanoid robot.

in response to a Decepticon called Soundwave who functions similarly, his 'primitives' being menacing surveillance robots. In a 1986 'Ladybird' book written by John Grant, one of Soundwave's cassettes accidently ends up in a teenage boy's bedroom, where his mother, tidying up, puts it into a box of tapes which the boy takes to a disco in the village hall. Put into the sound system the Decepticon tape transforms into a huge mechanical bird of prey: 'The dancers screamed as the sinister creature swooped over their heads.'[1]

This fascination with the hidden power of technologies, with the possibility that technologies somehow transcend their mundane functions, whether for good or ill, characterised the whole Transformers phenomenon. It was often thematically explicit in videos and comics. In a 1992 comic-book story called 'City of Fear', for example, a group of Autobots find themselves in the ruined city of Kalis – an urban industrial wasteland from the depths of which emerge the skeletal mechanical remains of 'dead' robots who have somehow been revitalised, zombie-fashion. The plot revolves around the question of how these zombie machines can function without their 'brain modules', according to the Autobots the site of their intelligence and compassion. The notion that these qualities of life can reside in machines sets up the tension on which the Transformers master-narrative depends: in an imaginary world in which virtually nothing organic remains do such values and qualities retain their meaning? It transpires that the mechanical zombies are being computer-controlled, as part of a plot to challenge the Autobots, and so a machine intelligence tempered with compassion once again triumphs over the merely technologically clever.

So densely are such layers of meaning laid down around the toys by other narrative manifestations, that there can be little doubting the fact of children's thoroughly mediated relationship with the toy objects themselves. Those objects become meaningful in relation to the narratively imagined world constructed around them. Children not extensively exposed, through various media, to the details of that world, are much less likely to find the toys of interest than those for whom a toy robot is a character with a readily available and complex narrative existence; play then becoming an acting out of scenarios appropriate to, and informed by, the available master-narrative as outlined above. Adults unaware, as most are, of the complexity of that narrative and its richness of detail, will be unable to 'read' the toy objects in those terms and will quite simply fail to understand what children are actually doing with the toys.

The peculiar nature of the object relation between child and toy created in this way is worth dwelling on. If, as some versions of object relations theory suggest, aggression is not the manifestation of an instinctual drive but a personally meaningful reaction to bad object relations in one's life, then the preoccupation with aggression in GI Joe/Action Force and Transformers becomes intelligible in a new way. The preceding summaries suggest that the aggressively pursued conflicts between the Joe/Action Force team and the Cobra terrorists (Chapter 3), or between Autobot and Decepticon, are broad narrative contexts within which an inner story is pursued – in effect, the story of what to do with the fact that aggression creates the very anxieties which aggression is then called on to 'solve'. Into the seemingly endless cycle of battle scenes in comics and videos, and played out with the toys, the complex master-narratives insert detail that both motivates the violence and renders it unmistakably incomplete as either explanation or solution. Put more simply, the child invited to enact a battle scene with a set of little toy robots would have merely the tools for imagining a mechanised battle, except that a more inviting narrative knowledge with a subtlety of 'history' and characterisation adds depth to what is superficially only an acting out of aggression for its own sake.

Object relations and aggression

Instead of aggressive toys being used to satisfy some instinctively aggressive urge in the child, there would appear to be a much more complex situation in which the child is invited to find within the represented aggression a narrativised object relation to substitute for bad object relations in the real world; object relations which in fact themselves stimulate the aggressive interests in the first place. Understanding a toy Autobot called 'Rumbler' as a character with his own role to play in the imaginary world sketched above is not at all the same thing as seeing merely a little toy weapon to bash about in play battles with others. That bashing about will occur in actual play of course, but it can hardly remain unaffected by the narrative knowledge which endows the toy with much of its attractiveness and significance in the first place. Mastering the complexities of that knowledge and thereby relating 'fully' to the toy object (or to the larger system of which it is a part) may offer substitute satisfactions for less complete object relations in the 'real' life of the child. If so, there should be clues in the very nature of the narrative knowledge which offers this substitution.

In fact it is abundantly clear that unsatisfactory object relations with the adult world are reflected in these narrativised toys. An adult world of organised terror and potentially dehumanising technology, of massive unnatural forces incomprehensible to the child, finds itself reconstructed into the more manageable terrors of Cobra or the Decepticons. The aggression which marks the very condition of unsatisfactory object relations (of the gap between that perceived reality and the values espoused before the child by adults – see Chapter 2) then becomes the context for narratives which both recognise that very aggression and yet also persistently explore its limits. A further example of the latter is found in the 'City of Fear' story from the *Transformers* comic.[2] In that story the Autobots are lead by Springer, a robot who is uncertain of his own abilities and is haunted by the memory of a dead friend and leader called Impactor against whom he never seems to measure up. When Impactor turns out to be among the zombie robots of Kalis, Springer has to confront the memory of his friend and his own uncertainty about having taken Impactor's place. The cover picture of this issue of the *Transformers* comic shows the two locked in violent combat. The point of the story, though, is to raise a series of questions about the nature of that conflict and indeed about the distinction between humanised and dehumanised technologies, in this case Springer and the zombie Impactor respectively, the one mindlessly aggressive, the other bewildered and forced into violence. It is important that when a child looks at his or her Transformers toys such things may be coming to mind.

Of course it can be argued that such 'depth' is merely the result of narratively convenient plot devices which allow an endless recycling of battle scenes. That is certainly true up to a point. In both *GI Joe/Action Force* and *Transformers* there is an inexorability about the descent into violence (part of a more general closure of possibilities which we will look at in more detail in the final chapter). Their violent purposes are an inescapable feature of the toys. Indeed they are their dominant feature. But once created, for whatever reason, the contextual 'depth' refuses to go away. While aggression is a Transformer toy's denotation, its connotation is unavoidably the narrative knowledge which explains its very existence and which refuses to let the violence be the whole story.[3]

In the toys, an obscuring and misleading adult world, in which espoused values are contradicted by aggression towards others and towards nature, is translated into a fullness of meaning, a graspable whole, a master-narrative. To work, to be effective, this has to contain the very anxiety-inducing features of the adult world that impel the child to seek these alternative object relations in the first place (hence terrorism, war and the supplanting of the natural by machines) – including the aggression which is both a response to that which obscures and misleads and a perceived feature of the adult world which does the misleading.

To take a final example from the Transformers toys, it is worth considering a line of small toys called the Constructicons. These consisted of little plastic models of heavy construction equipment – trucks, earthmovers, cranes, cement-mixers, etc. Introduced in 1991, these toys might have innocently offered children a miniature construction site to

30 At the heart of the Transformers there seems to have been an increasingly ambiguous relationship between children and technology. The innocent cranes and diggers of Meccano are now tainted with environmental menace. Here a simple little yellow mechanical digger transforms into an ugly and frightening Decepticon.

play with. But as images of such machinery ripping up the environment, destroying rain forests and replacing nature with concrete, now sit uneasily with the child's sense that clearing and building is just something that the adult world does, so the construction equipment transforms into menacing Decepticon robots. Thus aggression is located inside the very machinery of the construction site, the Transformers' master-narrative making imaginary sense of an ambiguity that the child might not otherwise be able to deal with in relating to imagery of real earth-movers and caterpillar-diggers, no longer mere objects of innocent awe as they once were for the children who played with Meccano.

Television and violence

So we come to the thorniest problem facing any account of the relationship between children and the media – that of violence, its representation and supposed effects. There is an evasive line on this problem, increasingly adopted within academic media studies – to suggest that there is just as much research evidence for there being no ill effects as there is of children being made more aggressive; in short that the jury is still out and is likely to remain so for some time. In fact, the best research now suggests another answer.[4] Given the complexity of the issues involved, however, there may be some merit here in opting for brevity rather than miring our own discussion in detail that can be picked up elsewhere.

The more interesting answer to the question of what effects TV violence has on children is that it is entirely context-dependent. The definition of 'violence' is itself context-dependent (do we mean news footage of a riot or cartoon characters bashing each other?). The ways children respond to a particular instance of violence are context-dependent: violence in an LA-based cop series will be understood differently by a child in Los Angeles and a child in rural Scotland. In other words the degree of 'reality' or 'fictionality' recognised in the representation (its modality in the jargon) will also be context-dependent. The specific meaning of a violent act on television will depend on how the narrative context and characterisations situate and explain that act: is it unmotivated, an act of revenge, an act of self-defence, etc.? There is a growing and convincing body of evidence about the inescapable significance of all these kinds of context-dependence.

That evidence includes work which clearly suggests children are discriminating in their understanding of contexts. Televised footage of Rodney King's beating by LA police in 1992 had the 'effect' of triggering violence (among many teenagers as well as adults) because of the complex context of its reception in that city (including the legal acquittal of the officers). In other contexts it was shocking, but not a cause of violence, as far as we know. The Danish Lego toy company's 1993 catalogue was criticised for depicting a little Lego-built car thief knocking over garbage bins as he careers down the street pursued by a police car and helicopter. Charged with encouraging joy-riding, it is more than likely that the only context recognisable to children will be the fictional television police series and that the child will consequently 'identify' with the pursuing police rather than with the thief. The image has the wrong modality (a fictional genre) to connect unambiguously with real joy-riding, never mind to encourage it – unless a child in LA, a very long way away from Denmark, finds it impossible to identify with the police and reads the image 'deviantly'. It is to that degree of local, specific determinants of meaning that research into 'effects' has to look. More generally, the contexts of family, peer group, neighbourhood and school will all influence how a child responds to violence on television. It is certainly possible to imagine a situation in which all these contexts conspire to create a child who, on seeing a particularly provocative piece of violence on television, goes out and repeats it. Such copy-cat events are rare and make the headlines, fuelling panic about 'effects' when their rarity should instead be telling us that such things seldom find such an unfortunate conjunction of supporting contexts.

This is the conclusion reached by Smith in *The Sleep of Reason*, about the murder of a child, James Bulger, by two ten-year-old boys in Liverpool in 1993. The trial judge speculated unwisely on the fact that one of the boys had watched a horror video, *Child's Play 3*, and this escalated into a full-fledged moral panic about the 'effects' of such material, in which an academic 'discussion paper' played a significant role. Smith quotes from the paper:

> 'Video Violence and the Protection of Children' was written by Elizabeth Newson from the Child Development Research Unit at Nottingham University, and was endorsed by a bewilderingly large number of 'psychologists, psychiatrists, paediatricians and others'. The paper made a direct link with the Bulger case and, in the course of a preamble, stated that we should 'try to ensure that Jamie (*sic*) is not just the first of many such victims'. It went on . . . 'However, child abuse, poverty and neglect have been a part of many children's experience over the years: indeed although neither Jon nor Robert could be said to have come from happy and nurturant homes, there was little evidence of the extremes of neglect and abuse that could be documented in any Social Service department. What then can be seen as the different factor that has entered the lives of countless children and adolescents in recent years? This has to be recognised as the easy availability to children of gross images of violence on video . . .'

Smith comments, 'Maybe it was only a discussion paper, but I found this a particularly depressing document. An ill-considered remark by the trial judge had made a minor sensation in the media and was now being given the credibility of an academic paper.'[5] Where the Newson paper downplayed the importance of context in order to 'find' a single blameworthy cause, the previous two hundred pages of Smith's book are devoted to explicating that context and in so doing to explaining the crime as a multi-factorial event within that context.

The issue of violence is, therefore, an important one, but it cannot be confined to the narrowly perceived problem of TV violence's supposed effects. We might be concerned, for example, with whether violence in reality is frequently the way of interacting with the world around them chosen by rootless, irresponsible individuals with no sense of

31 In 1993 the unfortunate Lego toy company got caught up in a moral panic about children's behaviour. A joyriding teenager made from Lego bricks attracted criticism of their catalogue, indicating how readily toys can be blamed for being causes of, rather than responses to, such problems. One British newspaper even went back to *Struwwelpeter* for its imagery.

commitment to the values of a broader community, as a result in part of all the social contexts that have made them what they are. Media representations of a glorified individualism that is its own source of authority, of an anomic, self-satisfied detachment from community, would then be more worrying, even if those representations did not include explicit violence, than some temporarily gut-wrenching scene of violent horror perpetrated by a fictional monster. The point is, in short, that the problem rests in our own understanding of violence and of its prevalence in our world, rather than in a medium which we can conveniently demonise. Violence on screen or reproduced in the imagery of toys may be unfortunate, but it's the misfortune of the symptom rather than the cause.

As such, violence and aggression in a television series like *Transformers*, and in the toys from which the series arose, are not fixed, given phenomena to be abstractly judged, but rather qualities of the context in which a scene from the animated series or a particular toy are situated – and from which they derive their meaning. What is noteworthy about *Transformers* is that the densely elaborated and open-ended context does not ultimately collapse into one metaphoric gun-toting figure who separates himself from that context in order to establish as supreme his own symbolic authority, and his right to defend it through violence. That sort of metaphor of rampant individualism, untrammelled by responsibilities, is of course all too common within a global popular culture still sustained by the shaky old Hollywood myth of heroism and powerful leaders, from Wyatt Earp to Rambo (partially interrupted only in the 1970s by a few years of revisionist self-questioning, an effect of a very particular political and industrial context). Refusal of that stereotype seems to be a characteristic of the most successful narrativised toys.

Of course we can regret that so much aggression finds its way into the narrative context of Transformers but, in a sense, this is only to regret that aggression is a preoccupation of our culture generally because there's so much of it about. The *Teenage Mutant Ninja Turtles* animated TV series and phenomenally successful toy range present us with a good opportunity to consider in more detail the question of how a cultural preoccupation with aggression is reflected and refracted in another densely narrativised context.

Turtlemania

The Teenage Mutant Ninja Turtles had their beginnings in Dover, New Hampshire, USA, in the winter of 1983, where two aspiring comic-book creators had got together and, calling themselves 'Mirage Studios', were looking for an idea for a comic.[6] Over-sized turtles with martial arts equipment emerged from a session of visual brainstorming by Kevin Eastman and Peter Laird. Launching their own black-and-white comic with only 3,000 copies per issue, Eastman and Laird would eventually see the concept grow into a cinema film, television animation series, pop-up storybooks, and a range of toys that dominated the marketplace for several years. A second line of comics, in colour and based on the animated series, was licensed to another publisher in 1988 to take advantage of the mainstream interest, while Mirage continued to publish the more quirky, downbeat original, reaching fifty issues by 1992. An investment of only US$1,000 by the originators in their first print run led to a runaway commercial success internationally for all concerned, especially Playmates, the Hong Kong toy company whose vigorous marketing drove much of that success.

According to Karl Aaronia, Playmates' marketing director in the United States, the company 'wanted to go into the boys area with some low-end high-value toys, and action figures really was the direction we wanted to go in. But we needed something new and different to fit into that category.'[7] In 1988, when Playmates Holdings obtained their licence from Mark Freedman, Mirage's licensing agent, Kenner had already firmly established the small 'action figure' as a successful feature of the toy market, following their commercial triumph during the previous decade with the Star Wars range. That success had demonstrated how 'value' could be added to fairly simple toys by association with versions in other media. The toys did not themselves necessarily have to be very elaborate or appealing in a self-contained way: they attracted by virtue of the meanings which a child would superimpose on them thanks to his or her familiarity with a television series, feature film or comic. The toys could, therefore, include relatively inexpensive items. Without the added value of total marketing through several media, toys had been tending to become expensive gadgets, often electronic, in order to stand out in a highly risky marketplace, thus raising the ante for players in that market. The so-called 'action figures', cheaply manufactured in China, were an altogether easier investment, enthusiastically embraced by many companies.

With simultaneous release of a television animation series and a more mainstream comic (from Archie Comics of New York), Playmates' Turtle toys stood out because of the instant recognisability generated by total marketing. The toys themselves consisted originally of only ten small posable plastic figures of characters from the comic. While attractively enough made, the idea of an upright green turtle wearing martial arts mask and pads is so inherently senseless that the toys could not possibly have appealed to children, except perhaps as a short-lived novelty, had it not been for the elaborately constructed meanings developed around the Turtle characters. The original comic appealed to a teenage and young adult readership and so did not itself create a prior interest in those characters among children. That interest was stimulated entirely by the multi-media narrative so clearly established in 1988.

What Eastman and Laird achieved with their original *Teenage Mutant Ninja Turtles* comic was a narrative with the kind of deep tap roots into

32 Thanks to an undercurrent of seriousness in Eastman and Laird's original comic, the Turtles implicitly raise issues about the relationship between individuality and group responsibility, helped by the deep roots of martial arts imagery. Broadcaster April O'Neil keeps up a running commentary on the assumption that somebody out there still cares. Who knows how much of this filters through to a child playing with plastic Turtles, but there is no doubting the complexity of the meanings that converge on these green misfits or their capacity for absorbing all sorts of themes from the culture at large. Cowabunga indeed!

popular culture that Lucas's original *Star Wars* film also had. This narrative was then available for adaptation into other media, including plastic. Peter Laird is of the same generation as George Lucas; Kevin Eastman is a child of the sixties. Michael Pye and Lynda Myles have explored how movie and television-saturated young Americans, born since the 1940s, understood that culture so well, grasped its shadows and light so intuitively, that they could revitalise it (and make a lot of money along the way) without even necessarily understanding fully what they were doing.[8] George Lucas and others of his generation construct narratives through which a popular culture refers mostly to itself and to audiences who live almost entirely within that 'reality' (including, as we will see in the next chapter, young video game designers at Nintendo). Peter Laird and Kevin Eastman have talked about their own childhoods in these terms – filled with Aurora plastic model kits of movie monsters and games played with toy *Man from UNCLE* guns. These are the 'superkids' described by Pye and Myles, launched out of suburbia with fantasies in their heads.

The Turtles fantasy has been reworked so often for different media that its basic premisses are utterly familiar – at least to very many children. There is an imaginary Japanese *ninja* clan known as 'The Foot'. Among this clan's teachers and spiritual leaders is Hamato Yoshi. But an unscrupulously ambitious pupil called Oruku Saki plots to usurp his master and by treachery succeeds in having him banished. Unjustly disgraced, Yoshi flees to the United States, where in despair he lives in the storm drains and tunnels underneath a city riddled with crime, corruption and pollution. There he befriends the rats and discovers four pet turtles, flushed down the drain by a child who no longer wanted them (in some versions this is described as an accident instead). Drains and sewers, however, can be dangerous places. From the industrial pollution of the city above leaks a glowing, radioactive slime. Called 'mutogen', this turns out to cause biological mutations in life forms exposed to it in sufficient quantities. Yoshi mutates into a rat-man, while the turtles take on some of Yoshi's characteristics, becoming semi-human and teenage-sized. From the slime of a city's effluent emerge the Ninja Turtles and their rat-like mentor. Meanwhile Saki has turned the clan into a global criminal organisation (cf. Cobra and the Decepticons) and has himself taken on the new identity of a masked villain called Shredder, whose schemes will bring him repeatedly into conflict with the Turtles.

All of this emerges gradually as the narrative unfolds in its various media. The Turtles' first appearance is when they venture out of the sewers to rescue April O'Neil, a crusading television reporter who wants to see the city cleaned up. The Turtles save her from a street gang who turn out to be in Shredder's employ. From then on April takes a personal interest in the Turtles' fight against crime in general and Shredder in particular. Their animated television exploits began running in Britain

33 Once accepted, the idea of teenage martial arts experts in the shape of turtles allowed any cultural reference points to be drawn in – so taking them into space was no problem. Indeed, in a spacesuit Raph could be mistaken for an escapee from the Star Wars universe.

in February 1990, screened by the BBC, and by May the press were reporting 'shortages' of the toys due to excessive demand in a market then judged to be worth US$500 million worldwide.[9] The series and toys had already enjoyed three years of success in the United States (screened daily on over 130 television stations for much of that period) and Fleetway Publications in London reprinted the first issues of the Archie comic in a 'Collectors' Edition' for the UK, to coincide with demand for the toys. The year 1990 also saw the release of the cinema version, consolidating the international marketing effort (but, although the film did spectacular business immediately on opening in the US, box-office interest was not sustained to the degree expected, perhaps for reasons we have already suggested in relation to 'Once Upon a Joe', an *Action Force* TV episode which did not have to work in the cinema, of course – it tried to occupy too self-consciously the space reserved for playing).

Powerplay: toys as popular culture

The BBC asked for the word *ninja* to be replaced by 'hero' because of the former's violent implications, but this change, reflected also in the UK versions of the comics, was merely cosmetic. The martial arts remained a defining feature of the Turtles' characters even when the BBC cut some of the detail from the fight scenes. Such tinkering could do little to stem the onslaught released by total marketing. Like *Star Wars* before them, the Turtles were inescapable.

Martial arts imagery

Just why the prominent martial arts or *kung fu* features of *Teenage Mutant Ninja Turtles* were so well received by children at the time is an intriguing question.[10] That aspect of the original comic clearly attracted Playmates Holdings of Hong Kong. Martial arts screen stars like Moon Lee and the actress Yakari Oshima (seen together for example in the film *Kickboxer's Tears*) are highly successful within Hong Kong's indigenous film industry, and martial arts films of the kind they appear in have long been popular there. Perhaps influenced by the cultures of Filipino and Chinese immigrants, there was a fashion for 'self-defence' of this stylised kind in California in the late 1960s, where Bruce Lee taught karate to a number of Hollywood actors, played bit parts and then starred in three Hong Kong-made films based around martial arts, followed by the Hollywood feature *Enter the Dragon* in 1973. After Lee's death later that year a somewhat morbid and faddish fascination turned him into a posthumous superstar, fuelling a continuing interest in the imagery if not the substance of the martial arts. Between 1972 and 1975 the television series *Kung Fu*, based around the fictional story of a Chinese immigrant on the American frontier in the 1870s, took clever advantage of that interest.

In the *Kung Fu* television series of seventy-two episodes, made for the ABC network and extensively sold overseas, David Carradine played Kwai Chang Caine, a Shaolin priest trained in martial arts in a Chinese monastery. There his teacher was Po, a blind old master of the feudal techniques of spiritual and physical discipline. Nicknamed 'Grasshopper' by his teacher, Caine completes his initiation but flees to the United States after killing a member of the Chinese imperial clan. Throughout his exploits on the new frontier, flashbacks to Caine's training in China fill in details of Po's philosophy and of the martial disciplines. Of course these provide the solutions to difficulties that Caine encounters in the barely civilised West. It would probably be sensible not to underestimate the effect of this popular series in disseminating a simplistic but vivid version of martial arts thinking and practice. Certainly a combination in the 1970s of the Bruce Lee craze and the long-running television series created a climate of interest which imported Hong Kong films on video would continue to take advantage of in the 1980s. The Turtles master-narrative draws thematically on the *Kung Fu* story of apprenticeship, as have other martial arts films and books.

Martial arts clubs (or groups as they prefer to be known) became established in many European and US cities during that period. A market grew steadily for instructional books, equipment, and magazines such as *Combat*, which reviews martial arts cinema (predominantly from Hong Kong), as well as covering the martial disciplines themselves.[11] From time to time such publications have carried speculation about the interests to which they cater, which sometimes seem to be merely a taste for ritualised violence but sometimes also a genuine fascination with philosophies of self-discipline. One writer, Taro Shindo, would appear to have got to the heart of it in arguing that the very notion of individualism is what is at stake here.[12] The martial arts dramatise the tension between individualism and collective discipline. For the Japanese or Chinese, the emphasis on individual empowerment can represent a symbolic transcendence of what Shindo calls the 'hive mentality', while conversely for the Westerner the same activity can represent a surrendering of unruly individualism to the discipline of a system or a group. Martial arts hold these things in a perpetual tension.

The *Ninjutsu* system has come to epitomize this tension. More than eight hundred years old, it is a stylised refinement of techniques developed by a Japanese sect of so-called 'stealers-in' or *ninja*, which arose among peasants who would not accept the dominance of the noble warrior class or *samurai*. Taking to the mountainous areas of Koga and Iga, they wore white outfits for winter camouflage and black for 'stealing-in' at night to villages: the black costume has come to be the *ninja* symbol today. A grandmaster in Japan now licenses instructors elsewhere in a network known as 'The Shadows of Iga'. In fact the Turtles use a variety of martial arts equipment, not just that appropriate to *ninjutsu*: the *nunchaku* or short fighting stick from the *karate* system, the wooden sword or *shinai* from the *kendo* system, etc. While it seems more than faintly ridiculous to relate the Turtles toys to this much broader cultural phenomenon of interest in martial arts, the imagery is clearly there and had to come from somewhere.

Blending individualism and collectivity

Taro Shindo's point about individualism is well taken. He sees the martial arts as deeply concerned with an uneasy balance between 'collective spirit' and 'individual will'. With changes in Japanese and Chinese societies, and young people questioning the old notion of obedience to the 'collective spirit', a popular culture of *kung fu* has offered a symbolic resolution. Derived from a Chinese term meaning roughly 'hard work and applied skills', *kung fu*, the generic term for the martial arts, has translated those ideals into a more individualistic context than the usual paeans to school and company which evoke them. With changes in Western societies, and young people evidently doubting that 'individual will' is enough to see them through (we might note teenagers seeking an abandonment of self in Rave), a popular culture capable of absorbing *kung fu* imagery has offered an alternative location for notions of work and skill capable of giving a more attractive sense of discipline and collective endeavour than those traditionally available (family, factory, firm or army).

So the *ninja* and *kung fu* imagery in general, with its ideal of freely chosen group-based discipline, condenses different ideas and sentiments according to the context, balancing as it does the individual and the collective and allowing each to escape some aspects of the other. This imagery was very much part of the popular culture within which Eastman and Laird set out to make their mark. The writer and director John Milius, a film-school classmate of George Lucas, has done a good deal to reinforce this imagery, writing it into the popular films *Apocalypse Now*, *The Wind and the Lion* and *Conan the Barbarian* as a glorification of the self-disciplined warrior. That represents perhaps its clearest appropriation for right-wing sentiments. Eastman and Laird ended up with something less politically sure of itself (except perhaps where its commercial potential was concerned).

Across the corridor from Milius in Hollywood for a time was Steven Spielberg, another superkid dreaming public dreams; but his were yearning for more conventionally liberal compromises in the interests of the happy ending. Conservative and liberal then coexisted in what

142

34 Martial arts imagery now seems to be one of the most powerful sources for popular culture. Even James Bond's son, invented for a TV series with spin-off books and toys in 1993, has a *ninja* outfit. And *GI Joe/ Action Force* (right) has steadily moved towards a fascination with the ambiguities of the *ninja*, set against the conventional image of the original soldier doll.

Pye and Myles called their 'playground' – a playground of themes and materials in which Eastman and Laird played freely. This takes us to some basic questions about the political nature of what resulted, even when applied to something as innocent as the real playground of toys and the latter's role in popular culture more generally.

In *Knowledge and Politics* Roberto Unger explores 'the context of ideas and sentiments within which philosophy and politics must now be practised' in post-liberal societies; that is societies in which the old liberal sureties, whether of left or right, no longer seem capable of telling us an adequate story about how to organise our lives and communities.[13] If the balance between freedom and responsibility is now bound up in dilemmas of mutually incompatible goals, and the values that once claimed to underpin available versions of that balance are increasingly in contest, then Unger rightly describes exploration of these ideas and sentiments as a 'prior task' before we can get to concrete practices of social and political reorganisation. On this level of generality, ideas and sentiments find themselves encoded in various ways: this was Raymond Williams's point in developing his concept of a 'structure of feeling' (see Chapter 1). Cultural artifacts have always been one way of encoding such things, of giving form to things that are as yet not settled and of putting them into play against the old ideas or sentiments, now mostly unsettled. Thus popular culture in the second half of the twentieth century is full of gun-toting conservatives and bleeding-heart liberals, some just echoes of a moment when those ideas seemed less problematical, others forced by the stories that make them what they are to suffer the dilemmas of uncertainty or the besieged reactions of overstatement. Symbolic resolutions of those dilemmas can then be achieved, perhaps by having it turn out all right in the end (the problem wasn't as real as we thought) or by striking up a precarious balance (the dilemmas are not insufferable after all).

Thus, in popular cinema and television, we have 'Dirty' Harry Callaghan or Hawkeye Pierce, Captain James Kirk or Doctor Who, *Wall Street* or *Grand Canyon*, *Rambo* or *Star Wars*, each offering its own refusal to acknowledge the inadequacy of the encoded ideas and sentiments or else starting to creak under the strain. Clearly the argument being set up here is that toys are not immune to such encodings, especially as toys are now intimately a part of that popular culture.

The Turtles: beyond post-liberal pessimism?

Unger identifies several dilemmas within the post-liberal structure of feeling or 'context of ideas and sentiments', of which three are especially pertinent here. All are concerned with the balance between individuals, groups and larger collectivities. The first: 'If there is a marked division of labour among groups, membership in each group will require the mastery of specialized skills or talents and the performance of particular tasks. Will not the group become an association of role players rather than a community of common purpose? And must not their specialisation, like their isolation, produce moral conflicts favourable to war?'[14] The second is concerned with what happens if higher-order organisational structures fail actively to absorb and contain lower-order groupings in society but merely coordinate or allow their separate existences: 'the weakness of the higher-order institutions would make it difficult to avoid the eruption of conflict among the base-line collectivities. This difficulty is merely the symptom of a deeper problem: unless the ideal of community is embodied in associations ever more extensive than the small group, the spiral may not only stop advancing but start to unwind'.[15]

The 'spiral' here is the process by which groups bind themselves together, sort out their problems in relation to each other, and continually distribute their evolving stabilities, solutions, values, 'upwards' to stabilise, and make a larger community of, the society as a whole. Its unwinding is made even more likely by the third dilemma: 'Every community sets its seal upon the social world; it orders the activities of its members and their relations to the members of other groups. If all groups are free to move into the territory of an established association or to exert influence upon it in other ways, the disruption of communal experience may be so frequent and far-reaching as to be destructive of community existence. Each organic group may have the power to pass a death sentence upon the others by simply intruding upon their internal forms of life.'[16]

Though abstractly stated, and perhaps hard to grasp, the very real post-liberal problems of the day are there: political correctness, the Salman Rushdie affair, US troops in Africa on 'humanitarian' missions, nationalism in a new Europe, the value-crisis around notions of childhood (moral panics about children's behaviour) and so on. Death sentences hang over forms of life, role-play supplants common purpose, the spiral of social energies unwinds and we panic about disintegration. The point, however, is this. The tap roots which popular cultural forms sink into fundamentally meaningful levels of social existence frequently prove, under closer investigation, to be in touch with ideas and sentiments given shape by dilemmas such as those Unger describes. In fact this is precisely what is meant by the rather pious vagueness of 'fundamentally meaningful'. This is where such meaning comes from – it is the structure of feeling theorised by Williams. Although the juxtapositions continue to look surprising and even somewhat darkly amusing, it is then absolutely necessary to set the *Teenage Mutant Ninja Turtles* beside such abstractly conceived dilemmas if we are to stand any chance of grasping what is really going on, what becomes representable here to children.

Indeed what is remarkable about the Turtles is that they represent, in a sense, all of the salient features of Unger's worst-case scenario in grossly exaggerated form. Here after all we are left with only a specialised group, role-players doomed to endless antagonisms with those from whom they differ (and how could overgrown talking turtles fail to differ from just about everybody?). Here too society is so insubstantial as to offer only an empty terrain across which opposing groups compete (who is the TV reporter April O'Neil actually addressing when she speaks to camera?). And what the Turtles are ultimately defending is their right to eat pizza leftovers in a sewer! Children are not offered here any sense of a broader community or more extensive associations. Similarly in *GI Joe/Action Force*, society when it is given a form is usually represented by victims. And again, specialised groups define themselves only according to their own specialness, their skills. There is no represented 'community of common purpose' to transcend the group – its internal coherence and its difference from other groups are all that matter. There, as a result, we have Unger's 'conflicts favourable to war'. So war is what we get.

Transformers pushed all of this to its limit, creating representations of both a total and endless war and a mechanisation of everything which says there is no room left for the soft sentiments of community and connection: the hard machine shells symbolise an acceptance of isolation and a refusal to be anything more than a role-player, an Autobot.

But, because these narratives unravel and de-centre themselves so extensively, there are other ways of looking at each of these things. The Turtles are trying to be more than they are; their 'teenage' isolation comes from the very fact of wanting to fit in, to contribute, not to return to the simple security of the glass bowl from which they came. April O'Neil keeps on talking to the camera, about crime, about cleaning up the city, about making things better, even though we get little sense of a community of viewers out there somewhere. It doesn't matter. She keeps on talking to them (as public service television does). The *GI Joe/Action Force* team persistently encounter contradictions inherent in the very narrativised terms of their existence. Otherwise there would be only one story to tell, and it would be an endless, mindless battle: instead there is the greater threat that brings friend and enemy together (for example the biological weapon story), or having to deal with the undesirable consequences of their own violence (for example the orphanage story), and so on. The Transformers repeatedly discover that, even for machines, issues of community can be very real (for example the zombie-robot story). These may seem like ridiculous contexts in which to think about such issues, but for children these contexts are the very stuff of an imaginative life. In playing with the toys these meanings are always potentially there. The child might be thinking only of killing the bad guys, but there is a very good chance that he or she (Transformers and Turtles appealed to boys and girls) will instead be experiencing the subtler effects of the master-narratives that other media have created around the toys. It matters what those meanings are, what kinds of sense are available, what sentiments interweave through those stories, what ideas emerge.

It matters that the toys described here and the extensive narrative contexts developed around them all take as their jumping-off point the bleakest features of a post-liberal reality: social disintegration, the iso-lation of groups defined by their own ritualised difference from each other, an *anomie* that justifies the existence of militaristic saviours, *ninja* experts and awesome technological solutions. Beyond this pessimism, however, the toys belong in a system of meanings with the potential to tell stories which transcend that bleakness, while nevertheless recog-nising it. Such recognition is vital to the effective object relations that play depends on if it is to be an antidote to bewilderment. The nature of the potential to go beyond a bleak vision of society is taken up in the remainder of this chapter, through the semiotic effects (our seventh set) by which toys provide a particular structure to this more general struc-ture of feeling.

A system of meanings

Toys have become a 'system', in the sense intended by semiotician Um-berto Eco when he refers to a system as 'a pure combinational structure . . . an interplay of empty positions and mutual oppositions'.[17] The brief history of toys provided here has suggested that toys have not always been a system in this sense; but that in recent years a number of key features delivered by that history to the contemporary concept of the toy have interacted quite obviously to produce such a system.[18] In particular, we have seen a convergence of narrativised spectacle (with roots in the peepshow and toy theatre), the doll as the adult world's reinvention of the child, and a continuing tension between, on the one hand, the notion of plaything and, on the other, a notion of the minia-ture replica. The emergent or 'new' toy is defined partly in relation to an idea of the 'traditional' toy, which in fact is a residual trace of the toy industry's beginnings in German wood-carving during the early 'artisan' phase of capitalism. The constructional toys, such as Meccano and the Erector Set, have come to seem the archetypal toys of the early twentieth century. Linking the plaything to the replica (play as the building of a replica), they evoked an expansive capitalism and growth in production, including predominantly the mass production which is itself mirrored in the tinplate toys that culminate in the toy cars rolling off the production lines.

The new concept of toy, inseparable from the culture of the media and the multinational phase of the toy industry, has evolved since the early 1960s and becomes most clearly visible in the narrativised spectacles of *Star Wars*, *Transformers*, the *Teenage Mutant Ninja Turtles*, *Mighty Morphin' Power Rangers*, and so on. The contextual factors involved are very much part of the history of childhood 'becoming visible to itself', as we have put it, which means the appearance of post-liberal, postmodern 'multiple choice' in this as in so much else. The complex multi-media worlds constructed around little plastic 'action figure' dolls give a new twist to the totemic function which toys have always tended to have. Instead of the powers of nature and man (*sic*) symbolically condensed in toy animals and soldiers, we now appear to have a more fragmentary, dispersed, context-related power – a power (to make meaning) displaced out into the structure of meanings that we can visualise as a system.

To be as clear as possible about what such a system is, we can in fact visualise it as a quadrat semiotic figure, semiotics being precisely the study of systems of meaning in this way – as combinational structures and 'empty positions', occupation of which turns the occupier into a sign.[19] So a particular toy, say a little Transformers robot, becomes more than just its plastic and metal parts when it occupies a position within this kind of system – it becomes a sign and, as such, carries complex meanings, including those we have already discussed. That it always already has those meanings tells us there is a sign-system of this sort already in place. We will fill in more detail, derived from previous analyses, as the chapter proceeds.

What the media culture of the late twentieth century has allowed, as we have seen, is an intertextuality capable of interconnecting toys within such a system.[20] Before that intertextuality, that dense overlapping and interweaving of texts in several media to constitute an

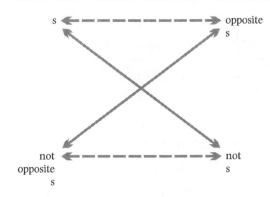

Figure 4 The interaction of semiotic constraints (after A. J. Greimas and F. Rastier)

endlessly self-referential popular culture, toys had far fewer channels through which the meanings of one toy might interrelate with the meanings of another. So Meccano referred mostly to the idealised construction sites of a real world. The Terminator 2 Bio-Flesh Regenerator toy refers entirely to meanings accessible to it through the intertextual channels of a popular culture: not just to a cinematic 'original' (of which there wasn't one for this precise object), but to the system of meanings which it shares with Transformers and all the rest, even with Barbie.

Contrasting the Terminator toy with the School Boot returns us to the earlier discussion of object relations in play. The School Boot is unmistakably a 'harmonising' toy, its imagery functioning in the way the steamboat did for Mark Twain's Ben Rogers – as a smooth blending of inner and outer worlds. For the child coping with a transition from home to school the School Boot is a marvellous reconciliation. The classroom is relocated magically into the comforting form of an old boot which is also a friendly-looking house. The mastery of tying the big, easy laces on the boot (an early triumph for all children) carries over, no doubt, into a sense of being able to cope with the bigger problem of going to school. But for the older child the Bio-Flesh Regenerator offers something much less harmonious. Putting a plastic robot skeleton into the machine where it becomes a spongy pink human figure, whose 'flesh' can then be peeled off again to reveal its underlying tubes and hinges, is hardly to discover a happy image of wholeness and integration. Before asking what kind of object relation this is, however, it is worth pursuing the related issue of how a society's view of itself can

35 From School Playboot (Matchbox) to Bio-Flesh Regenerator (Kenner): the harmony of the former seems nostalgic, the menace of the latter irresistible. Pulling the spongy flesh off the cyborg figure offers a weird pleasure.

constitute the outer world, then brought into balance with a child's inner world through the mediation of toys.

Images of society: the Britains farm

The Britains company's toy hospital from 1980, though only briefly in production, implicitly represented a celebration of forty years of progress towards the image of a healthy nation – first powerfully evoked in *Picture Post* magazine in 1941 when the new techniques of photojournalism were harnessed to a vision of a better Britain to be constructed after the war. The fact that 1979–80 was the founding moment of Thatcherite and Reaganite conservatism in the UK and the US, as supposed political antidotes to the loss of confidence centred on the global economic crises of 1973–5, serves to suggest that the Britains toy hospital represented a bit of doctoring for a nation's ailing self-image, and as such was essentially nostalgic. More than representing any reality of the time, it

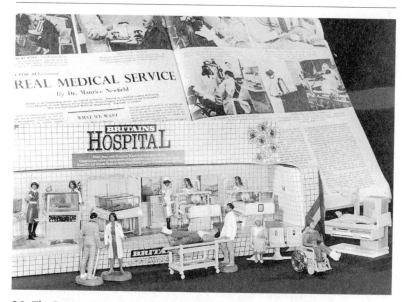

36 The Britains Hospital, what we want to think the National Health Service is still like, now seems to have more to do with a deep social symbolism (1941 *Picture Post* in the background) than with its play value. The ward is sunny, the equipment shiny and new, the staff look too happy to be exhausted and almost outnumber the patients.

evoked the post-war dream of a whole and healthy people. The Britains company's long-running representation of England as a farm has been even more effective as nostalgia.

Home Farm, the magazine for 'small and part time farmers', ran a promotional competition in association with Britains toys in its summer 1990 issue.[21] Under the question 'Have you ever wanted to encourage your child to help on the farm but didn't know where to start?', the magazine offered an enthusiastic editorial on the merits of the Britains farm range of toys. The notion of children helping on the farm was in stark contrast to moral panics about kids running wild on the streets. Interestingly, *Home Farm* magazine does not serve the mainstream farming industry; instead its appeal is to smallholders, self-sufficiency advocates and urban escapees for whom the idea of a farm has intrinsic appeal that far outweighs any commercial goals. The Britains farm toys were a nicely symbolic ally in this. The range evokes a perfect childhood

37 As mechanical earth-movers and superspray tankers edge in on the Britains Farm it looks as if its rural idyll is under threat. The range no longer includes many of the beautifully made plastic trees that once graced its miniature landscape.

image of the farm, all white fences, oak trees, free-range hens, shiny tractors and portly, jovial farmers. In fact, when introduced during the First World War, the Britains range itself was named the 'Home Farm Series'. It complemented the company's existing range of toy soldiers, offering an appropriately homely image of what the real soldiers were then supposedly defending – an idealised England of milkmaids and unspoiled pastures.

A Victorian inventor, William Britain (1828–1906) had founded what would become England's oldest toy firm to challenge Germany's almost total dominance in large-scale toy manufacturing.[22] To counter the success of the German toy soldier, made from solid lead, Britain had devised in 1893 a hollow-casting technique that allowed him to manufacture lighter, cheaper toys by 'slushing' a thin layer of liquid metal into a mould. From this initial success, Britains Limited emerged as something of a national icon – the epitome of market capitalism with a human face, based supposedly on hard work and creative energy. The founder's grandson, Dennis Britain, would see the firm develop successfully from the 1930s to the 1970s (when the farm range was consistently on the best-selling Christmas lists) and received the Order of the British Empire in recognition of his work. In 1984 the family firm was taken over by Dobson Park Industries, multinational manufacturers of electronic instrumentation, mining equipment and electric power tools, with an annual turnover now in excess of £200 million.[23] Dobson Park had also acquired Byron International, a company largely dependent at the time on one product range – the 'Petite' toy typewriters. By the time of their own takeover, 60 per cent of Britains Limited's production was for the export market, reaching over fifty countries.

In 1992, though, Dobson Park closed what had been the Britains headquarters factory in Walthamstow, East London, concentrating production at Petite's Nottingham plant and offering as explanation in advance the fact that 'competition on traditional toys and games continued to intensify'.[24] Ironically, in the same year, the company invited Dennis Britain back in a promotional exercise to endorse personally a 'centenary collection' of toy 13th Hussars and Royal Fusiliers: 'together, these two "favourite" regiments epitomise both the traditional "Toy Soldier" and the colour and splendour of the old British Army' (at a moment, significantly, when a public campaign was getting under way to save a number of regiments from post-Cold War closure by the British government). The glossy catalogue that carried those words also, even more ironically, reproduced an old photograph of a Britains factory floor in London in the 1930s. As well as the toy lines, Britains itself has been turned into an object of national nostalgia, playing on the obvious *double entendre* of the family name and evoking an earlier national stage of capitalism before the multinational.

In fact the 'toy' soldiers are now intended mainly for adult collectors, for whom the nostalgic look of what the company describes as 'traditional style' figures is precisely the point. The farm toys remain the mainstay of the children's range, backed up by smaller numbers of wildlife figures (a reduced range of what used to be called their 'zoo' animals) and various medieval knights, Cowboys and Indians, etc. It is in the farm toys that the Britains image, as itself a marketable international commodity, is clearly located. And the evocatively traditional 'home farm' is at the heart of that image. It is an image with its own identifiable historical roots.

The figure illustrates graphically what we all know to be the case: that since 1800 the English countryside has declined in terms of population share, percentage of population engaged in farming, agricultural contribution to the national income and national self-sufficiency in food production.[25] With those graphs at the bottom of their decline, the usage of the countryside for recreation has steadily increased since the 1950s. As the countryside has been inexorably shifted, for most people, from productive human habitat to visited spectacle, so too the imagery of an ideal existence on the land has grown in significance. One of the most striking early evocations of this kind appeared in the *Northern Star*, the

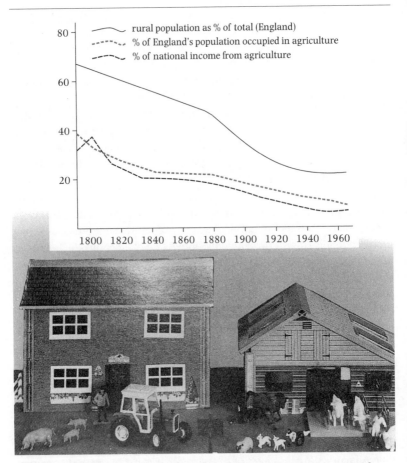

38 The Britains Farm has been forced to carry new meanings because the character of the British countryside has fundamentally altered (data source *The Changing Countryside*, Countryside Commission, 1985).

newspaper of the radical Chartist movement, in August 1846. It is an idealised picture of a farmed landscape, of nature and people in productive harmony. Its neat, roomy houses and friendly spaces, not too rigidly enclosed or over-committed to specialised agriculture, and very much 'lived in', are almost uncannily echoed in Britains' 'home farm' imagery of seventy years later, and in today's version. We have to remind ourselves of how unrealistic the Britains farm actually is – it embodies

154

39 An 1846 illustration from the Chartist newspaper *The Northern Star* looks like an advertisement for the new Britains farmhouse toy for younger children, its stylisation now more obviously locating the toy in a land of symbolism rather than in any real landscape.

instead this popular vision. But for the Chartists this was already an image deliberately constructed in contrast to the real conditions of the labouring poor in England. Their Charter for reform was intended to prepare the way politically for bettering the lot of 'the industrious classes'. The natural idyll of the countryside was supposed to have offered 'all the blessings of life that reasonable men could desire', in the words of one Chartist leader.[26] It never did, of course, but the point of the imagery was to underscore instead the harsh conditions awaiting those who were then being drawn off the land in such large numbers.

From the Chartist imagery of the 1840s to *The Country Diary of an Edwardian Lady*, a popular myth has evolved of a lost rural community. While economic historians have argued that the development of capitalist agriculture made the best of rural resources in the nineteenth century, where an older post-feudal rural economy was moribund and unable to sustain large numbers of people, the sense of a forgone potential lingers. The farm toys of Britains Limited have certainly helped sustain this popular myth for several generations of children. With half of Britains Petite's 1990 sales of £24 million occurring outside the UK, it seems that such a myth has widespread appeal. J. B. Priestley, who believed in these things, wrote of a 'characteristically English sense of community' (he thought he saw it in pubs, at cricket matches and at the Southern Railwaymen's Fruit and Vegetable Show) which the Northern Star's illustration of 1846 was undoubtedly also striving for. 'In spite of the Admass atmosphere, inflation, the all-round grab', thought Priestley in 1973, 'all this must yet exist even now, for there are deep roots here.'[27] In fact what exists is a desire for such 'roots', a desire which itself conjures up the very image of the Britains 'home farm', a corner of the social world which we look back at from an artificially fixed point of view.

A Pizza Hut in Barbie's shopping mall

What does the story of the Britains farm tell us about toys and culture? Certainly that powerful representations are at work; that toys can carry imagery deeply embedded in a cultural history. But, also, it raises the question of what happens when toys become a prime location for such representations. Is the nature of the representation altered? Did, for example, the myth of the rural idyll, of the 'home farm' at the heart of a mythical English community, change in some way as it found itself represented in little plastic milkmaids and saddle-back pigs? One way in which what we might call the representation's conditions of existence change is that a representation now has to take its chances in a market-place. This is a not insignificant point. Instead of lingering rather insubstantially in the culture, appearing sporadically in a Chartist news-paper, in the backgrounds of the new automobile advertisements in the early 1900s, in Shell petrol advertisements in the 1930s, in a wartime propaganda film like Humphrey Jenning's *Listen to Britain*, or on biscuit-tin lids in the 1950s, the representation finds for itself a more solid existence and takes its chances, to be bought and sold for pocket money. The commercial fate of the Britains farm in the hands of Dobson Park Industries is, therefore, entirely relevant here.

That company's Annual Report in 1991 indicated unfavourable pressure on their 'traditional' toy range, leading to closure of what had been Britains Limited's main factory, and signalled a shift of focus on to 'the significant success being achieved in the role play category'.[28] The latter had evolved from the toy typewriters of Dobson Park Indus-tries's other toy-manufacturing acquisition, Byron International. The first 'Petite' toy typewriter appeared in 1956, having emerged from the failure of a business typewriter line dating back to 1925. Influenced by the success of the 'Tom Thumb Typewriter' in the United States, Byron Business Machines gradually converted from the real thing to toy ver-sions, which then survived the demise of the original company and major restructuring in the 1960s. In the late 1970s Byron moved into other toy versions of adult machines, such as a licensed Singer sewing machine and a cash register. By the 1990s the range had expanded to

156

include more elaborate 'role play' or 'activity centre' toys, like their post office counter. The kind of thing that Dobson Park Industries appear to be pinning their hopes on for the late 1990s is their 'Pizza Hut'. A large plastic carry case folds out to form a pizza oven, tables, cash desk, cutlery counter, phone for takeaway orders, etc., all styled after the Pizza Hut chain of restaurants from which the name has been licensed. With such stable-mates in the Britains Petite division of Dobson Park Industries, the venerable Britains farm is confronted by the glaring reality of contemporary consumer culture, Priestley's 'Admass atmosphere'.

Already the proliferation of farm machinery in the Britains range has rather overshadowed the farm itself, with its cute animals and old-fashioned farm folk. The most recent additions, such as the digger and the superspray tanker, seem to have more to do with a prevalence of industrial imagery in toys generally than with the original farm. But the most telling shift in the balance between the traditional farm and new imagery is detectable in the fundamental differences between farm and Pizza Hut: for example, the fact that the Britains farm evidently belonged to a childhood pocket money culture of local toyshops in which a toy cow could be bought this week and a section of toy fence next, the barely economical production costs of such relatively cheap items being counterbalanced by collectors' long-term loyalty and by what the

40 As Dobson Park shift their emphasis off 'traditional' toys such as the Britains farm so their marketing, via the Petite brand name, concentrates on the 'mall culture' of Pizza Hut and the like, objects that refer only to other objects within the closed circle of consumer culture.

firm referred to in Dennis Britain's day as a commitment to 'pocket money purchasing power'. The Petite 'Pizza Hut' is more suited to the retail park culture of the 1990s, to the family visit by car to a toy warehouse from which the 'activity centre' can be carried home in its 'integral carry case', parents having paid for it by credit card.

In fact, the Pizza Hut toy carries that retail culture as its principal meaning. It belongs in Barbie's shopping mall. The Britains farm is a nostalgic image of wholeness, a harmonising object that condenses a complex sense of identity (individual and national) into its rural idyll. But the Pizza Hut opens on to a global superculture where stable images of that kind are much harder to find. Like so many of the toys described here, it does not itself offer the completeness of Twain's steamboat or the School Boot toy or the venerable Britains farm. The manufacturer's transition, from Victorian market capitalism through the period of industrial expansion to a multinational phase, mirrors that loosening or decoupling of meaning from the one good object and its subsequent dispersal into the system which it has been one of this book's goals to describe.

A semiotics of toys

That system can now be explicitly depicted as shown in Figure 5, filling in some key examples of the new toy. It takes its bearings, semiotically speaking, from the linchpin term 'asceticism'. As we have demonstrated, the history of childhood as a concept has, for the time being, installed that term at the centre of the demands our society makes of the child – to be good (which is what we really believe it to be) and convenient (which is what we very desperately want it to be). Alice Miller's deployment of these terms organises what she sees as the drama of being a child in this century – to engage in a pretence that disconnects the child from an understanding of the bad, which is to say ultimately from the century's own awfulness. But just as the Mr Atomic toy came back from Nagasaki, so too the century's other awfulnesses are sending parts of themselves back in the form of toys, by relating to which children may prove to be less bewildered than they might otherwise have been (the last chapter having offered detailed examples). The kind of object relation rendered possible for the child by these toys is new because our conclusion has to be that the whole system now carries

Toys and society

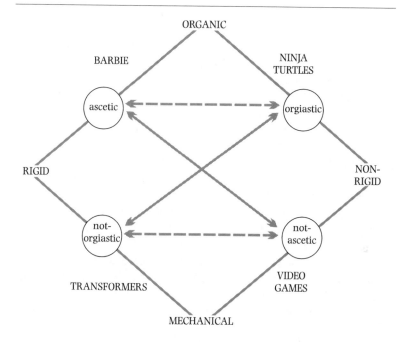

Figure 5 Toys and the interaction of semiotic constraints, filling out the skeleton semiotic system with representative samples of toys.

the 'harmonising' function (and even then only just). The single toy can no longer manage this, so the total system of meanings becomes the good 'object' in a sense; access to that system being a fundamental characteristic of an intertextual popular culture sustained by the media and a product of the resulting narrativisation. It is this system that many of these toys have the potential to open up for children.

In the interests of a summary, let us be programmatic in listing some of the features of the depicted system. There are three that should now be emphasised.

1 The great cultural reference points that have emerged from our description of toys, the organic and the mechanical, the 'rigid' and its alternatives, dramatise the very progress of capitalism – turning nature into raw material for machines, the increasingly rigid systems of mass production and then their supplanting by something

159

more flexible for which we don't yet quite have a concept – but it has a lot to do with information, with the 'soft' machines of digital electronics. And there are signs here also of the organic turning monstrous. (*Jurassic Park*'s hyped computer special effects got the best of both worlds in this respect.)

2 Male identity is persistently placed at the centre, at the point of intersection of these semiotic dimensions. The Picard toy from *Star Trek: the Next Generation* stands there: the starship captain as the contemporary version of Twain's steamboat captain. His identity is defined in relation to Whorf (animality), Data (the computer), the Borg (machine) and Deanna (Barbie). Why these toys can bear those characteristics will be familiar to anyone who knows the television series, but the toys condense and simplify (in the TV series, for example, Deanna is perpetually testing the limits of her traditional female role, Data his non-human nature, etc.). We could put the Luke Skywalker toy from *Star Wars* there and we would find a similar spread of other characters/toys along the available dimensions. The second chapter included additional examples that could now be similarly located.

41 *Star Trek: The Next Generation.* Playmates' toys (1993) emphasise the characteristics of control, animality, the machine, the computer and Barbie-doll 'femininity' in the appropriate figures.

3 The whole system now seems to revolve around male identity. The child and the woman wait in the wings while male identity takes centre stage. But the system of meanings *depends* on the child and the woman because they are the crucial form of difference in relation to which male identity defines itself. The other forms of difference include animality, the machine and the very essence of the new global reality that seems now to transcend both animal and machine – the quantum of information and its electronic carriers. The female child would then seem to be put in her corner with Barbie, while the male child ventures out from the central position to discover an identity defined in its very difference from these various forms of other: that might be the terrible logic of the system of meanings carried by today's toys. But *are* children positioned so precisely by this system of possibilities, like spectators offered only fixed points of 'identification'? Playing is not the same as being a spectator. Do children actually start out from these positions within the identified system? Do girls begin inevitably in Barbie's corner and find themselves fenced in there? Do boys begin in the centre? In the final chapter we will explore more complex ways in which players are in fact positioned.

So, before we give in entirely to that 'discovery' of a male-centred system (and haven't we always suspected that boys never grow up, that the world is damagingly full of boys' toys writ large?), it is important to recover an interpretative finding that the earlier detailed accounts of narrativised toys were meant to insist on. There is in the margins of cultural studies as a field the beginnings of a theorisation of metaphor and metonymy which deserves further work. Ryan and Kellner use it in their powerful study of Hollywood film (but consign its discussion to a footnote); I propose elsewhere a way of teaching about the media that heavily depends on a more explicit version; Kaja Silverman in *The Subject of Semiotics* provides the theoretical underpinnings but doesn't quite follow through in terms of its application. This study of toys has been partly an exercise in the application of that set of ideas.[29] As such, it is not the place to attempt a fuller theoretical exposition; but a brief summary will suffice to set up the book's final examples of what toys mean.

Metaphor and metonymy in toys

Metaphor and metonymy are the rhetorical strategies that play across a system of meaning such as the one described here. The strategy of metaphor clumps the meanings together into static, authoritative objects which lay claim to being *the* meaning in some idealised way. The strategy of metonymy disperses the meanings into fluid, more provisional and open-ended connections, with no single object claiming to encapsulate it all. Metaphor allows difference only as a way of establishing its object's identity in relation to what it is not; while metonymy affirms differences in their own right, although it tends to interconnect them. That is a necessarily abstract way of expressing these ideas; but a simple example, mentioned by Ryan and Kellner, should make it clearer. Treated metaphorically an eagle can come to represent the United States, freedom, the heights of achievement (the name of the first manned machine on the moon), etc. Treated metonymically, an eagle is related to other birds, to habitats, to ideas about species preservation, etc. In cultural terms, we have there the difference between a Clint Eastwood or Arnold Schwarzenegger character in a Hollywood movie and a soap-opera character on television – one pulls everything together to make a single kind of sense while the other tends to let everything unravel in its own way.

Now the importance of this theorisation of rhetorical strategies is that it allows us to recognise something significant happening to our male figure at the centre of the semiotic system we have identified. One strategy would have him pulling all the dimensions tightly around himself to form a monolithic image of male identity. The other strategy would let the dimensions play out more loosely, so that male identity comes into question to some degree in relation to the now more clearly established alternatives allowed for by the system as a whole. If we think of GI Joe/Action Man in this way then it all becomes more apparent. The original large GI Joe doll from 1964 to 1984 was superseded from 1982 by the range of small 'action figures'. As we have explored in detail, this was part of a more general narrativisation of toys triggered by *Star Wars* and developed into Transformers, the Teenage Mutant Ninja Turtles, etc. The original GI Joe stands as an image of isolated individualism, a straightforward representation of male identity around which the semiotic system we have described only weakly circulates and indeed into which it tends to collapse. The multitude of little GI

42 The 1993 re-launch of the large GI Joe, in the form of 'Duke' kitted out for a rerun of Operation Desert Storm in the Gulf, was only part of the revitalisation of war toys due to that conflict. Included here are French company Cesar's Saddam Hussein mask and Ertl's Stealth Fighter. The mobile missile launcher (second from right) was frequently seen in TV coverage from the Gulf. These small vehicles are from Lewis Galoob Toys of California.

Joes, each now with his or her own distinct identity, disperse themselves in less stable ways as a result of their complex narrativisation, and the system as a whole comes much more into play.

In Transformers, Teenage Mutant Ninja Turtles, and other examples, that process of dispersal even goes so far as to locate a new 'centre' temporarily on one or other of the semiotic dimensions. But if we remain with GI Joe we discover what appears to be a cyclical process, with the return of the large soldier doll in 1993. Fortified by the successful imagery of the 1991 Gulf War, an eleven-inch US sergeant in desert uniform with the nickname 'Duke' (connoting of course John Wayne and Hollywood heroics) would certainly appear to be a return to an unforgivingly aggressive and monolithic image of male identity. However the intervening narrativisation of GI Joe has bequeathed Duke a

163

43 Duke as Gulliver. The proliferating meanings and identities of the small GI Joes confront an attempted return to a simpler message about male identity.

significant companion. A large 'Snake-Eyes' doll stands beside him, representing one of the more deeply ambiguous heroes from the television series and comics. Although ostensibly one of the good guys, Snake-Eyes's imagery is a blending of conventional military connotations into Eastern *ninja* elements and, with his hooded face and scimitar, we even recognise the return of the Arab, the ostensible enemy of the Gulf War.[30] There can be no clearer example, perhaps, of how the new toys with their narrative or 'metonymic' complexity have allowed places for difference, for messier forms of identity, unravelled by phantasy, to take hold. Otherness now returns to unsettle even this sacred icon of male identity.

What this means for children we can (looking ahead to the figures in plate 46 specifically) perhaps depict more easily than say. If we take the kind of supremely metonymic and intertextual mixing which children can so easily do for themselves we end up with something like this: Willy DuWitt, a rather androgynous child from San Francisco, has stumbled into another dimension where he is confronted by a line-up of characters among whom it is difficult to tell the heroes from the

44 Along with the conventional soldier doll Duke, Hasbro released three others in 1993 – a second US Army figure, a hooded terrorist leader, and this one. Snake-Eyes was already familiar to children from the comic-book, his *ninja* imagery blending connotations of the other, the oriental, in what was ostensibly one of the good guys. The narrative elaborations of comic and TV series sustained and explored this ambiguity. Western popular culture has long been full of images of the scimitar-wielding, hooded oriental, a mythical figure now haunting popular accounts of a terrorist holy war against the West (such as Yossef Bodansky's here). Snake-Eyes would seem to have delivered literally into the hands of children something of Robin Morgan's 'Demon Lover': 'The explosions going off today world wide have been smouldering on a long sexual and emotional fuse. The terrorist has been the subliminal idol of an androcentric cultural heritage from prebiblical times to the present' (*The Demon Lover*, New York: Norton, 1989, p. 24).

villains.[31] There is Toxie, once an ordinary man called Melvin, who has been turned by toxic pollution into a swollen, bug-eyed creature. Beside him stands Nozone, a man who crashed his aircraft into a radioactive silo and emerged half-man, half-machine. The skeletal Terminator lurks as the very essence of that kind of cyborg. Then there is Bruiser, the giant baboon engaged in a space war against a race of giant toads. Finally, we have Dr Killemoff, the four-armed founder of Apocalypse Inc., dedicated to poisoning the Earth and causing mutated biological monsters. A great deal becomes representable there to young Willy and

45 In a remarkable story from December 1992, written by Larry Hama and drawn by Andrew Wildman, Marvel's *GI Joe* comic depicts Snake-Eyes struggling through the corridors of identity, in which there appears to be no escape from 'programming' and 'conditioning'. It is important to remember that such meanings are available to children in the intertextual world now inhabited by apparently simple toys, even if such stories too explicitly present what is at stake. The 'innocent' toys probably resonate more for children, with these implicit meanings, than the clever self-consciousness of the adult comic writer. Nonetheless, Hama's work was compelling.

to the child he represents. And although Toxie with his American flag is the nearest thing to a hero, he looks like a hero in deep trouble (both Nozone and Bruiser are good guys too, not that you can tell from looking at them!). Perhaps the best that we can say about these toys is that through them the child can confront some of the worst things the world has to offer and is just a little less likely to come away with the tired old stereotypical and prejudiced ideas that got the world into that mess in the first place. Otherness seems to have got into these toys to a degree that suggests a new way of thinking identity itself.

Jacques Derrida has suggested that we should understand the term 'identity' in a doubled way: 'for what we recall (to ourselves) or what we promise (ourselves)'. We should feel a specific identity 'among other things', not 'through and through' or 'in every part'.[32] These new toys, postmodern toys we can finally call them, offer many parts for the child to play and to feel, recalling an older more stable identity but also promising other things. That is the very nature of their metonymic narrativisation.

We might finally be pleased, then, about such an easily optimistic conclusion; until we remember that facing Willy beyond that toy line

46 An identity parade? The androgynous Willy looks perplexed amidst these phantasy companions. With whom should he identify?

celebrating identity and difference is the microworld colonised by Sega and Nintendo. Everything that has been opened up by the new narrativised toys with their open-ended stories, their contextual elaborations, their questioning of individualistic identity and of aggression as its only definer, seems to be under threat of being closed down again by the onslaught of video games. The microworld of the programmed games appears to turn all these toy identities into insubstantial sprites, makes the child adopt only one point of view and then blasts all the others to smithereens. Narrative contexts full of choices and options get programmed down into narrow levels and routes. Static, unreflexive, unthinking identity returns and, once again, it's in the form of the man with the biggest gun. What chance is there for Willy but to see there what he should become, reflected in that game screen? And little Willy's androgyny would give way to a male-supremacist point of view.

What we are left with is, in fact, a unique tension in the densely populated world of childhood. The narrativised spectacle of peepshow and toy theatre has ended up in both a TV world elaborated around toys and a video-game world that is itself a toy. The totemic power once invested in little animals and toy soldiers has migrated through toy machines into the ultimate machines, the TV and the video game; the former briefly offering a dispersal of the power to make meanings, the latter apparently a concentration and lack of choice. Images of self have shifted from the baby doll into a spread of possibilities, stretched between the mechanical and the organic, but now seem to be in danger of disappearing into that new definer of identity – the programmed artificial intelligence of the electronic self, metaphor of an ultimate but apparently imprisoned power. We need to look more closely at how the child is positioned as a player in all of this.

5

Video games and identities

Magazine advertisements for video games leave little room for doubt in the way they position the ideal spectator-player. 'Armed with only a laser gun, Ace must seek out and destroy . . .' is typical of one style of address, accompanied by a picture of a muscular hero clutching the scantily clothed Kimberly and blasting away at the villains with his ray gun. Or even 'A Worm's Gotta Do What a Worm's Gotta Do', with a picture of an erect muscular earthworm in spacesuit – blasting away at the villains with his ray gun. Such games, Space Ace and Earthworm Jim in this case, are typical 'shoot 'em ups'. Their appeal, just like that of the illustrated science fiction magazines of the 1920s and 1930s such as *Amazing Stories* that they sometimes visually echo, is directly to the adolescent male who doesn't know whether he is a hero or a worm, but recognises what a superhero costume and a big gun can do for him. A superficial glance at a boy clutching a game controller or an arcade console tends only to reinforce this impression of a narrowly defined male adolescent activity – as he blasts away at the villains with his ray gun. In fact, especially in the domestic market of Nintendo and Sega, much younger children make up a substantial proportion of players, both male and female, but there is a tendency to view this as a mere apprenticeship for the arcade life of the young male video game fanatic – and, therefore, to assume that girls drift off into other activities while the boys continue to stare and zap well into their teens.

Spectator or player?

In *Playing with Power in Movies, Television and Video Games*, Marsha Kinder explores the notion of a 'dual form of gendered spectator/player positioning'[1] in relation to postmodern media, centred specifically on television's intertextuality. In other words, TV has soaked up so many other forms of culture, and relayed them in so many endlessly repeated combinations and recombinations, that it can no longer (if it ever could) be thought of in the same terms as cinema – as constructing a stable position for the spectator, based on a fixed viewpoint in relation to textual unities achieved through highly integrated and coherent forms of audiovisual and narrative organisation. Along with such cinematic forms of organisation went processes of identification and pleasure that have been extensively examined using psychoanalytic theory. But those textual unities (or aesthetic coherence, in another vocabulary) and theoretical tools are now only applicable to one side, as it were, of the subject's position in relation to today's more hybrid media forms. A more playful set of processes is detectable on the other side. (So, radical film theory's interest in finding textual ruptures or tensions as signs of flexibility in subject positioning is now joined by other possibilities.)

This other side finds the 'spectator' also a 'player', something we are already familiar with from the way the new narrativised toys combine the spectator (TV, videos, comics) and the player (the toys themselves). In Kinder's more generalised sense, the player is riffling through ever more rapidly accumulating piles of cultural bits and pieces to construct some (fragile, transient) sense from them. This is describing life in a magazine culture, against the backdrop of MTV, or amidst the buzz of channel-hopping, or, for Kinder, in front of children's Saturday morning TV in the United States (which combines something of the magazine with the channel-hopping in texts deliberately designed to have these kaleidoscopic characteristics). Where this sort of position might be casually dubbed postmodern by others and then left as a description of how things simply are these days, Kinder more carefully twins the 'player' and the 'spectator' in order to explore the cultural and cognitive interaction between the 'idealised malleability', on the one hand, and the 'idealised unity', on the other.

Recognising that both are idealised serves to draw us back from the easy celebrants of the postmodern as endless and total malleability, but without finding ourselves standing instead amidst the cultural conservatives who hanker after lost unities. The cultural forms we are dealing with are marked by the tension between these two positions. Kinder is especially concerned with how cognitive processes may be similarly marked.

In thinking this through, very convincingly it has to be said, Kinder employs Piaget's notion of 'equilibration'. Piaget (though now much revised) was perhaps the foremost researcher and theorist of child development in terms of successive and well-defined stages. To quote from work of Piaget's to which Kinder does not refer: 'One of the problems raised by the complex expressions of cognizance and conceptualization characterizing our successive stages, is . . . the relationship between conscious finality and the equilibratory regulations open to the future during the passage from any one stage to the next . . .'[2] In Piaget's discussion of 'direction without finalism',[3] it is possible to find further evidence for an interesting hypothesis of Kinder's. She suggests that much of the 'equilibration' or cognitive reintegration achieved by children, as they negotiate their way between the idealised unities of spectatorship and the idealised malleabilities of playing, is actually achieved in the 'middle passages' as it were. In other words, some kind of balance is achieved in the narrative bits and pieces that have not yet been drawn towards the finalism of narrative closure. This is simultaneously the middles of stories, where everything is still up for grabs, the endless interchangeable 'middles' obtained by channel-hopping, and more subtle manifestations such as the 'sleep-bargaining genre' through which children ramble on playfully in a stream of consciousness narrative before an enforced surrender of self to sleep – the 'future' at stake here being nothing other than the morning. It is also the space of the metonymic elaborations described in the previous chapter.

This rediscovery of middles by Kinder (although I am emphasising this vocabulary in a way she does not) offers a great deal of scope for understanding otherwise perplexing features of contemporary culture – from late-night channel-drifting by adults (a kind of sleepy variant of channel-hopping which defers the moment of switching off) to a specific object of Kinder's own study, children's video games, with their abrupt beginnings, vastly extended middles and always remote finales (except in the sudden cutting short after an error, which returns the player to a 'saved' point earlier on). In such ways of dealing with contemporary culture, people are 'equilibrating' the player and the spectator. In a sense, it is the former that now keeps the latter alive, since to be a spectator without the resources of a player is now to have little purchase on the fragmentary accumulations of a culture which has itself become unremittingly playful and piecemeal.

Kinder folds all of this back into textual and narrative analyses of movies such as *Teenage Mutant Ninja Turtles* or video games like *Mario Bros.*, and finds 'playing', adaptability, an ability to mutate through the available identities of a consumerist mass culture actually thematised within those texts. This is an interesting analytical tactic, and it pays off through some real insights into how these cultural instances work; but it has the overall effect of finding the 'commercial supersystem of transmedia intertextuality'[4] inside texts. The child as consumer and the 'commercial empowerment'[5] on which it is being sold, reappear within texts as the pizza-eating Turtles saving the city or Mario munching magic mushrooms to gain super-powers. Those connections are undoubtedly there, and Kinder has done an excellent job of exposing them, but at a price. The price is a relocation of the 'player' inside the text as well; which reactivates the theories of subject-positioning that were applicable to cinematic texts and runs the risk of relocating the 'player' within those theories as merely a new variant. That may not be entirely without justification, but it is clear that 'playing' in Kinder's sense (as a variant of subject positioning) cannot be isolated from where most playing is actually done – in the world of toys.

The 'commercial supersystem' that interconnects toys, child-as-consumer, TV programmes, video games, etc. is no more inside texts than is the toy itself. The Turtles movie was the spin-off product from the toys in this case, not vice versa. To find all of these things inside a text, such as the movie, tells us a lot about the text, but is less informative about the 'supersystem' in which the text simply occupies one of many places. More specifically, it is important to think of 'equilibration' as not just a textual process (or a process at work between text and the subject position constructed by the text for its viewers). To rehabilitate the terms suggested in the first chapter, it is a process at work within the larger, more complex field of effects (of which a text is just one set).

Gendered playing or playing with gender?

Kinder, in referring to the 'dual form of *gendered* spectator/player positioning' (my italics), demonstrates that, while there may be productive interplay between 'spectator' and 'player', the gendering of both remains fixed.[6] The little girls' aisle in the toyshop remains filled with Barbies and brushable toy ponies, the little boys' with GI Joes and sci-fi machines. A bit of empirical observation of my own complicates this picture slightly: in the hours spent lingering suspiciously on such aisles while writing this book it became clear that both boys and girls frequent the 'boys'' territory, while only girls browse among the Barbies and ponies. The latter, in many toyshops, are placed within what is almost a retreat, a quieter corner, all pinks and pastels, to which mothers are often immediately attracted, while daughters head straight for the Power Rangers with their brothers.

This reproduces a pattern familiar from analyses of cinematic spectatorship. Since Mulvey's ground-breaking work, much feminist film theory has sought to make sense of the seeming paradox at the heart of female spectatorship – that either the female viewer identifies with the male protagonist or she 'masochistically' identifies with women who are objects moved around by the narrative rather than its motive force, images constructed to be looked at by the male protagonist rather than themselves owners and directors of the look.[7] No matter how much fiddling around contemporary cinema may do with gender stereotypes, 'strong' female leads, predatory women as 'voyeurs', and so on, this paradoxical positioning of the female spectator evidently remains stubbornly there within most women's sense of what goes on when they take pleasure from mainstream cinema.

Similarly, it would seem, the toyshop offers girls a kind of oscillation between boys' toys as in fact 'everybody's' and a minor place for girls only, which seems less exciting, less filled with totems of power and thrilling activity, more inherently passive (although not visually subordinate – the Barbie glitziness is often a dominant visual effect in toyshops).

The cinematic version of this oscillation, in particular, has proved challenging in terms of theorising more generally the processes of subject-positioning within culture at large. In a sense such positioning is itself what is meant by the term 'subject', where the institution of cinema is replaced by other social institutions (family, school, nation, etc.) and people find their identities given and fixed within (or subjected to) the areas of compelling overlap long established among these institutions: 'They are inserted from, and even before, birth into certain institutions whose characteristic rituals and discourses furnish them with their identity, and teach them to act so as spontaneously to reproduce the dominant social relations . . .'[8]

One of the areas of theoretical debate has been whether we can usefully think of those social relations as constituting, then, a pre-existing reality – abstractly a grand 'object' called ideology (formed, for instance, by capitalism and patriarchy). If so, this reality is then joined by every new 'subject' at the very moment, or endless succession of moments, of being fixed into place. But the thesis of the first chapter would suggest that the only reality is in those moments of fixing, that what we are dealing with are subject-effects, and that terms such as 'ideology' and even 'subject' itself run the risk of taking on too much reality, leading us to see less clearly than we might the effects that course through them.

Perhaps a better option is to think of these subject-effects (the fixing of identities) as operating at a slightly lower level than the 'effective surface' evoked by Raymond Williams, as a kind of substrate perhaps. We are interested here, less in tracking moment by moment in that substrate the complex processes by which someone's identity is called into place ('interpellated', in the theoretical vocabulary), than in what happens when identities then get caught up in the complex play of effects operative at this cultural 'surface'. Recognising that the subject-effects are always already taking place underneath, seems to be a prerequisite for asking what then goes on at the surface. Such a recognition is a crucial part of the theoretical project that has come to be known as the 'death' or 'critique' of the subject, the dismantling of pretensions to a unified subject that somehow stands free of determining forces. As a result of this critique we are not likely to mistake what we see at the surface as the actions of such free-standing subjects. But reducing one level to the other will miss a great deal of what actually is happening.

Vincent Descombes's essay 'Apropos of the "Critique of the Subject" and of the Critique of this Critique' outlines succinctly how the distinction being made here actually works. To establish the distinction he uses the term 'suppositum' (that which is supposed to be acting) to refer to the 'subject of action' as distinct from the 'subject' conceived as the place of identity-fixing.

> What can write a phrase with a quill pen? We can imagine, as acceptable answers: a human person (for example, *Napoleon*) or a personal organ corresponding to the means of the action (for example, *Napoleon's hand*). Now let us consider the same action, but under a different description, which could be, for example: *to sign a peace treaty with Austria*. This time, an acceptable suppositum for such an action is Napoleon, whereas the relation between Napoleon's hand and the action of signing the treaty is no longer as clear. Let us move finally to a third description of the same action, namely: *to reconcile with Austria*. For this description, Napoleon's hand is no longer a conceivable suppositum, whereas other entities now appear in the field of acceptable responses, for example: *the French Empire*.[9]

Whatever complex historical, social, economic and psychological facts impinged on the 'subject' Napoleon, whatever elaborate 'interpellations' called his identity into place, it is still necessary to ask such different questions as 'Who is writing with the quill pen?' and 'Who is reconciling with Austria?' These are identity-effects that rest upon the prior formation of Napoleon as ('ideological') subject but are not reducible to it (except perhaps in the case of a film about Napoleon being watched by someone who thinks he is Napoleon!).

This may seem like so much intellectual quibbling, but it takes us better equipped into a difficult area of cultural theory. The oscillation of the female cinema-goer (or toy-desiring little girl) between female and male subject-positions has been the cause of considerably energetic theoretical gymnastics in order to match an analysis of subject-fixing processes, psychoanalytically understood, with the varied positions that people then actually seem to adopt when living the 'oscillation'. The final chapter of Tania Modleski's *Feminism Without Women* clearly shows what is at stake.[10] Lesbian feminism, lesbian sadomasochism, male homosexual subcultures and the consequent range of views about pornography, choice, dominance and subordination have made it very difficult for the theoretician of the 'subject'. The practices and beliefs involved across that range of identities offer more extreme instances of 'oscillation', of people *apparently* jumping in and out of the available subject-positions. This has been described in theoretically vague ways as a form of 'theatricality' or in theoretically more precise ways as an 'erotics of inequality' (within which, for example, lesbian sado-masochism can eroticise domestic chores because the real threat of male force is absent). A lot of energy is expended, among feminist theorists and practitioners of these various 'oscillatory' identities, in rebuking each other for diverse forms of complicity with ideological subject-fixing.

If, however, we argue that the identity-effects involved are not reducible to those theorised subject-fixing processes, then we do not have to work so hard to make the theorisation of the latter capable of explaining *all* the odd things that seem to go on with the former. This is, in fact, another way of saying that social reality is not a text: the processes of subject-positioning identified through a sophisticated analysis of the cinematic text, for example, do not generalise outwards to explain identity-effects within social reality (who made peace with Austria?) without real tension arising between their explanatory capacity and the repositioning of the subject within an extratextual field where many other effects criss-cross endlessly.

To make this more concrete, we might think of the little girl 'oscillating' between the brashly aggressive Power Rangers aisle and the quietly reassuring Barbie aisle in the toyshop. Wherever she stands at any particular moment is not reducible to those subject-positioning processes which fix her somewhat more precisely in her spectatorial place when she watches a Power Rangers video or reads a Barbie comic. The toyshop aisle is intersected by a range of other effects – harmonising effects that operate through the experiencing of a 'toy' as she picks it up and finds it meaningful; relational effects that operate within the response elicited when she turns round to her mother and says 'look at this one!'; totemic effects that operate through the toys' evocation of powerful forces apparent to the child in the outside world; narrative effects that operate through the story contexts with which the child may be familiar; commodification effects, when mother says 'put it back, it's too expensive' or the girl counts her own pocket money and ranks the toys in terms of consequent accessibility or otherwise; and social semiotic effects that link toys to machines, animals and people, the child's basic classification of the world around her. The textual effects (through TV, video, comics, books, cinema) are just as important as any of those; but, while complex interactions exist, one set of effects does not reduce to another without some loss.

The consequence of several decades of sophisticated textual theorising (in literary theory, media studies and latterly cultural studies) has been a clearer sense, than with any other set of effects, of how subject-positioning works. The cost of the particular insights gained has been a tendency to export them to explain other, as yet less theoretically exposed, sorts of effect within the cultural field. I am not arguing that those subject-positioning processes are not operative there, but rather that, the farther one gets from texts, the more such processes become a sort of substrate on top of which other, highly important effects are also operative. The journey for a girl, out from a moment of transfixion in front of the TV set showing Power Rangers to the toyshop with its simultaneous choice between Power Rangers and Barbie, is a journey defined as much by those other effects as by the ones specifically operative in front of the TV. Acknowledging this has been a principal reason for pursuing the material of previous chapters.

Opening and closing

So what is emerging from this discussion is something like a substrate of subject-fixing processes on top of which a kind of opening and return, a prolonged 'middle' is operative. The former is the level of the drive towards closure, the end of the story, the drawing of everything into place – in a sense, then, also the place of sleep where all pretence of freedom and control is surrendered. The 'opening and return' is the postponing of sleep in the child's ramblings (Kinder's 'sleep-bargaining genre'), but also the place where playing supplements being a spectator, where stories supplant each other rather than ending, where metonymic elaborations are achieved and where identity-effects interact with other effects.

We can generalise this still further on the basis of previous work here on some of those other effects. There is a larger system of opening and closing detectable through toys. In their own world of relative helplessness, children reach out to toys in order to deal with bad objects they perceive around them and with themselves as secret 'bad objects'. As the media, predominantly TV, extend the reach of that perception, so the bad objects proliferate and toys along with them. The objection that this claim disguises the basic consumerist function of toys misses a key point – consumerism's crazy proliferation of 'goods' itself generates bad objects for the child in the form of endless things it cannot want because it cannot understand them. Toys are a training in consumerism precisely because they then function as a way of recuperating objects. In seeking among toys harmonising objects that hold the otherwise intolerable in place, in ways that can be coped with, children achieve a made equilibration. But the return, the 'closing' that is inevitably twinned with this 'opening', is when found equilibrations impose themselves, in the form of the very structures of power and inequality ('coping' reduced to domination and subordination) that give rise to many of the perceived bad objects in the first place (abusive adults, war, famine, threatening technologies, their own feelings, etc.). This is when identity-confining gendered subject positions reimpose themselves, and beyond them all manner of other familiar nastiness.

There need not be anything metaphorical in this vocabulary of opening and closing. Orrin Klapp, in *Opening and Closing: Strategies of Information Adaptation in Society* offers the metaphor of 'a gate swinging ajar or slamming',[11] but proceeds to define this process in highly

concrete ways, in terms of systems theory, in which 'opening and closing, by optimizing information, constitute a strategy of living systems
against entropy'.[12] So these can be characteristics of the semiotic system
identified in the previous chapter. Important to Klapp's definition is the
notion that opening and closing are not necessarily positive and negative respectively. Closing can be 'playback of valued parts' of the already
established, when opening has revealed too much to handle. We might
think of the child's demand for the repetition of familiar stories of wit-
ches, wolves or Power Rangers – the closing of repetition allows the
opening on to those terrors. Closing can help people fit in: 'It feels good
because it is the basis of resonance, meaning, and identity'.[13] The endless
return to gendered identities as formed within social structures of dominance and subordination can also be a return to the familiar. But too
much closing can become the 'entropy' of too much banality, boredom,
drudgery and constraint – the very things which impel children to
novelty, interest and play, which is undoubtedly why playing with toys
is such a clear example of opening.

What is of particular interest in this repeated swinging open of the
gate and its slamming shut again, is what comes back in along with
each cycle of opening and closing – in previous chapters it has been
suggested that a great deal can, such as Snake Eyes coming back with
Duke (the new post-Gulf War GI Joe toys) to unsettle his otherwise
all-too-evident complacency – a complex return in which Snake Eyes
has emerged from a 'multicultural' set of identity-effects traceable back
through the Ninja Turtles and Star Wars toy ranges. Or in the 1950s
the Fat Man bomb returned from Japan to the US in the shape of Mr
Atomic.

Where such things come from is where the many effects explored in
previous chapters – identity, harmonising, relational, totemic, narrative,
commodification and social semiotic effects – interweave in complex
ways. That is the terrain also of the structures of feeling which always
accompany clusters of effects and explain why things matter to people
(and where we have explored a postliberal, postmodern structure of feeling accessible to children). The opening is on to that terrain. The closing
draws it all back towards the subject-fixing processes that are continually operating underneath, limiting the range of opening that is possible
and making the return inevitable – precisely a foregone conclusion.

This way of thinking about a 'gap' between subject-positioning or
fixing, on the one hand, and identity effects, on the other, dramatically

alters our conception of agency (of who or what it is that acts practically in the world). It is important to emphasise from the outset, however, that nothing in the above chapters (in either the empirical explorations of effects or the framing theoretical material) suggests that subject-fixing is in any way inherently challenged by what goes on in the overlay of effects within various social domains, whether identity effects or any of the six other clusters of effects described here. The return, the closing, is always back to those subject-fixing processes. The point being made here is that subject-fixing is not an instantaneous event, a given without movement, without some dynamic characteristics (derived from history and context). Toys dramatise these dynamic characteristics (in one relatively accessible domain) and we have grasped them here in the notion of an opening and closing, a swinging ajar of the gate of 'ideology' and its slamming again. Indeed what perhaps makes the dead weight of the way things are seem so vicious at times is this regular slamming effect or violent reassertion.

Agency, in this account, is the overall configuration which relates subject-fixings and identity effects at any particular moment. It is constituted in the actual space and time and experiencing of that opening and return. Whether the girl comes away from the toyshop with a Barbie or a Power Ranger is the complex result of a particular configuration; it may not happen the same way the next time, or to a different girl in what appear to be the same circumstances. What this does mean, however, is that changing the configuration deliberately will change the result – this is a glimpse of how, for example, a critical pedagogy might function as a reconstructive intervention into configurations of agency. No supposed 'agent', whether educator or child, need be in possession of the totalising point of view, the perspective from which a configuration is recognisable as such, an 'outside' view from which the whole complex interaction of circumstances can be grasped and manipulated with a better set of arrangements in mind. But a reconstructive intervention from inside remains a theoretical possibility. Before considering that possibility further, it will be useful to complete our account of actual toys with some thoughts on the computer game and its enormous impact.

Mario and My Little Pony

The Famicom, or 'Family Computer', which Nintendo started selling in 1983, is now often cited as having changed the face of entertainment (it would be called the Nintendo Entertainment System in the West). In fact, it could only do what personal computers in general could then do; but Nintendo's marketing success was in downplaying the identity of their box of tricks as a computer and emphasising instead its identity as a toy. To this day, Nintendo consoles have computer system interface connectors tucked away under a little plastic cover, connectors that would allow them to function as processing units within more elaborate computer systems (even with telecommunications capabilities); but Nintendo, except for a few trials in Japan, have not yet decided to market their boxes in this way. So the success of the Famicom or Nintendo Entertainment System (NES), its 'Super' version (SNES), etc., have all relied on disguising the fact that they are computers behind the more playful guise of a 'games console'. The hardware developments have been those of the personal computer industry generally: thus, for instance, the SNES marked the widespread availability of 16-bit processors (processors with storage areas that can handle current program instructions in 16-bit groups, a 'bit' being the basic binary unit of information, the previous generation of processors having been 8-bit).

Nintendo's previous foray into video games in Japan had been in collaboration with Mitsubishi on the 1977 Color TV Game 6 (so named because it had six games permanently programmed into its microprocessor-based circuit board) and the expanded TV Game 15. The innovation which the Famicom borrowed from early US examples was the interchangeable cartridge for games software. The bigger, faster processors opened the way for the designers of that software to explore beyond existing definitions of 'games'. The early games were often variations on the theme of batting a point of light around – hence ball games of various kinds, from *Pong*, the first American game to be commercially successful, to the Color TV Game 6's variants of tennis. Nintendo already had some experience of how US-dominated popular culture could provide resources for striking a resonant chord with consumers: in 1959, when they were still a manufacturer of traditional Japanese playing cards, Nintendo's brash young president had made a licensing deal with Disney that allowed him to put their characters on new mass-produced, plastic-coated cards. The cards were advertised on Japanese television and sold well. That success undoubtedly demonstrated to President Yamauchi how 'playing' could profitably be linked to the imagery of a mass popular culture. Here was a powerful convergence, the social appeal of which did not have to be fully understood – so long as it worked commercially.

As they worked to open up the definition of video games beyond the bat-and-ball genre or the target-shooting routines that were really a variation on the same theme, Nintendo's designers would seem to have been intuitively drawn to the visual resources of a Westernised popular culture which their president already knew offered short- cuts to a mass audience.[14] According to David Sheff's research with employees from the time, Yamauchi created an unusually competitive atmosphere at Nintendo, rejecting the normal Japanese industrial emphasis on company spirit and overall teamwork in favour of setting young designers and engineers competitively against each other in small teams.[15] (Sheff interestingly relates this to Hiroshi Yamauchi's own background of estrangement from his father, succession to his maternal grandfather's business at an early age and the clean sweep with which he removed the older generation from that business to take complete control himself.) Yamauchi employed young men whose formative experiences were very much in the post-war world of US dominance, for whom a great deal of tradition had been left behind in the rubble and who looked to the vitality of a new popular culture for a sense of identity.

Although we need to take considerable care with any easy connections among the war, the bomb and the trivialised but none the less portentous overtones of the apocalyptic in Japanese variants of the mass culture of the century's second half, Yamauchi's young men were still, if only indirectly, what Robert Jungk has called 'children of the ashes': people who could hardly do other than have 'an ear for the undertones of fear and morbidity that the clatter of the new buildings . . . cannot smother'.[16] Of the late 1950s and early 1960s, Jungk wrote, 'It was only now that the secondary consequences of atomic radiation were beginning to become apparent in large numbers: these included damage to the brain mechanism, to the heart, to the pulmonary organs and to the circulation of the blood, as well as premature senility both physical and mental.'[17] Overlayed on the more direct imagery of deformation associated with the first victims, this generalised sense of lingering consequences renders entirely unsurprising a youthful determination to live within a zestful popular culture and at a pace that defies time, to affront at every possible moment the shades of brain damage and senility. While it may be simplistic to suppose that this is how individuals actually felt, there remains the distinct possibility of some such 'structure of feeling' (in Raymond Williams's sense) being present in the culture.

Jungk sadly noted the 'honourable repugnance' of the Japanese photographer who walked through the atomic devastation of Hiroshima but could not bring himself to take pictures. Jungk wished he had – perhaps there is another residually honourable repugnance, less important but still significant, that prevents us from too explicitly seeing a direct link between those awful deformations of people and place and the base stuff of a popular culture. And yet Japanese popular culture of the past fifty years, especially in *anime* and *manga*, has been a world filled with *charas* (a loanword from the English 'characters') and *mechas* ('mechanicals') whose violent interactions, in various environments disfigured by disaster, have seen the human body representationally twisted and squeezed into a series of bizarre transformations: the most notable dubbed CB, for 'child body', and SD, for 'super deformed'. If not snapshots of an original trauma these are undoubtedly pictures of an imaginary post-apocalypse, of primitive unstable energies inhabiting the familiar and reducing people to the level of children before them.

At that point, they are also simultaneously something far simpler. They have a distinct familial relationship with Disney's dwarfs and child–animal hybrids. CB *charas* have large heads and big eyes like Bambi; SDs are like the seven dwarfs. The end-results can be disturbing, with CB figures, for example, often combining child-like characteristics and conspicuous sexual endowments. Nevertheless, the Disneyesque connotations are there – but in the sense that a set of visual motifs from American popular culture has been reinhabited by something much stranger. Which is where Mario comes in.

Sigeru Miyamoto, the designer at Nintendo who originated *Super Mario Bros.*, the company's breakthrough game, relates Mario's world to his own childhood (in interview with Sheff).[18] Living in the countryside outside Kyoto, Miyamoto's family did not have TV when he was growing up, so favourite outings were regular train trips to the city to see movies – he remembers Disney films in particular, such as *Snow White*. He organised a school cartoon club and made his own elaborately drawn flick-books of animated drawings. At college he discovered American bluegrass music, such as the Nitty Gritty Dirt Band, bought himself a banjo and travelled to Tokyo to see American bands perform. He recalls his childhood pleasure at exploring the countryside around his home – the stream beds, caves and ravines – before the family moved into Kyoto. For Miyamoto, Mario was a combination of that exploring child and a consciously Disneyesque character, their convergence mediated by a sense of the ever-present popular culture introduced by the United States.

Employed by Nintendo at the age of twenty-four, on the basis of a portfolio of ideas for conventional toys, Miyamoto's first success was a 1981 video game called *Donkey Kong*, based on the misadventures of a gorilla and its owner, a chubby little man in overalls who would later become Mario. ('Donkey' was assumed to mean in English the same as the Japanese word for 'goofy', via a rather mistaken link with 'stubborn' – thus the perils of translation from a phrase book.) In the mid-1990s, a redesigned version of *Donkey Kong* would appear for Nintendo's then much more sophisticated consoles. In 1984 Miyamoto was promoted to head a new research and development division, Nintendo's fourth, continuing Yamauchi's strategy of encouraging inter-divisional competitiveness.

Riffling the resources of a now global popular culture, from Disney to *Alice in Wonderland* and *Star Wars* (he cites George Lucas as a major influence), Miyamoto came up with *Super Mario Bros.* and, from 1985 onwards, a series of linked games: *Super Mario Bros. 2 and 3* (like Hollywood sequels) and *Super Mario Bros. The Lost Levels* (*Raiders of the Lost Ark*, one of a sequel-series, is among Miyamoto's favourite films). At each stage he added more characters and increasingly elaborate environments. The whole sequence of Mario games broke definitively with the shoot-'em-up and ball games which, in his 1977 job interview, Miyamoto had told Yamauchi were unimaginative and insufficiently like movies. Over sixty million Mario games were sold and they were bundled together as *Super Mario All Stars* with the SNES console, emphasising the identification of Mario with Nintendo itself. Miyamoto is, therefore, the world's most successful games designer to date and his influence on the entire industry has been incalculable.

In the – by then well established – tradition of Japanese comics, Mario is a 'deformed' character: his head constitutes half his body, he has a bulbous nose and big hands. This visually combines some of the 'cuteness' of Disney characters with the child-bodied look of many other *manga* and *anime* figures. His clothes and 'character' rehabilitate this distortion: in plumber's overalls with big buttons and a jaunty red cap, Mario is intended to be an icon of ordinariness. This inhabiting of ordinariness by something stranger gives the Mario 'sprite', the manically mobile little figure on screen, a quality which Miyamoto has described as 'a trigger to again become primitive, primal . . .'[19]

In a much earlier analysis of Disney cartoons and their export to other cultures, Dorfman and Mattelart identify two kinds of child-shaped creature in this particular world. One kind is the innocent, the child as 'noble savage', often taking animal form, as in Bambi. The other is more resourceful – a child-bodied but clever figure such as Mickey Mouse or Donald Duck. It is the latter that, for Disney, offers a route into adulthood, while the Bambis or noble savages remain objects of pathos and patronising affection. In a 1971 summary of these alternatives, Dorfman and Mattelart come uncannily close to describing the world of Mario and other video game characters who were still several years away:

> Thus the child-reader has two alternatives before him/her, two models of behaviour: either follow the duckling and similar wily creatures, choosing adult cunning to defeat the competition, coming out on top, getting rewards, going up; or else, follow the child noble savage, who just stays put and never wins anything. The only way out of childhood is one previously marked out by the adult, and camouflaged with innocence and instinct. It's the only way to go, son.[20]

Mario is the one who shows cunning, comes out on top, gets rewards, goes up. All of these things are quite literally present in his interaction with the game environment. The implicit acknowledgement, by Dorfman and Mattelart, that there is a gendered mode of address here ('It's the only way to go, son') interestingly raises the question of whether staying put and not winning anything is also a gendered option, with the male and female positions all too obvious. Contemporaneous with the Mario phenomenon was My Little Pony, a toy line from Hasbro supported by TV animations and comics. It is useful to pause on this contrasting example from children's popular culture, as it clearly demonstrates how the alternatives identified by Dorfman and Mattelart have indeed migrated out from Disney into the culture at large.

The My Little Pony range of toys consists of colourful, chubby child-bodied 'ponies' with long, flowing hair (and little plastic combs). Initially 'grooming' toys for girls, cleverly playing on the notion of grooming a pony and taking care of one's own hair, My Little Pony has developed a more elaborate narrative to sustain the TV and comic variants. In a story from a 1989 comic, a group of the pony friends are excited by the arrival in Pony Land's idyllic glen of the Amazing Odzukins, circus performers represented as dwarfish figures who would look very much at home in Mario's world. It turns out that the Odzukin children have stolen apples from the ponies (because they stopped to play on the way to market and by the time they got there it was closed). Far from being upset, the ponies discover that the Odzukins use apples in their juggling act and provide them with soap balls as an alternative. This is perhaps a particularly convenient example, as it offers a clear contrast between the domestic idyll of the ponies and the more problematically 'adult' world of the Odzukin dwarves, but it does clearly show a characteristic of My Little Pony generally. The pony toys are very much images of the 'noble savage' evoked by Dorfman and Mattelart, feminised stay-at-homes who are not out there competing in the world but whose 'value' is in the domestic conviviality which makes Pony Land such a safe and reassuring place (where problems can be solved with soap!).

In contrast Mario is more of an Odzukin, a playful rascal who is determined to get on. That the massive sales of the Mario games must have embraced girls as Nintendo players, reminds us there is not an absolutely clear division here. While boys were unlikely to play with My Little Pony (if inclined to, the explicit gendering messages which surround the toys would soon put them off), girls have again the 'oscillation' here between something that is regressively gendered for them and something else, not quite 'themselves'. Underpinning the thematic and narrative elaborations, however, are the actual little bodies, whether peripatetic Mario or a chubby purple pony.

These bodies are distorted by the gravitational pulls, as it were, of the effects that intersect through them: from Disney cuteness (marked by the two alternatives suggested), through *manga*-type portents of the body invaded and under threat, to their function as manipulable commodities that have to attract children's attention. Then too, there are the connotations of animality or of doll-people, inherited from the history of toys as outlined in previous chapters. None of these intersecting effects 'explains' why a bloated little 'pony' with a child's face and hair or a dwarfish little man with oversized head are precisely as they are. On a simpler level for example, Mario was the product of design decisions based on how he would look as a tiny figure on a screen. But generally speaking, these are bodies marked by the multiple functions they fulfil within such a network of effects. In a sense they are dense little meta-phoric condensations of those effects.

What then of subject-positioning? The argument being developed here, on the basis of the book's previous evidence, is that another whole set of identity effects can be identified 'on top' of the subject-fixing processes that hold boys and girls in their socially and historically defined places. And these identity effects can only be fully understood if relocated within a complex configuration of other effects. To under-stand the computer game this way, it is necessary to think about how it actually feels to play *Super Mario Bros.*

Playing the microworld

There have been three particularly alert accounts of what happens when children play video games (amidst a plethora of half-baked no-tions): David Sudnow's *Pilgrim in the Microworld*, Patricia Marks Greenfield's *Mind and Media* and Eugene F. Provenzo's *Video Kids*. Sud-now's is by far the deepest and has not yet been bettered, even though the games he writes about (like *Breakout*, a 'classic') are very basic in comparison with Mario; the kinds of game which at that very moment Miyamoto was planning to supersede. Intrigued by behaviour in the arcades, where most video games were played before Nintendo really took hold with its home consoles and *Super Mario Bros.*, Sudnow begins as a detached observer, standing off and watching 'the strangest human conduct I've witnessed in a public place'. He sees 'right hands putting epileptic seizures to shame, while the rest of them just stares and cares, standing up, watching TV'.[21] One of the players is his son, and through him Sudnow gets drawn into playing the games.

His first encounter is with *Missile Command*, and I have replayed this encounter myself to get a feel for what he says about it. It is one of those 'bat and ball' type games, converted to represent missile launchers and anti-missile-missiles on one side with descending intercontinental ball-istic missiles on the other (the latter controlled by the computer and randomised for increasing difficulty). It is compulsive. You are defending cities from attack and if a descending missile gets through your defences, a city can just explode into a jagged outline of rubble. It is all at once extremely stylised and yet engaging. A horrible scenario, utterly un-disguised; yet Sudnow's conclusion?

But the pace of things. The speed. The fast twists and turns. The fireworks. The luminescence. Take a Polaroid picture on a street corner in Bombay, a ten-second kind, and inside of three there'll be fifty people hovering around, with a depth of curiosity so heavily smacking of worship you can see the reverence and fear in their faces, whether it's a picture of a dead body or their own child held up for a smiling pose. That doesn't matter. It's the thing in its fully emblematic significance, token of a new world and way of being. Watch them watch your ten-second Polaroid come up, and you can see them looking across the Atlantic. We were looking out there. Way out.[22]

Amidst all the frenetic activity on screen, Sudnow begins to find new sorts of rhythm and continuity, fluid movements carrying staccato bursts of activity but somehow superseding them and cutting through the detail with effective strokes, effective control – smooth improvisations, he calls them. Anyone who plays video games properly will recognise this feeling; it's crucial to getting beyond the frustrations of awkwardness with which one inevitably begins. And it has the effect at times of pushing the superficial cacophony of it all into the background while one enters into the game with a kind of focused momentum that is concentrated yet relaxed, aware of the rapidly changing details yet cruising through them. In *Missile Command* it is a matter of getting a feel for the way 'missiles' drop out of the sky and then scything back and forth across that space in a way which eventually feels instinctive. It's a small achievement, but Sudnow is right – it feels real. And by that point the connotations of nuclear war are barely there; playing has bypassed those 'meanings' on its way to a more direct experience defined by the game space in highly physical terms.

Sudnow explores these things in more depth, but that doubled insight remains: the 'snapshot' which these games are, of a coming world 'out there' somewhere (not for us the USA of Polaroid so much as the Japan of Nintendo) and simultaneously the physical enactment of a 'way of being' that seems able to cope. The Atari programmers Sudnow talked to were good at describing the structure of the microworlds they created, but tended to 'forget the action itself',[23] the way of being in the game that is indispensable to feeling at ease and empowered there. So too, we might add, today's army of magazine tipsters who feed kids clues about how to get on in this or that microworld. Those details are only the tactical foundation for being inside these games and being comfortable there sometimes.

The real tension in video games is between those moments of relative comfort and the inevitable moments of overload when it all becomes too much to deal with and 'Bam!', you're dead again. Part of the pleasure comes from pushing those moments of overload farther and deeper into the game, up several levels of complexity. The novice, especially the mildly curious adult, experiences the overload so quickly and so repeatedly that such satisfaction does not even seem possible. But it is, and it's a key to the whole thing. Sudnow speculates on some of the costs along the way: the 'neuro-tic fixation', the necessary programming of one's own actions; the training in an exclusion of the extraneous. He verges on suggesting, of the latter, that children are beginning to live in what McKibben would later call 'the age of missing information'[24] – all the contextual details that whizz by too rapidly, pausing to consider which leaves one too vulnerable.

Greenfield advises caution, however, in assuming that what goes on inside the games transfers to other situations. Dealing robustly, on the basis of empirical research, with the fear that children become 'addicted' to video games, she concludes that not unreasonable periods of time are spent playing with them on average, once the initial novelty has subsided. What is mistaken for 'addiction', she notes, is often the challenge of multi-level games and the satisfaction that comes from pushing deeper into the gameworld (which is very unlike the repeated fix of an addiction). Greenfield astutely links this to a specific cognitive demand, located in the fact that 'computer games require the player to induce the rules from observation'.[25] They are therefore very unlike the older board games with pre-determined rules and highly inflexible procedures. This observational induction process is a necessarily lengthy one, and is itself sufficient to explain why children may spend a great deal of time with a video game. A characteristic feature of a game such as *Super Mario Bros.* is that many features can only be discovered by trying things; there are hidden places to go and unexpected consequences that derive from actions which are not rule-bound in any obvious way.

Greenfield is especially concerned to explore the cognitive and motor skills which video game playing engages and to develop hypotheses about possible educational appropriations of game formats which might further develop such skills. It is that interest which leads her to doubt whether gameworld skills by themselves transfer to other contexts – she looks at various ways in which educational practices might, therefore, deliberately draw these skills out and relocate them. By implication, therefore, she is reminding us of what an enclosed, self-contained and highly specific form of activity video game *playing* actually is. The surrounding merchandise, the licensing and hype reintegrate the video game as part of a larger context, including more conventional toys. But the playing remains something distinctive.

Provenzo reconsiders all of this, post-Nintendo as it were.[26] He points out that game consoles have reached so many households, especially in the US, that the industry's ups and downs now tend to follow the graphs of population through the game-playing age-range (generally from six years of age to the mid-teens). That range produces sub-groups which are increasingly targeted and defined by marketing of 'lifestyle' imagery, within which games, movies, clothes, toys, foods, etc. are assembled into relatively homogeneous subsets of the culture at large. When this total marketing gets it right, in commercial terms, the pay-off for manufacturers of the various products has been immense. When one of those manufacturers has a product which in some way defines or sets the tone for the subset as a whole, their commercial power can seem unassailable for a time. This is what happened with Nintendo. What is especially interesting is the way that other manufacturers flock to the first signs of such a definer emerging – their own interests amplify and consolidate that first definitional moment, in order to create a commercially advantageous subset of products. So the defining contribution of the instigator does not have to be as comprehensive as it may later appear.

Provenzo lists the commercial evidence of Nintendo's success in the United States in the late 1980s and the marshalling of other products within the subset they defined. Such lists are familiar, as they themselves become part of the promotional 'aura' that surrounds the products: 16 of the top 20 toys in the US in early 1989 were Nintendo games or games-related products; total sales of Nintendo-related stuff the previous year had been US$1. 7 billion; by the middle of 1989 Nintendo games had an 80 per cent dominance of the video game market in the United States; by Christmas the Nintendo console or games were the single most wanted type of toy; and so on. Provenzo's detailing of all this is empirically valuable. In fact, though, it is a now familiar situation. The scale sometimes varies, but we have seen the same with Ninja Turtles toys or Power Rangers. The inter-media penetration is similar, so too the cereal box promotions or wallpaper. Listing the signs that make these 'phenomena' recognisable only takes us so far.

Provenzo notes that growing interest in educational appropriations of the video game format (Greenfield's aspiration) has now taken what is apparently a very concrete step forward through Nintendo's funding of a research centre at the MIT Media Lab to look into this. The centre's director, Seymour Papert, is highly respected for his constructivist theories of how children learn by building (objects but also conceptual structures), and well known for being the holder of a Lego-sponsored professorship through which he pursues these ideas.[27] It does seem, however, that between the now familiar high-profile market presence, on the one hand, and the new educational appropriations on the other, Sudnow's interest in how it actually feels to play these games is getting squeezed out.

Playing Mario well is a wonderful experience. Playing for the first – and second or third or tenth – time can be very frustrating. But when it starts to come right there is a bodily ease combined with a mental alertness that together support one's absorption (although it's hard to admit to in adult company) – into the Mushroom Kingdom with its happy clouds, jaunty music (by Nintendo's Koji Kondo, who has contributed much to the ambience of the games) and endlessly playful inhabitants, some good, some bad. It is not that one identifies with Mario (he's too minimal a figure) so much as that one begins to feel like a powerful intervening force on his behalf (in cinema this would be rather like identifying with the director – an extraordinary situation). One's whole effort is then directed into maintaining that influence, until the moment when the game shuts it down, either with some outrageous new trickery or by taking instant advantage of a player's momentary loss of concentration amidst familiar tricks. At which moment one simply starts again, usually from a point where one's progress had been smooth, before the trouble really began.

The overall set of goals is clear enough: physically to negotiate one's way through a land where an evil spell has rendered everything and everybody strange, a land of empowering mushrooms to be eaten, magic coins to be collected, fire flowers to be picked (with amazing consequences), a land of interconnected places in each of which things get more challenging. At the end of it all is Princess Toadstool to be rescued. This description, however, says very little about how the game feels to play or how its irresistible forward momentum catches a player up. One does not think about the story, about magic spells and princesses. Rather, these superficial meanings lend some recognisability to an environment that is actually more abstract when played from within, as it were. When playing, it isn't necessary to think about where Mario is going or why; one simply pushes him forward with the control pad (left hand) and jabs away at the action-generating buttons (right hand). As dexterity improves, the two-handed grasp on the controller fades from consciousness.

The narrative framework and matching environmental details (crevasses to leap, caverns to explore, walls to dismantle) have enough reality in the gameworld for falling off an edge to feel momentarily like falling over a cliff, for climbing up the screen to feel like climbing a vine, and so on. These are just enough to render the abstractions of forward momentum and dexterity-challenging obstacles more than mere geometry, but the grip of the thing is in that geometry, not in the personification of objects or detailing of places. Without the latter it would all seem thin and probably too schematic; but the actual process of absorption would be little different. *Super Mario Bros. 2 and 3*, and *The Lost Levels*, add narrative complexities and more characters as an excuse for more elaborate gameworlds, a denser geometry of place and action. Throughout there is a precarious balance between repetition and newness. One's progress depends on becoming familiar with how things work in these gameworlds; but one's interest depends on the unexpected constantly turning up. The genuine achievement of Nintendo's designers is in making this balance work, for players who are willing to spend the initial time needed to get into the gameworlds and develop some competence there. (When youthful games magazine reviewers rate games on 'playability' it is this balance that is at stake, and many new software companies have found it difficult to match the playability of Nintendo originals. That is largely what killed the original Atari-led boom in video games in the United States.)

To lapse for a moment into a personal perspective, I have tried hard to play Mario as innocently as possible, to set aside my reservations about the gender stereotyping that has me trying to rescue a powerless princess, or the violence that sees me hurling fire-balls at my enemies (although Mario does not seem to be a violent game at all, even without putting one's critical sensibility on hold). What happens, when this critical commentary gives way to total absorption, is that the very facts which one might have critically accused fade away as well. This is an intriguing experience. It is the replacement of the gameworld's thematics by its geometry, which is where the fully engaged action really is.

Nintendo played around with this in an early game called *Metroid*, in which the space-suited warrior at the end takes off 'his' helmet, spilling long blonde hair and revealing herself as a woman. Nobody really cared, probably because at the heart of the playing experience such things are only superficial detail.

So as a video game player, I would urge caution as to how we handle Provenzo's main worry in *Video Kids*, that the content of so many games is based on gender-stereotypes and violence. Setting aside the fact that many games do not employ gameworlds of this kind, it is clear that many do – but it may be that this is not so much the 'content' of a game as its decorative thematic surface. In 1972, when Atari introduced *Pong*, plastic overlays could be put on the screen to adapt the basic ball-game format to specific games, such as tennis or football. There is a sense in which those 'overlays' have just become a lot more elaborate and we have forgotten what David Sudnow discovered, that playing the things is something else entirely. (As he points out, there is a response to a photograph which renders the content irrelevant for a while – so too with other media.) The onlooker sees the bombs and ray guns and karate kicks, while the player feels the responsiveness of the controller, the forward momentum, the onset of a relaxed energy, a feeling of competence. As those feelings intensify, the surface thematics become much less apparent. This is not to suggest that a problem does not exist here. There comes a point with some games, undoubtedly, when the represented world so deliberately pulls the physical experience into its thematic content that the two are inseparable – *Street Fighter* and its clones are probably an example. The vividness of the violence and the way the gameplay is locked into the routines of that violence (a seemingly endless succession of hand-to-hand fights) is very different from the experience of playing Mario. It is closer too to the repeated fix of addiction.

What emerges, then, is a fact that should not be as surprising as it is. Video games are now as diverse as movies. We should be careful of too many generalisations. One of the dimensions of difference is the distance, in the experiencing of a game, between representational surface and the underlying geometry of playability. Where the former is reliant on gender stereotyping or violence, as is often the case, this degree of distance will determine the extent to which we should worry about a game's reinforcing consequences. At their worst, like a gratuitously violent movie which also victimises women or demonises certain racial identities, computer games are strongly reinforcing of these in-equalities and patterns of domination and subordination. At their best, computer games simply operate elsewhere for much of the time.

Opening and closing in the gameworld

I think there is enough evidence here to suggest that Mario (as a representative instance of the form) is an example of the 'opening' and 'return' hypothesised earlier; but, like all computer games, a perpetually fixed example. The opening is on to that 'elsewhere', the gameworld of possibilities and the experiencing of a kind of freedom in the accomplished dexterity that has to be developed to get properly out into that gameworld. An identity effect hovers around the figure of Mario as he jumps and darts about, but is really only an effect of contrast: of the difference articulated through the animals and machines which try to trip him up or knock him down; through the constant threat of a bewilderment about why the world should be full of so many things that happen outside one's influence; through the engagement of a structure of feeling that says the whole world is like this, going crazy beneath grinning clouds; through a residual awareness that every time one jabs at the control pad the whole multinational business of this global popular culture gets one more sustaining contribution. None of this, of course, is conspicuously there when a child plays with Mario; but both the child and the game are located there none the less. It awaits them both on their return, when the child is most fully a little gendered consumer again.

The return or closing is what happens when Koji Kondo's music signals another failure; and, as the game resets itself, inviting another attempt, the player becomes once again the boy being asked to show his dominance by rescuing the helpless princess. Or the girl being asked to accept that having control means being other than herself. It is at these repeated moments of return to the superficial meanings of the gameworld that a relatively innocent game such as *Super Mario Bros.* takes its place alongside *Street Fighter* and the like, as one small contribution to that massive structure of endlessly repeated domination and subordination, privileging and exclusion.

So the opening, the middle, the empowerment that sheds those regressive meanings, is replayed as a perfect ellipse by this new form of toy. The video game always takes the child out from the starting-point and back to it, to the point where the underpinning subject-fixing is always re-engaged. At its most open, as in Mario, the outward arc is played as real, experienced as a marvellous, playful freedom and capacity to cope. But there is always the return.

Mario takes the 'player', as part of the dual form of spectator/player positioning hypothesised above, and enacts the 'opening' and 'closing' characteristic of playing with all toys but *in a perfect way*. A perfect equilibration of spectator and player is achieved because programmed, ultimately fixed. The spectator becomes the player (the opening) but eventually falls back into place. So, from this perspective, part of the huge appeal of video games may reside in their perfect delivery of an experience which, while characteristic of playing generally, is seldom so neatly preserved. There is one more thing worth noting here as well. This programmed version of the opening and closing (which play, in a fundamental sense, actually is – but usually with less rigid programming) has about it a quality of the inhuman in the end. To return again to the anti-essentialism that we have been holding back in the interests of seeing certain ('essentialised') things as they are in the world, where things happen, it is possible to suggest that the child and the inhuman are not really so far apart. Instead of the inhuman quality of the video game's programmed play striking us as the very opposite of what children are, a surprising sort of identity comes into view instead.

Playing the other

. . . what if human beings, in humanism's sense, were in the process of, constrained into, becoming inhuman (that's the first part)? And (the second part), what if what is 'proper' to humankind were to be inhabited by the inhuman?[28]

The inhuman that inhabits us, according to Lyotard, is the child before development (child development but also the larger process of late capitalist advance) catches it up into both the habits that make it recognisably human and, at the same time, into a different sort of 'inhuman', into the grip of an increasingly technologised culture. The latter, of course, has much to do with the postliberal sense of confusion about what it means to be human, with the postmodern effect of living in a world of information to be scanned and skimmed, and with the sorts of thing that mutated the Turtles or set off a galactic war between two armies of smart Transformers: in short, a lot to do with the structure of feeling that explains so much about why these new toys matter to children today. It has confused us about what it means to be a child as well – which is to say, the relativity of all the historically available modes of relating to children has struck us forcefully with the coming into view of that history, thanks to the crisis-engendering sense that it is a history (along with so many others) which has come to an end. (It has not, of course; but the sense that it has is a defining feature of where we are now, owing to the complex circumstances we call postmodernism.) It is easy just to coast along with the tide. A recent magazine advertisement reads, 'Upon purchase of a Sega CD system, there may be a few questions you ask yourself about the future interdependency of man and machine, the emerging technological utopia, and our peculiar human desire for omnipotence.' Over the page it responds, 'But force yourself to get over any philosophical crap quickly, and just play the coolest system ever made.'

Playing the coolest system ever made, not Sega's or Nintendo's but the whole 'technoculture' of which they are a part, is something that we are all increasingly doing in the developed societies. The video game has put playing right at the centre of the system. This book has given rise, implicitly throughout, to a hybrid concept as a way of understanding what today's children are up to – that of 'object-relational interpellation'. I want to propose also, at least in outline, a critical–pedagogical response which might try to intervene in what they are up to. But we have to recognise that it is not just the kids who are at it.

Conventional toys are not the only mediatory objects in our lives; not the only objects to function transitionally for us, somewhere between the comfort blanket and things out there. Technological objects, from domestic audio systems to games consoles, from 'home cinema' TV sets to the Walkman, function similarly in many ways. It is not so much that they are toys for big boys and girls as that they generate a safe feeling when we give ourselves over to them. It is that harmonising feeling which connects them to toys. The intimacy extended to us by technologies capable of generating these transitional moments is experienced by so many people as so real that even cars, camcorders, portable phones, mountain bikes, computers, etc. have become meaningful beyond their content, as it were. They seem to hold things in a precarious balance for us, to perch us within moments of stability, of coping in a world of awesome forces. That they can appear also to be ways of getting on explicitly in the adult world is part of their flexibility. Advertising is parasitic on this, shaping, extending and making concrete (in trivial ways) that sense of meaningfulness, in order to sell more of it. But we make a mistake if we assume that it isn't there already in some basic way. Indeed, if we don't recognise this, there is then nothing behind commercial meanings for us to rescue – no way of relating to these things based on a better understanding of the effects that they have for us, and no better meanings for us to strive for. So the argument that today's toys merely train children to be good little consumers misses the point that within consumption adults may often be rediscovering the kinds of harmonising effect which toys once achieved for them.

It has been difficult, within recent academic cultural studies, to see the importance of what we might now term object-relational interpellations because of the grip taken on the field by the notion that ideology interpellates individuals from 'outside', as it were. Or, in the terminology we are familiar with, a subjectivity is a position inscribed (and endlessly reinscribed) within structures of subordination that are produced (and endlessly reproduced) within a given social formation. This has not strictly been the vocabulary of the present book, partly because it has become so routine elsewhere that there is no point in repeating it. Interpellation, or the summoning of the subject into the position prepared for it, can be examined in many ways: literary and media texts summon their readers in some such ways and have been extensively analysed to reveal these mechanisms; more recently notions of cultural identity have turned on the sum effect of the accumulation of many such summonings – and on borderline cases or various forms of hybrid or fragmented identity where the summoning has been historically resistible. Where an 'inside' is allowed, as by a post-Lacanian psychoanalysis, it is only in so far as language (or the 'unconscious structured like a language') operates in people as a pre-existing system which underpins their summoning into place.[29]

To suggest that some objects in the world hold us enthralled, not just because they are conduits for delivery of an ideological 'summons', a fix, but also because we summon forth from them a function as devices of enthralment, is to propose a more interested role for the subject than has been allowed in most cultural studies to date (and evokes the notion from psychoanalytic object-relations theory that pleasure is not an end in itself but a 'signpost' to a meaningful object). We would have to accept that such attachments are not fully explained when we say that they are something like affective implants installed in us by the operation of ideology.[30]

The position from which the affective attachment is maintained is undoubtedly produced ideologically (ideological interpellation, summoning into place); but I have been marshalling evidence here (in this particular corner of our culture) that the attachment itself involves something like a second, overlapping but not coextensive, field (object-relational interpellation). The difference between the two fields may vary enormously, from a tight superimposition (a dominating ideological fix) to a looser slippage of one field across the other like tectonic plates (allowing an opening of, or room for manoeuvre in, the subject's use of the objects concerned). It seems likely that the determining factors in the relation of these fields to each other will derive from the sites at which they are experienced – the concrete circumstances and actual places where attachments with objects are formed. In that sense the degree of movement between the two fields will have little if anything to do with individual agency, with choice or intention. Rather it has to do with where one is. This is certainly the case with children and computer games: this encounter is situated for them within the moment (or at its leading edge as it were) which we have been exploring throughout this book. The effects (analysed here in terms of seven sets) which define this moment at their intersection, situate the child's encounter with the computer game. This is precisely why it is a site that brings so much into view for us.

There is also the challenging fact that such a site reveals the 'inhuman' as the basis of its object relations. I am thinking again, particularly, of Lyotard's recent use of that term: 'The inhumanity of the system which is currently being consolidated under the name of development (among others) must not be confused with the infinitely secret one of which the soul is hostage. To believe, as happened to me, that the first can take over from the second, give it expression, is a mistake. The system rather has the consequence of causing the forgetting of what escapes it.'[31]

Lyotard offers the notion of development, in this broad sense, as proceeding forward and narrowing in, while there remains the possibility of a backward movement that opens out: 'Development imposes the saving of time. To go fast is to forget fast, to retain only the information that is useful afterwards, as in "speed reading". But writing and reading which advance backwards in the direction of the unknown thing "within" are slow.'[32]

To go fast is to forget fast: in the present context this evokes all too clearly the relationship between children and toys today. In writing this book I have been keenly aware of writing about the quickly abandoned. I have seen Transformers or Turtles lying apparently unwanted even while I was struggling to understand their appeal. What Lyotard is calling development is, in fact, that graph or rapidly ascending curve superimposed on adult–child relations in Chapter 2 (Figure 1). As everything gets pulled towards the vertical, which is to say that change simply becomes so rapid as to be a constant, it is as if toys can only really function momentarily. That is in any case the logic of consumerism – buy it and then look elsewhere for the next fix. It is also, however, a commentary on how children now experience time, their own place in it and the transitory nature of each attempt to grasp what is happening out there.

Lyotard is concerned to describe three sets of memory-effect, three 'temporal syntheses' in relation to which we can understand technology's effects on our handling of human time and the processes it sustains. The first is habit. Lyotard offers the succinct, and not unfamiliar, description of culture as consisting of 'nebulae' of habits controlled by structures. Habits are 'commanded' (through what we now term ideological interpellation) and they have been substantially 'unanchored' in space and time by new technologies – their close contexts have been supplanted: from steamboat to starship, we might say.

Beyond habit lies the possibility of a second synthesis – a more voluntary or knowing recognition and identification of what has led to the here and now. This is the beginning of a process of reflecting, one step beyond mere living according to habit; but the new technologies have intensified and expanded what was already a 'scanning' process. The reflective scanning of situations and moments has been generalised to the point where remembering becomes data acquisition on a powerful scale, with its own continuing momentum: 'More knowledge and power, yes – but why, no'.[33] For today's children the very scale of data acquisition required of them may make slowing down and reflecting almost impossible to achieve – without assistance. The momentum that carries them from Transformers to Turtles to Power Rangers to whatever, is simultaneously the momentum of the consumerist drive and, where these things are meaningful to children in the ways suggested here, the momentum of minds trying to keep pace.

Habit and scanning, then, mark out the dimensions of where and how people, kids included, live their culture. What is new and suggestive in Lyotard's analysis (only imperfectly sketched here) is his proposal that there is a third form of synthesis which he cryptically evokes as being 'to pass beyond the reminder of what has been forgotten'[34] or, more colloquially, as 'a resistance to clever programmes'.[35] That phrase powerfully aligns, for us, the video game with the very rising curve of development, with simultaneity and rapid change as experientially grasped by children.

What I want to do now is borrow the idea of a third synthesis and suggest how it might work in relation to the specific terms of this book, however banal this renders the application of Lyotard's subtle formulation. The 'forgetting of what escapes' the system of development concerns the child, as Lyotard reminds us. The secret 'inhuman' which evades the inhuman system (modernity, development, technology) is the 'miserable and admirable indetermination' of the child, which always, however briefly, has a pre-human existence, if we understand 'human' to be a descriptive term for the accumulated effects of the ideological interpellations that structure the child into human habits. The contention should then be supportable that the farther back towards the 'inhuman' child that we go, the more visible will become the interpellative process. In more concrete terms, I have been suggesting in this book that what becomes especially visible is the process of object-relational interpellation which answers the summons of ideological interpellation, as we have understood it up to now. Toys (to which children respond with an absolute, though transitory, openness about their own enthralment) make object-relational interpellation much more visible than it is later, when densely overlaid by adult habits.

The final point, then, to be made about, for example, the Star Trek toys is this. A little plastic figure of a balding man is not especially enthralling in itself. These toys invite an emotional attachment, a response, in part because of the way they unpack the idea of the 'father' into a semiotic space marked out by other figures. (In part, also, because of the narrative associations derived from TV – but those are themselves links in the metonymic chains that make the toy figures meaningful by generating a semiotic space.) Together these figures play around the

47 Mario's All Stars are extended here to include a pile of toys that is simultaneously a pile of identity effects. From left to right: Cat Woman (from *Batman*), the Borg (from *Star Trek: the Next Generation*), Ripley (from *Aliens*), Trini the female Yellow Ranger (from *Power Rangers*), Cheetara (from *Thundercats*), Gemini (from *Gladiators*), Picard (*Star Trek*), Patch (*My Little Pony*), Nozone (*Toxic Crusaders*) and Willy (*Bucky O'Hare*). It is not at all clear where a child's allegiance might lie, and the combined effect is more than the sum of the parts. This is not a harmonious ensemble of differences: Ripley points her big gun at Picard, while Cat Woman and the Borg have their own plans.

ideological installation of Picard/father as organising centre, as the controlling point of identification. The child, though, is insufficiently 'humanised' (Lyotard's striking insight) simply to want to be Picard – instead he or she wants to be Nozone or a pony or the monstrous Borg. How to want such things is something we may tend to forget as adults, especially white male adults. To 'be' any of the embodiments of otherness (not patriarchal white male, not the controlling presence) is literally to play with the process of ideological interpellation, even though that process sets the limits on how far one can playfully deviate off centre as it were.

It can be argued that the narratives of *Star Trek: The Next Generation*, the television series, depended precisely on endlessly opening up those questions (is Troi's intuition inherently 'feminine'? is Data human?) only to secure the repeated settlement of them around the dominant figure of Picard on the starship's bridge, ultimately embodying the authority which settles such questions. But the toys are not the TV series. The child who carries around a little plastic Borg as an object of totemistic attachment is identifying with the monster, the 'inhuman', in a way that is never explicitly allowed by the conventions of the TV series. Mundane as this example is, it points us to an understanding of object-relational interpellation that can be applied more generally.

We have then a specific demand to make of a critical pedagogy when it intervenes in this particular area – that it should *support* in some way the kind of practice which Lyotard theorises as necessary to that third synthesis, what he terms *anamnesis*, borrowing from psychoanalytic vocabulary.

Anamnesis is the recall and working through of an event – its thera-peutic reconstruction. In this context it comes to mean a critical–pedagogical practice that reconstructs what it is given to work on. Lyotard refers to it as 'the *other* of acceleration and abbreviation',[36] meaning a practice resistant to those tendencies we have evoked through such notions as the inevitable 'closing' of the video game – the paradigm, in a sense, of life in a rapidly developing technologised cul-ture, on a developmental curve rising towards the vertical. If the child's own inherently reconstructive practice with toys has been proposed as a sort of everyday emanation from the source of an alternative to acceleration and abbreviation, it may fall to us ultimately to suggest how that alternative might be realised, and worked through, within critical–pedagogical practices.

Toys demonstrate how some objects generate a semiotic space that is more supportive of, or open to, reconstructive elaboration than others. If we understand the processes of development ('the ideology of the present time' as Lyotard puts it) as beginning with child development, then it is unsurprising to find that the process of object-relational inter-pellation at that early stage is not yet fully 'humanised', in the sense of not yet being fully synchronised and matched to, or absorbed by, the ideological interpellation. The child is much more likely than the adult to play at being a Borg, an other. Generalising from this, we need to identify resources in the culture more widely that offer similar support and then develop ways of doing reconstructive work on and through those resources with learners. In this regard, as we have suggested, the metaphoric and metonymic axes of representation footnoted by Ryan and Kellner in *Camera Politica* may well be a useful guide to the most responsive cultural resources, broadly speaking the metonymic.[37] It is in a distinctively metonymic move that the playing child is capable of bringing home the uninvited guest, as Duke came home from the desert with Snake Eyes.

The playing child, then, is not necessarily confined at first to the gendered positions we have identified – Action Man at centre stage, Barbie looking on from the wings. The playing child is not a mere spectator in relation to the staging of that system of positions, of difference, is not simply called to identify with the appropriate occupant of a predetermined position. As inhuman, in Lyotard's sense, or as Alice Miller's bad, ugly, angry, jealous, lazy, dirty, smelly, opportunistic, inconsiderate, domineering, sadistic little other, the child is capable of loving *all* the occupants of those different positions on the system which we have been exploring here. And those positions are not occupied by smiling representatives of harmless and innocent diversity – what the child loves at any one point is just as awfully, intransigently other as he or she is. Because not yet fully human (developed), the boy is not in that central position, the girl is not in that marginal position. Those positions are the terrible truth that is waiting for them, but on their playful way children can and do love the other. Because they are other themselves, for a brief moment.

The fearful gendering forces, the developmental forces (because in this way of looking at it, development is something that happens to children, not a process of natural growth) close in so rapidly on the playing child that we adults risk not even noticing the brief moments of opening to otherness which are occurring. The toys we have been examining here are the vehicles of both processes – the opening and the closing. The video game achieves this in the most perfectly repeated cycle. That is toys' paradoxical function as both objects which matter to children and consumerist things. What we need now is a critical pedagogy (not just in school, but a pedagogy which involves children, parents, even cultural theorists, in a collective remaking of our attitudes to toys) capable of enlarging the moments of opening to otherness, of 'promise' in Derrida's terms, as distinct from mere 'recall'. But not an intervention which spoils things for children.

Figure 6 Alan Leslie's model of the 'metarepresentational' possibility in play (reproduced from *Psychological Review*, 94, 412–22: copyright 1987 by the American Psychological Association; reproduced by permission). For the present argument, the left-hand side shows how 'closing' is effected', whereas the right-hand side shows the means through which 'opening' can be achieved.

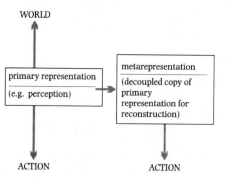

To suggest how this might be done, I want to end by proposing a generalisation of Alan Leslie's model of what he calls the 'metarepresentational' possibility in play.[38] Leslie's model, as reproduced, is meant to function as a precise description of certain kinds of observable play in young children. But I want to take the liberty of superimposing on it a more general description, based on the ideas of the present book. The left-hand side of the model is how 'closing' is effected. Here the way things are in the world results in play actions that simply reflect them – boys wave big guns, girls play at being nice, properly domesticated mothers, nothing changes. The right-hand side is how 'opening' is achieved. Here toys become 'decoupled copies' of things in the world, still allow children to deal with those things, but through narrativisation and metonymic elaboration offer scope for their reconstruction – boys might make mock of people with big guns, girls might make mock of subordinate mothers. The potential action which results is what we (as adults concerned to place toys within the learning that children do) will have to latch on to in devising a supportive critical pedagogy, attuned to the subtleties of the toy world. Where that might take us remains to be seen.

Notes

Introduction

1 Children's culture as an adult construction, and the 'impossibility' thus represented, is explored in Jacqueline Rose, *The Case of Peter Pan: or The Impossibility of Children's Fiction*, Macmillan, 1984.
2 An excellent example of recent work on the texts of contemporary culture for children is Cary Bazalgette and David Buckingham (eds), *In Front of the Children: Screen Entertainment and Young Audiences*, BFI, 1995. See also Ellen Seiter, *Sold Separately: Parents and Children in Consumer Culture*, Rutgers University Press, 1993.

Chapter 1

1 The theoretical approach adopted here has two major points of reference: Foucault's summary of his approach to 'discourses' in Michel Foucault, *The Archaeology of Knowledge*, London, Tavistock, 1974; and the first section, 'Cultural Studies: Theory, Power and the Popular', in Lawrence Grossberg, *We Gotta Get Out of this Place: Popular Conservatism and Postmodern Culture*, London, Routledge, 1992. Although not precisely faithful to Grossberg's terminology, the first chapter of the present book is fundamentally 'Grossbergian'. Also highly influential has been a chapter from Raymond Williams's *Marxism and Literature*, cited below.
2 Dan Fleming, *Media Teaching*, Oxford, Blackwell, 1993.
3 *Ibid.*, pp. 77–80.
4 For the concept of 'modes of experience' see Michael Oakeshott, *Experience and its Modes*, Cambridge, Cambridge University Press, 1933; and P. H. Hirst and R. S. Peters, *The Logic of Education*, London, Routledge, 1970.
5 Raymond Williams, *The Politics of Modernism*, London, Verso, 1989, pp. 130–31.
6 It is clear from Schneider's inside account of children's TV and associated marketing in the US that 'picking a hit' is by no means a certain activity: Cy Schneider, *Children's Television*, Lincolnwood, Illinois, NTC Business Books, 1989.
7 Grossberg, *We Gotta Get Out of this Place*, see particularly pp. 47–52.

Notes

8 For a summary of usages of the term 'discourse' and its analytical deployment in a way that emphasises the social, see John Fiske, *Television Culture*, London, Methuen, 1987, pp. 14–15 and *passim*.

9 Grossberg, *We Gotta Get Out of this Place*, p. 80

10 *Ibid.*, p. 81.

11 Alan O'Connor, *Raymond Williams: Writing, Culture, Politics*, Oxford, Blackwell, 1989, pp. 83–4.

12 Raymond Williams, *Marxism and Literature*, Oxford, Oxford University Press, 1977, pp. 128–35.

13 *Ibid.*, pp. 133–34.

14 *Newsweek*, 8. 8. 1994, p. 42.

15 *Ibid.*, pp. 42–3.

16 This generated the predictable newspaper coverage: see for example 'Power Rangers have mums and dads in a spin', *Sunday Post*, 11. 12. 1994, p. 19.

17 Helen McCarthy, *Anime! A Beginner's Guide to Japanese Animation*, London, Titan, 1993. Also useful for background information is the recently relaunched magazine *AnimeUK*.

18 See *AnimeUK*, vol. 1, no. 1, 1995, pp. 20–3.

19 Frederik L. Schodt, *America and the Four Japans*, Berkeley, Stone Bridge, 1994, pp. 137, 174, 177.

20 Karl Taro Greenfeld, *Speed Tribes: Children of the Japanese Bubble*, London, Boxtree, 1994.

21 *Ibid.*, p. 14.

22 Andrew Goodwin, *Dancing in the Distraction Factory: Music Television and Popular Culture*, London, Routledge, 1993, p. 94. Mulvey's early, influential work on the 'look' is found in Laura Mulvey, 'Visual pleasure and narrative cinema', *Screen*, vol. 16, no. 3, 1975.

23 Greenfeld, *Speed Tribes*, pp. 240–1.

24 Goodwin, *Dancing in the Distraction Factory*, p. 96.

25 Stephen Kline, *Out of the Garden: Toys and Children's Culture in the Age of TV Marketing*, London, Verso, 1993.

26 *Ibid.*, p. ix.

27 *Ibid.*, p. 13.

28 *Ibid.*, p. 320.

29 *Ibid.*, p. 321.

30 Myriam Miedzian, *Boys Will Be Boys*, London, Virago, 1992; Eugene F. Provenzo, *Video Kids: Making Sense of Nintendo*, Cambridge, Mass., Harvard University Press, 1991.

31 Kline, *Out of the Garden*, p. 323.

32 *Ibid.*, p.339.

33 *Ibid.*, p. 350.

34 Brian Sutton-Smith, *Toys as Culture*, Gardner Press, New York, 1986.

35 *Ibid.*, p. 243.

36 *Ibid.*, p. 242.

37 *Ibid.*, p. 251.
38 Cedric Cullingford, *Children and Society*, London, Cassell, 1992.
39 *Ibid.*, p. 146.
40 *Ibid.*, p. 147.
41 *Ibid.*, p. 155.
42 *Ibid.*, p. 156.
43 *Ibid.*, p. 157.
44 *Ibid.*, p. 159.

Chapter 2

1 There is a very useful analysis of Christmas as popular culture and family ritual, including the ritual of gifts, in the Open University coursebook *Popular Culture: Themes & Issues 1* for the now defunct course U203, Milton Keynes, Open University Press, 1981. The role of photography on such occasions is explored in Jo Spence and Patricia Holland (eds) *Family Snaps*, London, Virago, 1991, especially Part 1, 'The child I never was'.

2 The Bethnal Green Museum of Childhood in London, a branch of the Victoria and Albert Museum, has an excellent display on the early German toy industry.

3 *Thunderbirds* is a puppet-animation and special effects series that first appeared on British television in 1964. Although the series is owned by US company ITC, producer Gerry Anderson's own company Century 21 licensed games, toys, records, books and comics based on *Thunderbirds*, which dealt with the science-fiction exploits of an international rescue organisation. The original series ran for three years. Licensing is now handled by a London agency called Copyright Promotions.

4 One of the most popular of a new breed of cynical superheroes, the Punisher first appeared in the comic *Amazing Spider-Man* in 1974. A heavily armed urban vigilante and Vietnam veteran, he now appears in three monthly comics from Marvel Comics in New York and as an 'action figure' toy. Doctor Who, a liberal-minded tourist in time, was the science-fiction star of a long-running British television series which began in 1963, becoming a household name and something of a television institution. Numerous toys based on the series have appeared over the years, including Doctor dolls and replicas of Daleks, his long-standing enemies who looked like giant salt-cellars.

5 Throughout the book I have relied for most examples either on my own collections or, as here, on museums – of which the most informative have been the Bethnal Green Museum of Childhood in London and the London Toy and Model Museum at Craven Hill.

6 The concept of 'popular culture' is implicitly explored at many points in this

book but, among the numerous other academic explorations of the field, a particularly readable introduction to the idea that popular culture in general is playful is John Fiske, *Understanding Popular Culture*, London, Routledge, 1991. Less optimistic theoretical treatments can be found in Colin MacCabe (ed.), *High Theory/Low Culture*, Manchester, Manchester University Press, 1986, especially MacCabe's own essay 'Defining popular culture'. MacCabe notes 'profound mutations in the geopolitics of entertainment' (p. 10). In a very modest way, my concern to understand today's toys is marked by a sensitivity to such mutations, as I think they have made toys more powerful definers of the child's world than ever before. But I am keen to retain some place for Fiske's optimism.

7 Semiotics (or semiology), the study of sign-systems, is a useful field for the student of popular culture, and the present text draws freely on what is by now a respectable tradition of cultural semiotics. Roland Barthes, *Mythologies*, London, Paladin, 1973, remains the most entertaining introduction, while a rigorous grounding is offered by his *Elements of Semiology*, New York, Hill and Wang, 1967, and by Umberto Eco, *A Theory of Semiotics*, Basingstoke, Macmillan, 1977. Applications of the method are usefully collected in Marshall Blonsky (ed.), *On Signs: a Semiotics Reader*, Oxford, Blackwell, 1985.

8 The most successful introduction of a toy is represented by sales of Teenage Mutant Ninja Turtles toys in 1990, the previous most successful launch having been the Transformers range of toy robots. But Barbie's consistent and long-term market presence remain unmatched.

9 Throughout, my comments on Barbie have been informed in general by information in Mattel Toys' 1991 trade publication *Billion Dollar Barbie*. However, Mattel would not allow the more specific statistics from their extremely thorough analysis of Barbie's market position to be published.

10 Sue Sharpe, *'Just Like a Woman': How Girls Learn to be Women*, Harmondsworth, Penguin, 1976, p. 78.

11 The trilogy of Twentieth Century-Fox films, *Alien*, *Aliens* and *Alien 3*, have offered cinematic science-fiction's dark and disturbing side to counterbalance the optimism of the *Star Wars* trilogy. The 1979 original set the tone by surrounding fragile human bodies with menacing, intrusive technologies and reptilian alien monsters. *Alien 3* in 1992 saw the female protagonist Ripley (Sigourney Weaver), the focal point of the entire trilogy, die to evade the horrors of both.

12 Fredric Jameson, *Postmodernism, or, The Cultural Logic of Late Capitalism*, London, Verso, 1991, p. 300.

13 *Thundercats* was produced by Lorimar-Telepictures in the United States, shown by 132 stations there in its first season, 1986, and then sold worldwide, supporting a very profitable toy range which remained widely available in Britain in 1992, with the animations still running on satellite TV. In the US, Lorimar offered broadcasting stations a share of the toy profits

in their area if they screened the series. The animated series of 1983 *He-Man and the Masters of the Universe* (handled by the Saatchi and Saatchi agency in Britain) was the first to establish clearly the animated TV series as a form of extended advertisement for toys that were already in the shops.

14 *El Aquelarre* by Goya, Museo Lazaro, Madrid.

15 This relationality of signs is the absolutely fundamental message of contemporary semiotics and sets it apart from older conceptions that held to a notion of meaning as a given, an essence, something to be detected in the sign rather than a product of signs' interaction. See for example Barbara Hardy's notion of novelistic 'truthfulness' in *The Appropriate Form*, London, Athlone Press, 1964, and contrast it with the semiotically-informed deconstruction of 'truth' by Barthes in 'Textual analysis of a Tale of Poe', Marshall Blonsky (ed.), *On Signs*, Oxford, Blackwell, 1985, pp. 84–97. The shift effected here is taken for granted throughout the present text.

16 *Jurassic Park*, 1993, an Amblin Entertainment production for Universal Pictures, based on the novel by Michael Crichton. The film's sophisticated effects work gave dinosaurs their best cinematic roles to date and triggered a wave of marketing dino-mania.

17 Nick Fury, archetypal cigar-chomping US Army sergeant, was the bullish hero of a comic from Marvel, New York, which ran for a decade from 1963. In 1983 He-Man appeared in an animated TV series as a 'sword-and-sorcery' version of the muscular tough guy so beloved of American popular culture. In Hollywood cinema Arnold Schwarzenegger has played both military and fantasy incarnations of the same basic figure in different guises in recent years.

18 There have been British and US versions of *Gladiators*, the former made by London Weekend Television since 1992 and supported by a newsstand magazine, fan club and spin-off goods (T-shirts, etc.).

19 *Captain Planet and the Planeteers* (TBS Productions and DIC Enterprises) was an animation series made in the United States and televised in Britain in 1992. The name Gaia is derived from the 'Gaia hypothesis' proposed by James Lovelock – that the planet functions as a self-regulating holistic system.

20 David Sudnow vividly describes the world of the video arcade in *Pilgrim in the Microworld*, London, Heinemann, 1983, to which we return in the final chapter.

21 The first series of *Beverly Hills, 90210* was broadcast in 1991–2, created by Darren Star and produced by Spelling Entertainment, California.

22 *For Women*, vol. 1, no. 6, 1992, London, Portland Publishing.

23 For a useful discussion of the games market see Gail Counsell, 'Will they ever reach the end?', *The Independent on Sunday*, 20. 6. 93, pp. 8–9 Business Section.

24 For a worried discussion of the effect on childhood of this system, and beyond

it the modern media in general, see Neil Postman, *The Disappearance of Childhood*, London, W. H. Allen, 1983.

25 In addition to the works quoted in the text, the following are representative of the wealth of material available on play: Catherine Garvey, *Play*, 2nd edn, London, Fontana, 1991; Iona and Peter Opie, *The Lore and Language of Schoolchildren*, London, Paladin, 1977; Kathleen Manning and Ann Sharp, *Structuring Play in the Early Years at School*, London, Ward Lock Educational, 1977; Virginia M. Axline, *Play Therapy*, New York, Ballantine Books, 1969. Citing journal references would open up a vast bibliography but, as most of the worthier findings reported in journals reappear in book form at some stage, I have chosen to keep things tidy by referring to a number of overview works instead, especially the following.

26 Jeffrey H. Goldstein (ed.), *Toys, Play and Child Development*, Cambridge, Cambridge University Press, 1994, p. 6. The bibliography here is an excellent guide to material in the research journals.

27 *Ibid.*, p. 9.

28 *Ibid.*, p. 29.

29 *Ibid.*, p. 129.

30 *Ibid.*, p. 107.

31 *Ibid.*, p. 111.

32 *Ibid.*, p. 77.

33 *Ibid.*, p. 28.

34 *Ibid.*, p. 13.

35 A. M. Leslie, 'Pretense and representation: the origin of "theory of mind"', *Psychological Review*, 94, 1987, 412–22.

36 Some sense of the very different positions on human culture adopted by the humanist psychologist and the cultural materialist can be derived from Carl Rogers, *Carl Rogers on Personal Power*, London, Constable, 1978, and Alan Sinfield, *Faultlines*, Oxford, Clarendon Press, 1992. The former argues for empowerment of the individual through coherent personal growth, while the latter argues that power resides in impersonal social forces which construct an imaginary coherence within which the individual, however uneasily and resistingly, grows into whatever society makes possible.

37 Erik Erikson, *Childhood and Society*, London, Paladin, 1977, p. 197.

38 Erik Erikson, *Toys and Reasons*, London, Marion Boyars, 1978, p. 57.

39 The role of feelings in cognitive development has received increasing attention in recent years. See for example: Richard Jones, *Fantasy and Feeling in Education*, London, Pelican, 1972; Peter K. Smith and Helen Cowie, *Understanding Children's Development*, Oxford, Blackwell, 1988, especially Chapter 5 'Play'; and Margaret Donaldson, *Children's Minds*, London, Fontana, 1978. The 'exploration–play cycle', as depicted by Nunnally and Leonard and reproduced on p. 126 of Smith and Cowie's book, is an important theoretical formulation which is implicit at many points in my own general discussion of what is going on in play. The cycle depicts a kind of

cognitive determination to draw new things into one's experience and understanding.

40 Erik Erikson, *Childhood and Society*, London, Paladin, 1977, p. 189.

41 *The Next Generation* was a revival of the original *Star Trek* series of 1966–69. The first series of the revived version was completed in 1988 under executive producer Gene Roddenberry, who had been responsible for the original. The new cast of characters on the starship is headed by veteran British actor Patrick Stewart, playing the ship's captain.

42 A pupil of Freud, Melanie Klein (1882–1960) was the pioneer of child analysis. A good introduction to her work is Hanna Segal, *Klein*, London, Fontana, 1979, and the object relations approach in general is excellently summarised in Stephen Frosh, *The Politics of Psychoanalysis*, Basingstoke, Macmillan Education, 1987, Chapter 4 'Instincts and objects'. But throughout the present text I have relied much more extensively on the comprehensive Jay R. Greenberg and Stephen A. Mitchell, *Object Relations in Psychoanalytic Theory*, Cambridge, Mass., Harvard University Press, 1983.

43 Greenberg and Mitchell, *Object Relations*, p. 135.

44 *Ibid.*, p. 134.

45 John and Elizabeth Newson, *Toys and Playthings*, London, Allen and Unwin, 1979. Fifteen years later Elizabeth Newson was being widely quoted in the British press for her views about the unhealthy impact of a meretricious popular culture on the moral standards of children – part of a general moral panic centred on cases of violent crimes by children.

46 *Ibid.*, p. 15.

47 *Ibid.*, p. 19.

48 *Ibid.*, p. 91.

49 The uses, conscious or otherwise, to which 'playful' readers and audiences put fiction has received increasing attention since the appearance of a 'reader response' criticism, often informed by psychoanalysis. For a general introduction see Elizabeth Freund, *The Return of the Reader*, London, Methuen, 1987; and then, more particularly, Elizabeth Wright, *Psychoanalytic Criticism*, London, Methuen, 1984, Chapters 6 and 7, where the author moves from object relations theory to theories of the reader's textually-dependent subjectivity. Wright's discussion of play offers important points of contact with the present work – especially her interpretation of Green's ideas.

50 Alice Miller, *The Drama of Being a Child*, London, Virago, 1987. Born in Poland in 1923, Miller was educated and lives in Switzerland, where she completed psychoanalytic training, but now questions many of the fundamentals of the Freudian approach and of analysis generally. In 1988 she resigned from the International Psychoanalytical Association. In a lengthy and useful interview in *Omni*, March 1987, pp. 72–83, Miller quotes the analyst Edward Glover to make the point that the child is naturally 'opportunistic, inconsiderate, domineering and sadistic' and that 'the baby for all

practical purposes is a born criminal' (p. 80). The terrible gulf between that reality and our expectations of children is blamed by Miller for many ills, both personal and social.

51 *The Drama of Being a Child*, p. 30.

52 The periodisation of 'modes' in adult–child relations, of which the nurturing mode is the latest, is derived from Lloyd deMause, 'The evolution of child-hood' in de Mause (ed.), *The History of Childhood*, London, Souvenir Press, 1976. De Mause's own view that the nurturing mode is the best that history can come up with does not have to be accepted as a precondition for employing his periodisation.

53 *The Drama of Being a Child*, p. 48.

54 *Ibid.*, p. 91.

55 *Ibid.*, p. 42. Alice Miller's 'chamber' evokes the perverse adult world of sado-masochism with its advertised 'bed, breakfast and dungeon' (or 'cuffs, whips, paddles, gags' – the toys on offer at Westward Bound in the West of England): *For Women*, vol. 1, no. 6, 1993, p. 109. See also James Miller, *The Passion of Michel Foucault*, London, Harper Collins, 1993.

56 Myriam Miedzian, *Boys Will be Boys*, London, Virago, 1992, p. 268.

57 David Sudnow, *Pilgrim in the Microworld*, London, Heinemann, 1983, pp. 4–9.

58 Elizabeth Matterson, *Play with a Purpose*, 3rd edn, Harmondsworth, Penguin, 1989, p. 185.

59 *The Drama of Being a Child*, p. 32.

60 The edition of *Struwwelpeter* I am referring to is from my own collection. Published by George Routledge and Sons in London, it is undated, but probably late nineteenth century. *Nightmare on Elm Street*, New Line Cinema Corporation, 1984, spawned a series of comics and follow-up movies, culminating in *Freddy's Dead: the Final Nightmare* in 1991.

61 *Edward Scissorhands*, 20th Century Fox, 1990, directed by Tim Burton, whose Batman films would, however, stimulate a huge range of toys and other merchandise.

62 This displacement of an older notion of 'society' by that of a 'social forma-tion' is indebted to Louis Althusser, *For Marx*, London, NLB, 1977, where the term 'structure in dominance' describes the new kind of totality being proposed – an uneven interconnection of parts, dominated by the capitalist economic system, but not reducible to it and not necessarily uncontradic-tory across its constituent parts. Hence social 'facts' and attendant meanings, such as family and childhood, are unstable and alter their char-acter at different points in the structure: for example in family snapshots as against in the law courts.

63 See, for example, Ken Richardson and David Spears (eds), *Race, Culture and Intelligence*, London, Penguin, 1972.

64 Lloyd de Mause (ed.), *The History of Childhood*, London, Souvenir Press, 1974. Philippe Aries, *Centuries of Childhood*, London, Jonathan Cape, 1962,

was the first major historical account of childhood as a social invention ('childhood' not being quite the same thing as 'children').

65 Emmy Elisabeth Werner, *Cross-Cultural Child Development*, Monterey, CA, Brooks/Cole, 1979.

66 The index of information growth used here is the number of scientific journals: see D. J. de Solla Price, *Science Since Babylon*, New Haven, Yale University Press, 1961. This is an index of 'development' as we will use the term in Chapter 5.

67 The whole matter of 'postmodernism' is not easily assimilated in a few phrases as here. The interested reader might begin with Peter Brooker (ed.), *Modernism/Postmodernism*, Harlow, Longman, 1992, and proceed to Margaret Rose, *The Post-modern and the Post-industrial*, Cambridge, Cambridge University Press, 1991.

Chapter 3

1 Museums have been indispensable sources of information and examples for this study. In addition to the toy museums of London, already acknowledged, the British Museum has been an inexhaustible resource for examples of early playthings, totemic objects, etc. For the toy theatres and peepshows described in this chapter the Bethnal Green Museum of Childhood in London proved invaluable.

2 Peter Baldwin, *Toy Theatres of the World*, London, Zwemmer, 1992.

3 The new sorts of theatrical relationship between narrative and spectacle in general are explored in David Bradby, Louis James and Bernard Sharratt (eds), *Performance and Politics in Popular Drama*, Cambridge, Cambridge University Press, 1980, Part 1: 'Spectacle, Performance and Audience in Nineteenth-Century Theatre'.

4 For a succinct summary of Orientalism, the Western construction of the Orient, set in the context of discussion of Foucault's work, see Edward W. Said, 'Criticism between culture and system', in *The World, the Text and the Critic*, London, Verso, 1983, especially the closing pages.

5 Jonathan Swift, *A Modest Proposal for Preventing the Children of Poor People from being a Burthen to their Parents or Country*, pamphlet, published in Dublin, 1729.

6 Victorian sentimental painting of children, such as William Powell Frith's *Many Happy Returns of the Day* (1856), was very usefully set in the context of broader trends by the important Manchester City Art Gallery exhibition 'Innocence and Experience: Images of Children in British Art from 1600 to the Present', 19 Sep.–15 Nov. 1992, which I found highly informative in relation to de Mause's hypothesis of historical modes of adult–child relations.

Notes

7 Mary Hillier, *Automata and Mechanical Toys*, London, Bloomsbury, 1988.

8 A good summary of the development of this type of toy is Basil Harley, *Constructional Toys*, Princes Risborough, Shire Publications, 1990.

9 Ernest Mandel, *Late Capitalism*, London, Verso, 1978.

10 The 'inhabiting' of a contemporary object by a history, particularly where historical time is not representable in any other way, has been theorised as a distinctive feature of the postmodern: see Fredric Jameson, *Postmodernism, or, The Cultural Logic of Late Capitalism*, London, Verso, 1991, especially pp. 18–25.

11 E.g. the *Official Price Guide: Star Trek and Star Wars Collectibles*, 3rd edn, New York, Random House, 1991.

12 Throughout the discussion of *Star Wars* merchandising I have relied heavily on one definitive source: Stephen J. Sansweet, *Star Wars: From Concept to Screen to Collectible*, San Francisco, Chronicle Books, 1992. Sansweet is Los Angeles Bureau Chief of the *Wall Street Journal*, and was allowed privileged access to the Lucas organisation, resulting in a unique account of the new 'spin-offs' business.

13 Michael Ryan and Douglas Kellner, *Camera Politica: the Politics and Ideology of Contemporary Hollywood Film*, Bloomington, Indiana University Press, 1988.

14 *The Six Million Dollar Man*, ABC network, 1973–78; an adventure series based on the fictional creation of a 'cyborg' man, part human but with machine 'enhancements' – an appropriate subject for a toy.

15 A fascination with anthropological detail and imaginary cultures has characterised another area of play – fantasy role-playing, of which *Dungeons and Dragons* has been the most influential example. Players adopt characters and scenarios from extensive background documentation and sit around a table with maps and other aids, talking their way through an adventure with guidance from a games-master. The richness of detail in the many 'systems' now available is quite astonishing.

16 Sansweet, *Star Wars*.

17 François Truffaut, *Hitchcock*, London, Paladin, 1969, pp. 157–60.

18 Quoted in John Somerville, *The Rise and Fall of Childhood*, Beverly Hills, Sage, 1982, p. 93.

19 My discussion of the Asian toy industry draws heavily on the business magazine *South*, especially the December 1989 issue, which ran a number of features under the cover-story 'Toytown on the Move'.

20 General information about the toy business in Hong Kong has been drawn from Kevin Rafferty, *City on the Rocks*, Harmondsworth, Penguin, 1991.

21 *Asian Toys Magazine*, vol. 14, January 1991, p. 40.

22 *Ibid.*, p. 41.

23 Rafferty, *City on the Rocks*, p. 187.

24 For information on toy retailing in Britain I have relied on material provided by the British Toy and Hobby Association (BTHA), a trade organisation;

e.g. their *Yearbooks*, especially the expanded 1992 edition 'The Toy Industry in the United Kingdom'.

25 Birgitta Almqvist, 'Educational toys, creative toys', in Jeffrey H. Goldstein (ed.), *Toys, Play and Child Development*, Cambridge, Cambridge University Press, 1994, pp. 46–66.

26 Eric Clark, *The Want Makers*, Sevenoaks, Hodder & Stoughton, 1988, pp. 185–197.

27 I am grateful to the many exhibitors who offered me information at the 1991 British International Toy and Hobby Fair at Earls Court, London. This section is based on those formal and informal interviews.

28 See for example the BTHA *Yearbooks*. The facts in this section have been obtained from the 1991 and 1992 editions.

29 *BTHA 1992 Yearbook*.

Chapter 4

1 John Grant, *The Transformers: Laserbeak's Fury*, Loughborough, Ladybird Books, 1986, p. 29.

2 *Transformers Autumn Special*, Marvel Comics, 1992.

3 The very basic semiotic terms 'denotation' and 'connotation' (literal and associational meaning) are explicated in Roland Barthes, *Elements of Semiology*, Hill and Wang, 1967, pp. 89–94.

4 For a general overview see Barrie Gunter and Jill L. McAleer, *Children and Television: the One Eyed Monster?*, London, Routledge, 1990. But I am drawing particularly on the three-year, five-country research programme (USA, Australia, Finland, Israel, Poland) reported in L. Rowell Huesmann and Leonard D. Eron (eds), *Television and the Aggressive Child: a Cross-National Comparison*, London, Lawrence Erlbaum, 1986.

5 David James Smith, *The Sleep of Reason: the James Bulger Case*, London, Arrow, 1995, p. 242.

6 Useful background information on the Turtles can be gleaned from interviews in *Previews* June 1992 and *Model and Toy Collector* no. 3, 1990.

7 *Model and Toy Collector* no. 3, 1990, p. 17.

8 Michel Pye and Lynda Myles, *The Movie Brats*, London, Faber & Faber, 1979.

9 *The Guardian*, 19. 5. 90, p. 3

10 A good if entirely uncritical introduction to the whole 'martial arts' phenomenon is Peter Lewis, *The Martial Arts*, London, Tiger Books, 1987.

11 *Combat* monthly, Martial Arts Publications.

12 Taro Shindo, 'The Japanese martial mind', *Combat*, March 1993, 58–9.

13 Roberto Mangabeira Unger, *Knowledge and Politics*, New York, Free Press, 1976.

14 *Ibid.*, p. 285.

15 *Ibid.*, p. 286.
16 *Ibid.*, pp. 286–7.
17 Umberto Eco, *A Theory of Semiotics*, Basingstoke, Macmillan, 1977, p. 36.
18 Modernity has culminated in a global 'system' of social and cultural inter-connection: see John Tomlinson, *Cultural Imperialism*, London, Pinter, 1991. But see also Stephen Toulmin on how that 'systematization' has simultaneously undermined itself: *Cosmopolis*, Chicago, University of Chicago Press, 1990. The seemingly rather insignificant system of toys is a good case study in how cultural 'systematisation' locks meaning into a common grid but also makes representable in the very form of that grid things that might otherwise not be so accessible to thought and feeling. See also the next entry. The complex economic and cultural phenomenon of postmodernism tends to reactivate the multiple choices on which the grid was superimposed.
19 The brilliant contribution to semiotics evoked here, and used subsequently in this chapter, is A. J. Greimas and F. Rastier, 'The interaction of semiotic constraints', *Yale French Studies*, no. 41, 'Game, play, literature', 1968, 86–105, where the authors rediscover the medieval 'square of opposition'.
20 This intertextuality in relation to children is explored in Marsha Kinder, 'Playing with power on saturday morning television and on home video games', *Quarterly Review of Film and Video*, vol. 14, nos. 1–2, 1992, 29–59. Kinder's book is discussed in the next chapter.
21 *Home Farm*, no. 88, June/July 1990.
22 For a wealth of information on the Britains company I am indebted to their Marketing Director Tony Crump.
23 Dobson Park Industries, *Annual Report*, 1991.
24 *Ibid.*, p. 7.
25 John Blunden and Nigel Curry (eds), *The Changing Countryside*, Bromley, Christopher Helm, 1985.
26 A speech reported in the *Manchester Guardian* in 1838 and quoted in A. Briggs (ed.), *Chartist Studies*, London, Macmillan, 1962.
27 J. B. Priestley, *The English*, London, Penguin, 1975, p. 224.
28 *Annual Report*, 1991, p. 7.
29 Michael Ryan and Douglas Kellner, *Camera Politica*, Bloomington, Indiana University Press, 1988, pp. 312–13; Dan Fleming, *Media Teaching*, Oxford, Blackwell, 1993; Kaja Silverman, *The Subject of Semiotics*, Oxford, Oxford University Press, 1983.
30 On culturally sustained Western images of the Arab and their mixture of attraction and repulsion see Edward Said, *Orientalism*, New York, Pantheon, 1978.
31 The sources for these toys are as follows: Willy DuWitt and Bruiser are from the 1992 animated TV series *Bucky O'Hare*, Continuity Graphics; Toxie, Nozone and Killemoff from the 1992 animated TV series *Toxic Crusaders*,

Troma Inc.; and the Terminator cyborg from the 1984 Hollywood film *The Terminator*.

32 Jacques Derrida, *The Other Heading*, Bloomington, Indiana University Press, 1992, pp. 82–3.

Chapter 5

1 Marsha Kinder, *Playing with Power in Movies, Television and Video Games*, Berkeley, University of California Press, 1991, p. 10.
2 Jean Piaget *et al.*, *Success and Understanding*, Henley, Routledge & Kegan Paul, 1978, pp. 225–6.
3 *Ibid.*, p. 228.
4 Kinder, *Playing with Power*, p. 3.
5 *Ibid.*, p. 38.
6 *Ibid.*, p. 10.
7 See, for example, Laura Mulvey, 'Visual pleasure and narrative cinema', *Screen*, vol. 16, no. 2, 1975, 6–18; and Annette Kuhn, *Women's Pictures: Feminism and Cinema*, London, Routledge & Kegan Paul, 1982.
8 Michael Moriarty, 'Ideology', in Elizabeth Wright (ed.), *Feminism and Psychoanalysis: a Critical Dictionary*, Oxford, Blackwell, 1992, p. 169.
9 Vincent Descombes, 'Apropos of the "critique of the subject" and of the critique of this critique', in Eduardo Cadava, Peter Connor and Jean-Luc Nancy (eds), *Who Comes After the Subject?*, London, Routledge, 1991, pp. 131–2.
10 Tania Modleski, *Feminism Without Women: Culture and Criticism in a 'Post-feminist' Age*, London, Routledge, 1991.
11 Orrin E. Klapp, *Opening and Closing: Strategies of Information Adaptation in Society*, Cambridge, Cambridge University Press, 1978, p. 18.
12 *Ibid.*, p. ix.
13 *Ibid.*, p. ix.
14 The USA did not restore Japan's sovereignty until 1952. The impact of the American occupation is well documented in Meirion and Susie Harris, *Sheathing the Sword*, London, Hamish Hamilton, 1987.
15 David Sheff, *Game Over: Nintendo's Battle to Dominate an Industry*, Sevenoaks, Hodder & Stoughton, 1993. I have used Sheff's research extensively in this chapter.
16 Robert Jungk, *Children of the Ashes*, London, Paladin, 1985, p. 334.
17 *Ibid.*, p. 335.
18 Sheff, *Game Over*, pp. 39–56.
19 *Ibid.*, p. 51.
20 Ariel Dorfman and Armand Mattelart, *How to Read Donald Duck: Imperialist Ideology in the Disney Comic*, New York, International General, 1975, p. 47.

Notes

21 David Sudnow, *Pilgrim in the Microworld: Eye, Mind and the Essence of Video Skill*, London, Heinemann, 1983, p. 7.

22 *Ibid.*, pp. 18–19.

23 *Ibid.*, p. 150.

24 Bill McKibben, *The Age of Missing Information*, New York, Plume, 1993.

25 Patricia Marks Greenfield, *Mind and Media: the Effects of Television, Computers and Video Games*, London, Fontana, 1984, p. 100.

26 Eugene F Provenzo, *Video Kids: Making Sense of Nintendo*, Cambridge, Mass., Harvard University Press, 1991.

27 Seymour Papert, *Mindstorms: Children, Computers and Powerful Ideas*, Brighton, Harvester Press, 1980, represents his foundational work.

28 Jean-François Lyotard, *The Inhuman*, Oxford, Polity, 1991, p. 2.

29 All of this is extremely well summarised in the chapter 'Principles of Post-structuralism' in Chris Weedon, *Feminist Practice and Poststructuralist Theory*, Oxford, Blackwell, 1987, which could usefully be supplemented for a student of the field by Terry Eagleton (ed.), *Ideology*, Harlow, Longman, 1994, a reader with all the indispensable background texts needed to under-stand and develop Weedon's summary.

30 See also Robert M. Young, 'Transitional phenomena: production and con-sumption', in Barry Richards (ed.), *Crises of the Self: Further Essays on Psychoanalysis and Politics*, London, Free Association Books, 1989, pp. 57–72.

31 Lyotard, *The Inhuman*, p. 2.

32 *Ibid.*, p. 3, translation slightly modified.

33 *Ibid.*, p. 54.

34 *Ibid.*, p. 54.

35 *Ibid.*, p. 57.

36 *Ibid.*, p. 3.

37 Michael Ryan and Douglas Kellner, *Camera Politica: The Politics and Ideology of Contemporary Hollywood Film*, Bloomington, Indiana University Press, 1988, pp. 312–13.

38 A. M. Leslie, 'Pretense and representation: the origins of "theory of mind"', *Psychological Review*, 94, 412–22

Index

Index

Index

Index

Index

Index